Happiness and the Limits of Satisfaction

Deal W. Hudson

Rowman & Littlefield Publishers, Inc.

ROWMAN & LITTLEFIELD PUBLISHERS, INC.

Published in the United States of America
by Rowman & Littlefield Publishers, Inc.
4720 Boston Way, Lanham, Maryland 20706

3 Henrietta Street
London, WC2E 8LU, England

British Cataloging in Publication Information Available

Library of Congress Cataloging-in-Publication Data

Hudson, Deal Wyatt.
Happiness and the limits of satisfaction : by Deal W. Hudson.
p.   cm.
Includes bibliographical references and index.
1. Happiness.   I. Title.
BJ1481H83   1995   170–dc20   95-42149   CIP

ISBN 0–8476–8139–4 (cloth : alk. paper)
ISBN 0–8476–8140–8 (pbk.: alk. paper)

Printed in the United States of America

The paper used in this publication meets the minimum requirements of
the American National Standard for Information Sciences—Permanence
of Paper for Printed Library Materials, ANSI Z39.48–1984.

For Theresa

Contents

Acknowledgments

Anyone who writes a book on happiness needs the help of friends. I am fortunate to have had much help from mine. I would like to thank them all, but especially Matt Mancini, Brenda Steele, Jeff Wallin, Carolyn Farrar, Vincent Colapietro, Dominic Balestra, Russell Hittinger, Peter Pagan, Ted Naff, Samuel Casey Carter, Lillie Robertson, Marion Montgomery, Anthony O. Simon, Mortimer J. Adler, and John Van Doren. I am also thankful to the Earhart Foundation for its generous support.

Earlier versions of some chapters were previously published in the following:

"Can Happiness Be Saved?" in *Jacques Maritain: The Man and His Metaphysics*, ed. John F. X. Knasas (Notre Dame: University of Notre Dame Press/American Maritain Association, 1988), 257–63.

"Maritain and Happiness in Modern Thomism," in *From Twilight to Dawn: Jacques Maritain on Culture and Civilization*, ed. Peter Redpath (Notre Dame: University of Notre Dame Press/ American Maritain Association, 1990), 263–76.

"Contemporary Views of Happiness," *The Great Ideas Today* 1992, ed. John Van Doren and Mortimer J. Adler (Chicago: Encyclopaedia Britannica, 1992), 171–216.

"Comprehending Anna Karenina: A Test Case for Theories of Happiness," *International Philosophical Quarterly* (September 1992): 287–97.

"The 'Anguish of Beatitude': Happiness and Pain," in *On Memory*, ed. Erasmo Leiva-Merikakis (Atlanta: Scholars Press, 1993), 51–61.

Introduction

> As far as its name is concerned most people would probably agree: for both the common run of people and the cultivated men call it happiness, and understand by "being happy" the same as "living well" and "doing well." But when it comes to defining what happiness is, they disagree. . . .
>
> Aristotle, *Nicomachean Ethics*, 1095 a 15-20

Psychological happiness has become an unquestioned first principle of the present age. As a result, the cultivation of satisfaction, pleasure, and emotion now take precedence over the nurturing of moral and institutional character. There is nothing new about this view of happiness except for the fact that many of our generation seem to have forgotten its dangers and deceptions.

Few people remember that happiness was once understood in an entirely different way than it is now. The view of happiness known as eudaemonism began in the sixth century B.C. and lasted well into the eighteenth century. According to this tradition, named after the Greek word for happiness, *eudaimonia*, the mere claim to satisfaction is considered neither unquestionable nor irrefutable proof of a person's happiness. In other words, there is no state of feeling, enjoyment, pleasure, or self-consciousness that qualifies as happiness, whether to "feel good," to enjoy "peace of mind," or to be "satisfied."

Someone who understands happiness in the tradition of eudaemonism treats all claims to a happy life, including personal satisfaction and pleasure, as an occasion for moral appraisal. A happy person must be, in some sense, a morally good person. Judgments regarding happiness are based on character and action; they attempt to recognize a person's well-being as opposed to well-feeling.[1]

This book is about these two competing conceptions of happiness, whether we must choose one or the other, or whether some

bargain can be struck between them.[2] Those readers who cling tight-
ly to the promises of well-feeling will be challenged to loosen their
grip and reflect on its personal and social impact. For those readers who long ago gave up on happiness as an appropriate concern
for morally serious people, this book will help explain to them how
the idea of happiness has fallen to such a lowly state. It challenges
their dismissal with a reminder that the present meaning of happiness, although firmly entrenched, is the product of a relatively recent consensus.

The popular assumption that happiness is well-feeling can be
challenged by tracing the reasons for its gradual emergence out
of eudaemonism. A critical reconsideration of happiness in the light
of its history may persuade some advocates of well-feeling to
waver, in spite of the present consensus. There is no reason to believe that the wisdom of the past cannot be retrieved. To return to
the ancient meaning of happiness is not to say that the Greeks
lacked pleasure seekers, but to say that they knew successful pleasure seeking was not important enough to be the mark of a happy
life.

This book begins with a critique of well-feeling but culminates
in a description of happiness as an activity of loving and realizing
the real human good. As the principal condition of happiness, love
is the virtue of the will disposing a person toward an envisioned
goal of realization. The earthly realization of the good—gradual,
interminable, imperfect—entails both joy and suffering. The human
good gives priority to goods of the soul and the common good, since
without them the other goods, those of the body and external goods,
are misused. This realization that we can call a life happy is relative to an individual's natural capacity and historical circumstances.
Therefore judgments about happiness should be made in the light
of individual differences in capacity and circumstance. As it has been
said, "To whom much is given, much is required." These advantages and disadvantages in the pursuit of happiness include factors
of native endowments, family and community nurturing, education,
wealth, and economic opportunity. Happiness belongs to those who,
given their humanity and their circumstances, have distinguished
themselves to their friends by their steadfast and successful commitment to the life they envision.

In order to make the case that happiness is presently misunderstood a number of issues must be considered. First among them is
the relation of the happy life to morality; second is its relation to

the pain of misfortune. Readers accustomed to the present usage of happiness as well-feeling will already feel some misgivings about the appropriateness of referring to *the* happy life at all, given that happy lives, they assume, do not resemble one another beyond reports of self-satisfaction. Undoubtedly, the popular memory of the close connection between ethics and happiness has receded.

It is time to ask whether the psychological conception of happiness, given its present dominance, can bear the conceptual and existential weight placed on it (Part I, "Apprehensions"). In other words, can *well-feeling* remain our *happiness*? One might ask why there should be any doubts about its adequacy. The reason is simple: the concept of "happiness," in spite of present divergences from the classical tradition, still plays a large, though somewhat unrecognized, role in the habitual ways we direct our lives. This can be explained only by the residue of eudaemonism that still informs our thinking, despite the broad acceptance of psychological happiness (Part II, "Assessments").

The continued pursuit of happiness, in all of its forms, pervades the dispositions and decisions that direct private life and public policy, so that even in its vaguest conception, happiness shapes who we are and what kind of people we want to become. Some have argued that it would be best to excise all vestiges of a moral idiom from our language about happiness. To some extent, and especially for many schooled in this subject, this aim has been carried out for good or ill. By using the perspectives of classical and medieval happiness, this book draws attention to the dangers of valuing personal enjoyments and satisfactions to the exclusion of all other considerations of a happy life (Part III, "Reconsiderations"). A commentator introducing a study of St. Augustine on happiness has stressed the relevancy of the historical account: "We may in the process be reminded of something missing from the present, something we need to be reminded of. Now as then, it is a matter of determining a responsible concept of man and his realization."[3]

Nevertheless, it must be admitted that our culture is far removed from the perspective of the Greek and Latin cultures that regarded happiness—*eudaimonia*, *beatitudo*, and *felicitas*—as the summum bonum, the greatest good of human life. The ethics and politics of these cultures routinely prescribed, though not without disagreements, catalogues of virtue and codes of law with human happiness in mind (Chapter 4, "The Shadow of Eudaemonism"). Although we rarely appeal to these older traditions, we still find that such considerations about what will make us happy are at the core of our discourse, our thinking, and our choices about friends, family, lovers, work, play, politics, and religion.

The word happiness carries a heavy, and increasingly ignored, weight in our moral and political vocabulary, perhaps all the heavier because it is ignored. This residual trace of *eudaimonia* gives this project its initial plausibility, but in the long run it will take much more to broaden our reigning notion of happiness than an appeal either to the conventions of ordinary language or to the vestiges of a moral tradition, no matter how revered and sensible they may be. A eudaemonistic conception of happiness will be successfully revived, in my opinion, only by learning the lessons taught by the historical emergence and eventual renunciation of well-feeling (Chapter 3, "The Rejections of Psychological Happiness").

Despite its philosophical rejections, well-feeling made its way easily in those cultures that were increasingly concerned with charting the domain of subjectivity, the prerogatives of freedom, and the importance of affectivity. The new conception of happiness slowly became identified with the substance of happiness itself, first eroding the ancient tradition, then finally replacing it. In the face of well-feeling, the legacy of eudaemonism failed to dominate the moral consciousness of postmedieval culture. The reasons for this failure are many, but important among them is the inability of eudaemomism to articulate the place of suffering in the happy life (Chapter 8, "Happiness and Pain"). This failure was exacerbated in the Renaissance and Enlightenment, when the medieval happiness of heaven was translated into expectations about the terrestrial sphere (Chapter 9, "The Imperfection of Happiness"). The keys to correcting the problems of eudaemonism are to reject excessive intellectualism in the classical depiction of human nature, to affirm the imperfect nature of earthly happiness, and to recognize the central role of love in the dynamism of a happy life (Chapter 10, "The Passion of Happiness"). The present volume, therefore, not only exposes the dark side of well-feeling as a paradigm of human realization, but also treats the weaknesses in the tradition of eudaemonism itself.

Happiness may be conceived in terms of well-being or well-feeling or combinations of the same, but most thinkers have agreed that the *desire* for happiness cannot be avoided. Whether it is conceived in Freudian terms as gratification of instinctual urge, in Lockean terms as the sum of pleasures outweighing that of pains, or in Aquinas's terms as the intellectual vision of God, the pursuit of happiness appears to be an intractable fact of human nature. As a consequence, significant developments in the notion of happiness have evolved through a newly emerging view of human nature and society.

The development of democratic forms of government, for example, with their appeals to a principle of happiness for all, has created the expectation that whatever happiness may be, it must be made available *somehow* for every citizen to possess. If one asks what kind of happiness can be made available to everyone, well-feeling seems an obvious candidate. Americans are officially guaranteed the pursuit of happiness as one of their "inalienable rights." Our understanding of what Jefferson and the other Founders intended has proven to be a lasting puzzle: did he mean a happiness of well-feeling or something close to that? Jefferson's intellectual formation was shaped by both modern and premodern views of happiness and human nature—classical and Enlightenment thinkers. His ambiguous position in the history of the happiness question clearly presages our own dilemma (Chapter 5, "The Enigma of Jefferson's 'Pursuit'").

Happiness, love, justice, and freedom are the ideas that help us frame the meaning of human nature and the array of institutions that serve to ensure human survival and to encourage its flourishing. As the consensus on human nature has been lost, more and more ideas are often approached with an agnostic frame of mind, as in the question, "Who can say what happiness is for me?" In the meantime, and in spite of both the obscurity and the resistance, many people are turning to the self-help formulas of visualization and other mood-altering techniques, which at least have the advantage of making them feel better (Chapter 1, "Popular Views of Happiness"). All the while, unexamined notions of happiness remain embedded in our patterns of life. Perhaps its meaning is vaguely assumed because the word itself is so commonly spoken, yet this vagueness is precisely the problem because mistakes about happiness that stem from this vagueness can misdirect lives and wreck communities (Chapter 2, "The Case of Anna Karenina").

The increasing number of books and articles on happiness indicate a revival of interest in the subject. Today we are witnessing not just theories of the self-help variety but systematic treatises for specialists in philosophy and the social sciences. Readers will look in vain for much uniformity in these books about the meaning of the word *happiness*; a diversity of views has always existed in spite of systematic attempts to encompass the subject. The many meanings attached to the idea of happiness is the perennial challenge for authors and readers. Aristotle himself, whose *Nicomachean Ethics* remains the nemesis for all new theories of happiness, constructs his philosophical portrait of the happy life with the variety of popular opinions in mind: "Some say it is one thing and others another, and often the very same person identifies it with different things at different times: when he is sick he thinks it is health, and when he is poor he says it is wealth."[4] Perhaps the most influential treatment of happiness in modern times, Locke's *Essay on Human Understanding* (1689), also exhibits familiarity with the miscellaneous definitions of happiness in the marketplace: "For as pleasant Tastes depend not on the things themselves, but their agreeableness to this or that palate, wherein there is great variety: So the greatest Happiness consists, in having those things, which produce the greatest Pleasure. . . . Now these, to different Men, are very different things."[5]

Even though philosophers attempt to adjudicate among competing conceptions, they usually have recognized that happiness means different things to different people. To witness this awareness, one only has to glance through the Renaissance dialogues on happiness, in which characters representing conflicting views argue among themselves,[6] or through the standard catalogues of false happinesses that were prevalent in classical and medieval philosophy. A good example is St. Thomas Aquinas, who in his catalogue treats wealth, honor, fame, power, bodily goods, pleasure, psychic goods (e.g., knowledge). These are the primary "created" ends that people mistakenly pursue for the sake of happiness.[7] Aquinas, in devising such a list, carries forward a long tradition of bringing moral and spiritual discriminations to bear on claims to happiness, but the attempt to distinguish true from false happiness, to "correct their palates," as Locke puts it, does not blind the philosophers to the normal vagaries of pursuing happiness in everyday life. Some philosophical versions of happiness, however, as we shall see, may disassociate themselves from the concrete realities of day-to-day existence.

The evidence of renewed attention to the idea of happiness comes after a century of relative neglect. The tradition of reflection on happiness, which sought to distinguish the true from the false and to understand its nature and its causes, was a central preoccupation of philosophy, one of its "great ideas," until the middle of the last century. Furthermore, the reasons for the decline of interest in happiness lie deeply embedded in the earlier historical evolution of the concept itself. As the idea of happiness is beginning to preoccupy philosophers once again, however, critical attention to the popular and reigning notions of happiness remains scarce (Chapter 7, "A Typology of Recent Philosophical Views"). It was once thought that philosophy itself could not do anything else: St. Augustine wrote, "For man has no other reason for philosophizing than that he may be happy."[8] As a matter of fact, this renewed interest in happiness may be as important for revitalizing philosophy as it is for the very culture the philosopher seeks to serve. Happiness, as will be seen, may have lost much of its former currency among philosophers, but it is an idea that remains at the heart of our culture's self-understanding. So, too, philosophy has lost much of its relevance, its vital point of contact with everyday life.[9]

Certainly, another reason for revisiting the idea of happiness is its unique place in the cultural legacy of our collective past. Many values that were fundamental to the development of Western thinking about the human person and society relied heavily on the meaning attached to the happy life. Concepts of Greek and Roman virtue, medieval beatitude, Renaissance humanism, Enlightenment pleasure, and nineteenth-century political economy—as well as this century's happiness of well-feeling—all depended upon an accepted and articulated meaning of happiness for their influence, but even this inventory does scant justice to the importance of happiness, either as a professed ideal of moral and political conduct or simply as the most desirable of personal experiences. The sheer amount of historical reference on the history of happiness will undoubtedly resist the most relentless scholarly sifting. When Howard Mumford Jones wrote *The Pursuit of Happiness* (1953), he rightly remarked that a "history of happiness would be not merely a history of mankind, but also a history of ethical, philosophic, and religious thought,"[10] to which we must now add the burgeoning literature about happiness found in the social sciences. An investigation into the idea of happiness should not seek to avoid the story of its origins and evolution. The present study will attempt to jog some historical memories in order to set present claims about happiness into clear relief.

Broad statements such as those above may serve only to remind us of what we already know. What may be less apparent, given the general lack of historical knowledge, is the degree to which the meaning of happiness has changed and the consequence of that change. The widely accepted notion that happiness is a psychological state has prevailed for so long that people are surprised when they are reminded that happiness once had a more complex meaning.[11] It would be difficult to overstate the bafflement and the resistance of today's college students to considering the prepsychological conceptions of happiness. What frustrates their understanding of the Greek notion of *eudaimonia* or medieval *beatitudo* and *felicitas* is the strongly ethical content and tone of these earlier accounts. Once it becomes clear that, according to the dictates of this earlier tradition, persons cannot call themselves happy unless their lives satisfy some minimum moral requirement, students often become indignant, saying, "How can anybody tell me that I am or am not happy?" The fierceness of this response bears witness to the common unwillingness to examine our use of words and to submit our moral reasoning to the authority of an established tradition. We are more comfortable using morally benign words and phrases, such as *satisfaction, contentment,* and *peace of mind,* for which we are not likely to be called to account.

At first glance, a major problem in talking about happiness is the confusion caused by its two common and vastly different usages. In the first place, we utter the word *happy* to describe momentary and passing states of feeling or contentment. The occasion of being happy in this sense can result from anything from an unexpected snatch of beautiful music on the radio to a long-awaited visit with old friends. These experiences can be long or short, intense or serene, and can sometimes be reawakened by our memory of them. We can call ourselves happy at these times either because we are enjoying the presence of an object or immersion in an activity that delights us or because we are relieved by the removal of some burden or occasion of discomfort. This is not the type of happiness addressed in this volume.

Rather, attention is focused on the way happiness is used to justify the shape of our individual and corporate lives.[12] These justifications are heard when we report on how we estimate the success of our lives taken as a whole and whether we recommend a certain kind of life to others. "Am I happy?" is a question that can require appraising a job, a marriage, children, friends, and parents, as well as issues of personal lifestyle, moral values, and religious belief. As a consequence, questions about happiness can be explosive; they can signal the prelude to self-examination, decision, and change. Sometimes we ask ourselves if we are happy; sometimes one another. The latter case can be ticklish, because in the context of suffering, the question "Are you happy?" can seem the most prying of all, because it implies another question: "Do you want to remain in your present situation and work it through to a resolution?" Answering the question involves much more than a report on a state of feeling or even contentment, although that may enter into it. Life's fundamental commitments—our family and friends, our work, our responsibilities of citizenship—are not always the occasion of "felt" happiness, yet they are most assuredly, as will be argued, a part of a "happy life."

Happiness continues to serve as a dominant value in the ordering of both private and public life. In public and political terms the idea of happiness undergirds the concept of human rights in most Western nations, from the French "Declaration of the Rights of Man" (1789) to the United Nations "Universal Declaration of Human Rights" (1948). The promise of a public happiness is the "promissory note" that ignited and fueled the explosion of revolutionary ideologies.[13] In the United States, the right to "the pursuit of happiness" has been interpreted throughout the history of constitutional jurisprudence and continues to enter actively into the formation of public policy.[14] Such examples could, of course, be multiplied, and each of them serves to support the plausibility of Aristotle's original dictum that happiness (*eudaimonia*) is the final end for the sake of which everything else is done. "Honor, pleasure, intelligence, and all virtue we choose partly for themselves . . . but we also choose them for the sake of happiness, because we assume that it is through them that we will be happy."[15]

In ordinary conversation there should be no confusing the happiness of a "summer's day" with that of a life lived well, but problems arise when we do, when the value attached to a momentary pleasure or mental satisfaction assumes the place once afforded to the overall appraisal of a person's life. These problems range from specific issues of moral and political judgment to our ability to question the controlling images and metaphors regarding what constitutes a desirable human life, for example, when material consumption is elevated to the status of the highest good.

In both the ancient and medieval worlds philosophers representing different traditions agreed on the necessity of objective criteria for judging the content of a happy life. These "objective" conceptions of happiness, such as classical *eudaimonia*, allowed that an individual's life could be held up to the light and undergo the scrutiny and judgment of others concerning that person's claim to happiness. All of these criteria, particularly the requirement of moral virtue, have been largely rejected with the exception of one—the satisfied mind. Whether or not the possession of this subjective state is enough to justify calling a life happy, either our own or another's, is the central question addressed throughout this book.

Notes

1. The term *well-feeling*, suggested by Vincent Colapietro, is intended to cover subjective states of pleasure, enjoyment, positive moods, positive attitudes, satisfaction, contentment, peace of mind, and so on. *Well-being* can include well-feeling but not vice versa. Well-being always includes the possession of moral goodness, but may also include nonmoral goods or may extend to global appraisals of an individual life.

2. Richard Kraut develops this contrast but comes to a different conclusion in "Two Conceptions of Happiness," *The Philosophical Review* 138 (April 1979), 167–97. Another similar protest is made by Richard Taylor in "Ancient Wisdom and Modern Folly," *Midwest Studies in Philosophy* 13 (1988), 54–63, again toward a different outcome.

3. Werner Beierwaltes, *Regio Beatitudinis: Augustine's Concept of Happiness* (Philadelphia: Villanova University Press, 1981), 13.

4. Aristotle, *Nicomachean Ethics*, 1095 a 23–24 (6–7); page numbers in parentheses are to the Martin Ostwald translation, which is used throughout (Indianapolis: Bobbs-Merrill, 1962); hereafter cited as NE.

5. John Locke, *An Essay Concerning Human Understanding*, 2.21.55, ed. Peter Nidditch (New York: Oxford University Press, 1975), 269; page numbers are to this edition.

6. For example, Lorenzo Valla, *On Pleasure/De voluptate*, trans. A. Kent Hieatt and Maristella Lorch (New York: Abaris Books, Inc., 1977); and Ellis Heywood, *Il Moro*, ed. and trans. Roger Lee Deakins (Cambridge: Harvard University Press, 1972).

7. St. Thomas Aquinas, *Summa Theologiae*, 1-2.2.a.1-8. Reference will be made to the translation by the Fathers of the English Dominican Province, 3 vols. (New York: Benziger Brothers, 1947); herafter cited as ST.

8. St. Augustine, *The City of God*, 19.1 (671–72); page numbers in parentheses are to the translation by Marcus Dods (New York: Random House, 1950), which is used throughout.

9. A recent survey of ancient ethics makes a similar point about the advantage of a moral theory that begins with the commonsense concern for virtues, character, and happiness; see Julia Annas, *The Morality of Happiness* (New York: Oxford University Press, 1993), 10, 455.

10. Howard Mumford Jones, *The Pursuit of Happiness* (Cambridge: Harvard University Press, 1953), 65.

11. Jones, *The Pursuit of Happiness*, 65.

12. For relevant examples, see Robert Bellah, Richard Madsen, William M. Sullivan, Ann Swidler, and Stephen M. Tipton, *Habits of the Heart: Individualism and Commitment in American Life* (New York: Harper & Row, 1985).

13. Ghita Ionescu, *Politics and the Pursuit of Happiness: An Inquiry into the Involvement of Human Beings in the Politics of Industrial Society* (New York: Longman, 1984).

14. See Jones, ch. 2, and Charles Murray, *In Puruit of Happiness and Good Government* (New York: Simon and Schuster, 1988).

15. NE, 1097 b 1–5 (15).

Part I

Apprehensions

Chapter 1

Popular Views of Happiness

One of our great English writers, V. S. Naipal, a native of Trinidad, once published a brief but illuminating comment on happiness in *The New York Times*.[1] In explaining his preference for European civilization he credited the "guiding principles" of the West for discouraging the kind of collectivist terror seen in the spread of religious fanaticism throughout the Muslim world. Naipal singled out "the beauty of the idea of the pursuit of happiness," an idea his Hindu grandparents would not have understood, as containing the locus of his attraction to the West.

> It is an elastic idea; it fits all men. It implies a certain kind of awakened spirit. . . . So much is contained in it; the idea of the individual, responsibility, choice, the life of the intellect, the idea of vocation and perfectibility and achievement. It cannot be reduced to a fixed system. *It cannot generate fanaticism*. . . . (emphasis added)

Naipal's adoring tone is surprising. Granting the contrast with Muslim fundamentalists, his comments reveal nonetheless a certain naiveté of the role played by the idea of happiness in Western history and thought. One only has to point to the uses of happiness (*bonheur* and *felicité*) in the politics of the French Revolution and its legacy, spreading out from Jacobin rhetoric to infect the subsequent nineteenth-century political ideologies of Marxism and Stalinism that followed, to see that the "pursuit of happiness" was quickly channeled into totalitarian and collectivist manifestos.[2]

In fact, the very notion of the perfectibility of human beings and society mentioned by Naipal has generated highly volatile debates

3

in nearly every generation since classical antiquity.[3] Most of these
disputes were not played out on a public stage as large as the French
Revolution, yet they have had effects just as deep and lasting, and,
some would say, just as dangerous. The idea of happiness has generated not only highly recognizable public forms of fanaticism, but
also more commonplace ones, for example, in the absolute insistence regarding the utter privacy and inscrutability of claims to
personal happiness. Ambivalence, rather than unqualified adulation,
might be a more prudent response.

We meet these claims not only in our first-person reports, that
is, our claims of personal happiness, which will be discussed later,
but also in our attempts to settle practical disputes about other people. These third-person discussions often employ stock phrases, such
as, "As long as they're happy!" Appeals to happiness as a justifying principle permeate our everyday private conversation as well
as our public conversations carried on through news broadcasts and
talk shows. The setting in which the phrase is uttered is often the
same: two parties are either at odds or in a quandary about what to
think about somebody's behavior or lifestyle. Reasons are given back
and forth for their differences of opinion or for their confusion, until
finally one, with a tone of indisputable finality, expresses a sub-
junctive confidence in their future happiness.

Usually, these words bring an end to the conversation, as they
are intended to do. The bottom line having been reached, both parties agree to disagree or simply let the matter work itself out. Rarely
does the dispute go any further; it has become the custom not to
challenge someone else's claim to personal happiness. How often
is a challenge heard—outside the classroom, that is—to spell out
just what someone means by being *happy*? Our current assumptions
governing moral disputes discourage inquiry about this foundation-
al issue—anyone's claim to personal happiness is beyond reproach.

Conflicts arise, therefore, the moment one begins to raise questions about the content or cause of another person's happiness.
Immediately, the interlocutor, or even the merely curious, may well
be assailed with claims about the right to seek happiness, to define
it, and to enjoy it in his or her own way. No one, it seems, has the
authority to inquire beyond our common wish for everyone's "happiness." Further investigation will be met with the quickness of a
reflex action, one that defends the inscrutable and utterly private
territory within each person's life in which he or she pursues and
hopes to enjoy this end. Fanaticism like this in personal life can be

destructive and discouraging, running as it does throughout the daily intercourse of society and having been institutionalized in public policy.

One may ask why this claim of privacy should be considered destructive. Why consider it an objection to Naipal's tribute? The reason is simple: while making an appeal to the most desirable of life's outcomes, we are disallowing even the possibility of understanding and evaluating the happiness of others. By doing so, we have cut people loose from their moorings in their community and from their friends—we say, "Seek your happiness without our interference or our objections: *we* cannot know *you*, therefore we cannot help you." We have thus become agnostics about happiness in others, while still believing in its justifying power over the shaping of individual lives, especially the self. Each person is a law of happiness unto himself or herself. The possibilities of self-deception, aided and abetted by one's personal view of happiness, are endless. The ascription of living a happy life loses its public intelligibility and, instead, provides us with an excuse justifying any type of pursuit.

Such an unsavory situation elicits some obvious questions. If the idea of being happy still carries such momentous weight in evaluating our lives, should we not at least think about the kind of happiness we are recommending to others? Is it not entirely possible that our muteness in the face of the common appeal to happiness has involved us implicitly in disasters that we may have helped others, and ourselves, to avoid? Or do the responsibilities of friendship stop at specifying the limits of what kind of lives legitimately may be called happy?

Admittedly, this is a very large undertaking; it is but one more challenge to the liberal individualism taken for granted in contemporary society. The "inalienable right" to pursue happiness is viewed by many as the right that guarantees noninterference and, in particular, the right to avoid those who want to impose their view of happiness on others. Such endeavors appear as invasions of privacy to those who consider happiness a subjectively constituted state that nobody has the authority to enter or to question.

In this light, investigations of personal happiness also appear judgmental and presumptuous; they seem to overstep the boundaries of what can be known about the mystery of a human life and its subjective regions in particular. Of course investigations of happiness run the same gauntlet of criticism as other cardinal ideas on which we base our lives, such as love, justice, and freedom. Perhaps there is no way to address this resistance to examination without employing the indirection of a novelist.

Those who speak directly, however, need to explain (1) what is at stake if the present agnosticism continues; (2) what led us to adopt this belief; (3) what alternative views of happiness are available; and (4) what the reasons are for adopting another viewpoint. The crucial issue is that we admit that in its present usage *happiness recommends a way of life* and, therefore, cannot be considered immune to public scrutiny. By recognizing that the privatized happiness of well-feeling still plays a public role, we can overcome objections against treating it as a topic for philosophical reflection.

We need to begin by questioning the present willingness to ascribe happiness to almost any situation in which a person professes to be satisfied. This disposition can be compared to those times that were not so flagrant in descriptions of happy lives. For example, it has been suggested that this contrast can be observed in the difference between the happiness we wish for our children when they are young and our wishes for them when they grow older.[4] Our wishes for young lives do not include lives filled with divorce, drug use, infidelity, violence, and so forth; our early wishes exclude what appear to us then as obstacles to a happy life.

As children, however, grow older and disappoint our highest expectations, as we did those of our parents, our ideal of happiness becomes more flexible by becoming more subjective. We end up caring more about our children's mental and emotional state than certain states of character and external affairs—"As long as they're happy." The issue of what behavior or event *causes* happy feelings recedes. The popular usage of happiness has begun to run along the lines used toward the grown-up children.

Does this mean that the idea of happiness has been misshapen by the pressure of disappointment and a loss of hope? Many people would say that parents merely have become realistic in their expectations for their children. Children's lives are not perfect, and they have never conformed to parental dreams (not that fulfilling parent's dreams would make children perfect!). If realism is not taken into consideration when talking about happy lives, one risks assigning unhappiness to all but a very few—making happiness an unrealizable ideal. Too often this extreme has not been avoided, and all norms of judgment about happiness have been abandoned, but agnosticism must be avoided as well; it breeds a cynicism that justifies almost any action or any way of life under the umbrella of personal happiness.

This kind of uncritical tolerance becomes possible when being happy is reduced to nothing more than subjective satisfaction. Issues such as personal character, values, attainments, responsibility, and citizenship pale in the light of the overarching concern for inner contentment and freedom from pain. While no one doubts the desirability of these states, we may ask whether they should really be valued apart from the issue of how they were obtained. Satisfaction in what? Peace in what kind of circumstances?

In the present rush to feel and think positively about ourselves, we sometimes forget that it is often dissatisfaction and even pain that spur us toward the kind of introspection and moral correction that hope in the future requires. As shall be seen, the totally privatized happiness of subjective satisfaction has encouraged the narcissistic individualism already documented in American culture. There is no doubt that well-feeling has had a major role in preparing and maintaining the American mind for its drug culture as well. A drug "high" represents the moral paucity and personal tragedy harvested by the flowering of well-feeling as our ideal of the best human life.

It could be argued that the utterance "as long as they're happy" is simply a way of wishing people well, of accepting and of supporting their choices, and of hoping that they turn out well. Certainly these are good intentions, but the actual outcome needs reconsideration. Isn't it true that in many cases these words become a way of avoiding the more difficult job of grappling with the probable outcomes of our life choices? Or is it a way of remaining content with our own confusion about the purposes of human life? Are we actually helping other people, or ourselves, by using happiness in such a blind fashion? The idea of happiness was never meant to be applied as a kind of moral anesthesia to any situation that was too close to call. If this has become the reigning usage that is already too firmly embedded in the linguistic terrain to uproot, then perhaps we should consider putting a stop to wishing happiness for our children and our friends.

Fortunately, this is not yet the case. There are clear indications that people are ready for another look at happiness and its pursuit, that society is questioning those ideals and social arrangements that inflate the value of individualism, encourage the breakup of communities, and scoff at the purposes laid before us by the inherited paradigm of a common humanity. The mere wish for happiness in any form will soon lose its unimpeachable status.

Indeed, before proposing the ideal of happiness as the key to appreciating the attraction of the West, Naipal should have noticed that some contemporary developments suggest a more sober tribute. As shall be seen, Thomas Jefferson and the other American philosophers and jurists who gave happiness and its pursuit pride of place in the founding documents were aware of its shortcomings, in part because they were aware of the long and varied history of happiness as an ideal. By reflecting on the pursuit of happiness in light of its critics and its history, one can avoid Naipal's mistake of overlooking the dangers that infest the enjoyment of this American privilege.

From what has been said, it would seem that the topic of happiness is very difficult to address: conversation about it inevitably comes to an impasse. As we will see, warnings about the Western pursuit of happiness have been forthcoming for more than two hundred years; the message is basically that happiness has become an excuse for a self-consuming decadence and a disdain for public responsibility. A short stroll through the local bookstore, replete with books, tapes, and videos promoting how to be happy, suggests little awareness of the danger in pursuing happiness. Everyone from New Age channelers to old-style positive thinkers make a business out of selling personal happiness; they speak in unison of happiness without moral or social reform, a life of lasting pleasure and satisfaction resting contentedly in its own thought of itself.

For better or for worse, the idea of happiness is now firmly ensconced at the heart of popular culture; to which many will reply, "What is wrong with that?" If happiness is for everyone, if its pursuit is everyone's right and its end everyone's purpose, then surely it is natural that happiness be as widely discussed as possible. Is this objection just another example of a conflict between high and low culture, the professoriate trying to reclaim one of its lost privileges? To the contrary, one could argue that the privatization of happiness by its transformation into well-feeling has destroyed forever the eudaemonistic ideas of personal virtue, public citizenship, and the contemplative life.

Psychological happiness seems made to order for a democratic and inclusive age; it provides everyone equal access to the most desirable of human experiences, one no longer the sole province of the scholar, the monk, or the world-denying saint. The actual consequence, however, has been the placement of personal happiness into the less reliable hands of the self-help vendors, those purveyors of intellectual fashion.

Whatever one may offer as a critique of these popular views of happiness, it must be kept in mind that over the past fifty years the discourse of academic philosophy, and that of the rest of the humanities, has grown increasingly inaccessible to the ordinary layperson. Only a few decades ago there were notable philosophers who did not consider it beneath themselves to address the layperson. Perhaps their space on the philosophy shelf has been taken over by the self-help authors. Even if someone were to take the trouble to look into the literature about happiness among philosophers and social scientists, the ordinary reader would very likely find it difficult to follow. From this perspective at least one could say that the burgeoning literature of "pop happiness" is filling the vacuum left by academics who now write only for one another.

The problem remains that most popular writing about happiness lacks historical and critical perspective. The reader will look in vain for any awareness of the eudaemonistic meaning that happiness carried for two millenia. Various sorts of well-feeling have emerged without challenge as the norm for happiness in the popular literature, a development that has effectively reversed the historical relationship of happiness to well-being: the ancients argued whether or not *the* happy life required anything other than moral virtue, for example, pleasure—while our contemporaries sometimes wonder whether any criterion other than psychological satisfaction is needed.

If one were to accept the popular assumptions about the nature of happiness, the most germane question would be whether we should call satisfaction "happiness" when it lacks ethical justification,[5] but this would require accepting the notion that happiness itself can be wholly identified with a satisfied state. It would seem that this identification was the watershed event in the history of the concept.

The paradigm of subjective happiness or well-feeling has trivialized the notion of a happy life. Indeed, the philosopher who some would say is the most responsible for the present situation, John Stuart Mill, was himself apprehensive about the consequences of his own utilitarian approach to the issue of happiness. Although he argued that happiness is to be identified with maximizing pleasure, especially the high pleasures such as mental satisfaction, he remarked that it was "better to be a human being dissatisfied than a pig satisfied; better to be Socrates dissatisfied than a fool satisfied."[6] Mill's inability to stem the tide of pig-happiness encouraged by his own principle of utility epitomizes the problems facing popular versions of happiness: how do you begin with the identification of happiness with well-feeling and then seek to qualify it through the addition of an ethical justification? The criterion that once was considered the foundation of a happy life now has become an addendum.

If happiness has itself become identified with satisfaction, it still contains traces of its eudamonistic background. To be judged happy once required the embodiment of some moral value. The criterion of value that has replaced moral virtue in the imagining of a happy life is the idea of *positive* living. Although such expressions as "being positive" or "thinking positively" are taken almost for granted, they are useful in understanding the popular meaning of happiness. Such expressions became common in American culture with the popularity of figures such as Norman Vincent Peale, whose amalgamation of Protestantism, psychoanalysis, and Madison Avenue was a virtual talisman for several generations of middle-class Americans. Peale's books are filled with prescriptions for upbeat resolutions to the unconscious conflicts that keep us from drawing on the energy for a successful and happy life. Reading through Peale's books, one is struck by their geniality, their confidence, and their capacity to soothe the anxious inquirer. It seems almost mean-spirited to take issue with them, or with the entire genre for that matter.

Peale typically promises a lasting happiness by overcoming subconscious emotional conflicts. Healing the subconscious through psychiatric help and a religious faith can solve any problem and help the way to financial prosperity.[7] In considering what, if anything, could possibly be wrong with such a message, we must also bear in mind that numerous people report that positive thinking helped them find the happiness they sought. Peale's prescriptions are so simple and his promises so grandiose that one wonders, however, how much *un*happiness they may have generated.

His promises are refuted everyday by the tragic realities of the world, that not all are born into a class with relatively easy access to prosperity, that some are born without health and all of their faculties intact, or, that our most earnest efforts can be subverted by bad luck. In fact, given that Peale's readers were being made supposedly invulnerable to life's tragic, uncontrollable dimensions, one wonders how much his books actually created a dialectic of denial and disappointment when the experience of life actually forced unsuccessful people to admit their finitude. One wonders also how many of Peale's success stories came at the cost of disengagement with any realities that prompted negative thoughts.

Peale's method was and still is typical of self-help writers, a thin layer of old wisdom, in his case Protestant Christianity, bent and twisted to suit the intellectual fad of the day—psychoanalysis (itself barely recognizable next to Freud)—and finished off with stirring illustrative stories about successful people, once miserable but now happily reunited with their subconscious energies.

The formula has hardly changed in the half century since positive thinking came on the scene. Dennis Wholey, television host and self-help writer, recently recruited more than fifty celebrity contributors, from Leo Buscaglia and Willard Scott to Richard Simmons and Malcolm Forbes, for his reflection on *Are You Happy? Some Answers to the Most Important Questions in Your Life*. Once again the accent is on simplicity of means and availability of ends. "No one finds happiness after a long search," the author declares at the outset, but he then follows this statement with a comment that exemplifies the amount of self-contradiction readers of these books must be willing to allow:

> Happiness comes to us as the direct result of positive self-worth, personal attitudes, specific actions, and the way in which we relate to other people. Freedom to be ourselves, good feelings, satisfaction, contentment, peace of mind, joy, laughter, and happiness are the rewards of life. They are available to us for the doing—not for the wishing, asking, or demanding.[8]

This supposed clarification is followed by a confirming illustration, this time Wholey's own story of overwork, ambition, and alcoholism redeemed by the happiness of overcoming his inner conflict and selfishness.

In the aftermath of his recovery Wholey began talking to people about happiness, finding out that

> There seem to be two kinds of people: positive or negative; happy or sad; participants or spectators. Happy people are optimistic and know

that feeling good is the way you are supposed to feel. . . . Unhappy
people always seem to want something different. . . . [They are] con-
sumed by anger and resentment. They are critical of others; they live
in fear; they worry and they procrastinate; they wallow in self-pity and
depression; they try to change other people instead of themselves.[9]

Even the skeptical reader can recognize the good sense in these
words and in other similarly good advice throughout the self-help
approaches to happiness, but first one should notice the unquestioned
assumption of happiness as well-feeling and second, the thick black
line painted between those who have the know-how to feel good
and those who do not. Serious problems arise with both character-
izations.

The prevailing psychological wisdom is no longer Freudian, so
the jargon throughout Wholey's book is less psychoanalytic than it
is a mishmash of suggestions for unconditional love, acceptance,
responsibility, and commitment. These are of course all good ideas
for any life, happy or not, but the overall coherence of Wholey's
approach begins to break down when he fails to notice that his pre-
scription of feeling good has been strongly qualified by his ab-
horence of self-centeredness, which we are told is an obstacle to
happiness. As it turns out, Wholey has complete confidence in the
providential structure of our moral affections—that self-centered-
ness will bring misery. For the readers, who have been encouraged
to pursue good feelings before all else, it may not be intuitively
obvious that selfish acts always lack emotional relish.

Again, the issue is not with his recommendation of living for
others, but with his assumptions that we will always receive good
feelings as a result and that those who are selfish will always be
punished with negative feelings. As with the case of Peale, neither
the world nor human emotion work quite so providentially for forces
of good and against the forces of evil. To say that your conscience
should be your guide is not the same as saying that well-feeling
should be your guide. Wholey and his fellow contributors clearly
want happiness to follow from a generous and active character, but
they fail to take into account that well-feeling, that is, the satisfied
mind, can and does belong to the wicked as well as the good.[10]

Popular accounts of happiness want to have it both ways; they
want the happiness of feeling good and they want it to be the fruit
of socially beneficial behavior, but they do not want to let these
criteria interfere with their account of what happiness is. This constitutes evidence for the trivialization of happiness in popular cul-

ture. No one wants to restrict the happy life to the parameters of the morally good life, but many are willing to restrict happiness to what is regarded as *positive*. The notion of positivity as a value, like well-feeling itself, is morally neutral; it can be conjoined to diverse kinds of characters and actions. A criminal can pursue a crime in a positive frame of mind in order to ensure its outcome. He can then experience the well-feeling of successfully planning and executing, say, a burglary, not to mention possibly enjoying the illegal act.

In fact, the appearance of psychological happiness shorn of all its moral limitations came into being alongside the notion of positivity as a value. Philosophers and scientists of the nineteenth century used the term positive to represent a rejection of the abstract ideals of speculative philosophy and a move toward a concrete and social form of thinking. A positive philosophy aimed at transforming human behavior and human institutions. The mathematical connotation of positivity, in addition to that which is actually concrete, implies the possibility of quantification, thus making the world susceptible to empirical and historical investigation.[11] Auguste Comte, the French philosopher whose work is most identified with the emphasis on positivity, attempted to use that connotation as a program of social pragmatism. The idea of the positive took on the meaning of value, however, which has resulted in the idolatry of techniques capable of bringing about desirable effects and shortcutting the creation of stable foundations, whether in personal or national character.

For the practitioner of happiness, these techniques offer ways of creating and maintaining mental and emotional "highs" that are free from the nagging inhibition of depression, guilt, or remorse. In his survey of the positive-thinking tradition in America, sociologist Donald Meyer traces the evolution of these techniques from the nineteenth-century psychology of the "mind cure," through the movements of Christian Science and Unity, to their entrance into the Protestant mainstream represented by Peale and Robert Schuller.[12] Much of what Meyer discusses concerning the "psychology of auto-manipulation" and its methods of "mental photography," which is now called "visualization," is directly applicable to popular American beliefs about psychological happiness, its conditions, and its causes.

Positive thinking, as Meyer shows, encourages its adherents to turn inward for all the answers to their discontent; consequently, positive thinking risks denying the tragic, implacable character of much evil and suffering. It also tends to overlook the therapeutic and instrumental value of suffering. By their withdrawal into the self, positive thinkers buy contentment at the cost of contact with reality, particularly the very social reality that Comte sought to elucidate. The notion of happiness generated by this tradition insulated the self from the disturbances of the world. As William James writes, "Happiness, like every other emotional state, has blindness and insensibility to opposing facts given it as its instinctive weapon for self-protection against disturbance."[13] One can ask whether the kind of self-deceiving figures seen in Tolstoy's *Anna Karenina* and Flaubert's *Madame Bovary* would now find themselves saved from their tragic fates by the application of mind-cure, and positive-thinking techniques. Perhaps that way out has already been shown to lead toward the even greater blindness of Willy Loman in Arthur Miller's *Death of a Salesman*.

This confidence in a self-induced happiness achieved through "positivity" is the common denominator in the enormous popular literature on happiness, but some people will inevitably say that it is easy to pick on examples such as Peale and Wholey; surely there are more sophisticated examples of such writing. Three of the best in the genre, using a nonempirical approach to happiness, were written between the two world wars. They represent in its most elegant form what Meyer would call the mind-cure approach, and, it should be noted, they foreshadow the position that academic theorists would adopt in the 1950s and 1960s.

Bertrand Russell could certainly not plead ignorance to the classical tradition of happiness. Yet when he wrote *The Conquest of Happiness* he held that the cardinal virtue underlying happiness was not prudence, or love, or moderation but *zest*—"the most universal and distinctive mark of happy men."[14] His book does not lack good advice about enjoying one's work, family, and hobbies, avoiding "Byronic unhappiness" and everyday worry, and cultivating independence of mind and individual responsibility. He regards himself as a hedonist whose recommendations are largely the same as those of the moralist, but who thinks that the "state of mind" should be stressed over the "act" that might lead to the state.[15] Russell rejects the stability of moral character or the universality of a moral standard in favor of unpremeditated moral impulse. Indeed, the state of happiness is a "conquest" of the energetic and independent minded over forces of moral and spiritual gravity in the world, particularly those of organized religion and its doctrines of guilt and original sin.

More recently, Russell's attitude toward traditions of authority has been expressed once again by Paul Kurtz, who describes happiness as a "Promethean" endeavor to promote our "power" as a person. Kurtz, who is well known as a defender of secular humanism, supports his argument with the familiar language and inflated promises of self-help: "As man enters the Space Age, the possibilities of adventure for the soaring human spirit are virtually unlimited."[16] Rhetoric of this kind, which seems to evade the tragic implications of personal limitations, misfortune and social conditions, is typical of happiness books written for the popular market. Personal freedom allied with personal preference is writ large as the key to self-satisfaction.

Another tendency of these books is to cloak their techniques in the language of magic and mysticism. The novelist John Cowper Powys was not shy about taking his philosophy of self-exaltation to a broader market. His *Art of Happiness* represents in many ways the apotheosis of the positive thinking approach. Powys encourages his reader to use "the magic of the mind" to produce the "Ichthian" and "panegyric act" of "de-incarnation," which is happiness.[17] Indeed, Powys wholeheartedly recommends the very act of dissociation that Donald Meyer warned against among the prophets of the mind-cure: "Project your soul from your troubled brain, or *pretend* to yourself that you project it."[18] Few writers in this genre are as open and consistent in pressing the logic of a self-induced happiness to its conclusion. For Powys happiness has nothing to do with the perfection of natural capacities: happiness is artificial and can be furnished by any kind of mental trick that provides us release from painful reality. This book is filled with recommendations of a total reliance on will and imagination without any apparent concern for the possible cost of personal denial and social isolation.

The same trust in the efficacy of "mental magic" over circumstances is seen in a French contemporary of Powys and Russell, the philosopher Emile Chartier. Chartier, under the pseudonym Alain, wrote a series of newspaper articles about happiness for the general public. Ninety-three of them were published in a book that, like Powys's, recommends practical techniques on how to "will one's happiness, and create it."[19] His suggestions range from better posture to wearing a constant smile to never dwelling on or even talking about one's misfortunes. Most of all, Alain insists, one should never allow sadness to detract from sociability: "Everyone seeks to live, not die; and everyone seeks out the living—by that I mean those who *say* they are happy, and who *appear* happy. What a marvelous thing human society would be if everyone put his wood on the fire instead of sniveling over the ashes."[20] Alain's notion of encouraging happy lives resembles, as does Powys's, a somewhat twisted version of Stoic tranquillity. We are directed to cultivate mental and emotional repose through close attention to mundane tasks combined with self-conscious methods of controlling thoughts, images, and moods. Tranquillity is achieved not as the concomitant of virtue, as for the Stoics, but as the result of technique.

Of course, any criticism of these books risks sounding harsh: Why question the wisdom of such positive sounding advice? What harm can there be in managing our daily habits of thought and action in ways that result in more good cheer about our lives? Such books, and now tapes and videos, have a devoted following, and admittedly, possess some practical solutions to transitory problems of mood and fatigue, but the absence of any serious consideration to the moral consequences implicit in their recommendations leaves a large gap between these books and their classical counterparts. Folk nostrums and personal prescriptions for feeling good reduce the human desire for happiness to a craving for subjective satisfaction.

It is obvious to anyone who follows these trends that self-help techniques for momentary psychological relief raised to the level of a philosophy of happiness cannot satisfy that desire for happiness for very long. Most of these books suffer from an overmagnification of basic common sense. In other words, these authors take what in small doses is good advice and make too large a theory out of it, one that simply cannot do all the philosophical work required by the subject of happiness. And despite those who claim these books do help, there is the sad fact that most of them will quickly go out of print, while the unhappy reader eagerly waits to consume the next one.

It has been shown that, as a consequence of its association with psychological satisfaction, the simple mention of the topic of happiness is met with either skepticism or disdain and dismissal. Some consider talk about happiness a veiled excuse for doing whatever one feels like doing, regarding happiness as a morally unstable guide for living. They claim that the pursuit of happiness not only trivializes more sober and earnest purposes of life, but that also it risks introducing an unbridled and potentially aggressive self-centered-ness into our moral judgment and action. In an age when happiness is being hawked by just about everyone, it is difficult not to give some credence to these warnings. The hucksters of happiness promise a happy life without moral reform, a life of lasting pleasure and satisfaction resting contentedly in its own thought of itself. This seems to be precisely the message that many people want to hear and are willing to pay for.

The evidence indicates that the problems inherent in the overlapping traditions of happiness as the summum bonum and as psychological satisfaction have bequeathed an explosive conflict of meanings to the present age. What has become the unacknowledged greatest good in the public mind—subjective satisfaction—has been shown since the last half of the eighteenth century to be a questionable moral and political end. How and when happiness slipped free of its ethical moorings in classical thought and became an "Ichthian act" of "personal power" is impossible to pinpoint. It has not gone without comment, however, that some kernel of the same ambiguity was built into the American character at its foundation. Exactly what was Jefferson proposing by a right to the "pursuit of happiness"? It must be evident how radical the difference would be between his meanings if Jefferson had the eudaemonism of Aristotle clearly in mind along with the "greatest amount of pleasure" happiness of John Locke and Frances Hutcheson.

The problems inherent in the psychological happiness of well-feeling are not limited to the middlebrow quality of self-help literature or to the techniques of dissociation encouraged by positive thinkers; those problems underlie much of the disorder and suffering of our private life, and they help explain the reluctance to sacrifice the energies aimed at private consumption for the sake of service to the common good.

Notes

1. *The New York Times*, 5 November 1990, op-ed page.
2. Ghita Ionescu, *Politics and the Pursuit of Happiness: An Inquiry into the Involvment of Human Beings in the Politics of Industrial Society* (New York: Longman, 1984), 105–12.
3. See John Passmore, *The Perfectibility of Man* (London: Gerald Duckworth, 1970).
4. Richard Kraut, "Two Conceptions of Happiness," *The Philosophical Review* (April 1979): 189.

5. In his recent *summa* of happiness Wladyslaw Tatarkiewicz, while showing an obvious affinity for both eighteenth-century hedonistic and twentieth-century psychological accounts, argues that satisfaction must nonetheless be justified; see *Analysis of Happiness*, trans. Edward Rothert and Danuta Zielinskn (The Hague: Martinus Nijhoff, 1986), 15–18.

6. J. S. Mill, *Utilitarianism* (Indianapolis: Bobbs-Merrill, 1957), 14.

7. Norman Vincent Peale and Smiley Blanton, *The Art of Real Happiness* (New York: Prentice Hall, 1950). For a critique of Peale and more recent self-help figures, see Wendy Kaminer, *I'm Dysfunctional, You're Dysfunctional: The Recovery Movement and Other Self-Help Fashions* (New York: Addison-Wesley Publishing Company, 1992).

8. Dennis Wholey et al., *Are You Happy? Some Answers to the Most Important Question in Your Life* (Boston: Houghton Mifflin Company, 1986), 3.

9. Wholey et al., p. 6.

10. This point, of course, is the substance of Kant's critique of eudaemonism; see Chapter 3.

11. For a succinct overview of this development, see Abraham Edel, "Happiness and Pleasure, *Dictionary of the History of Ideas* (New York: Scribner's, 1973), 374–87.

12. Donald Meyer, *The Positive Thinkers: Popular Religious Psychology from Mary Baker Eddy to Norman Vincent Peale and Ronald Reagan* (Middletown, Conn.: Wesleyan University Press, 1988; revised ed.).

13. Cited in Meyer, 322.

14. Bertrand Russell, *The Conquest of Happiness* (New York: Horace Liverright, 1930), 158.

15. Russell, *The Conquest of Happiness*, 247.

16. Paul Kurtz, *Exuberance: An Affirmative Philosophy of Life* (Buffalo, N.Y.: Prometheus Books, 1978), 21.

17. John Cowper Powys, *The Art of Happiness* (New York: Simon and Schuster, 1935), 69, 95.

18. Powys, *The Art of Happiness*, 47; emphasis added.

19. Emile Chartier, *Alain on Happiness*, trans. Robert D. and Jane E. Cottrell (New York: Frederick Ungar, 1973), 248; originally published in 1928 as *Propos sur le bonheur.*

20. Chartier, *Alain on Happiness*, 245–6; emphasis added.

Chapter 2

The Case of *Anna Karenina*

"Happy families are all alike; every unhappy family is unhappy in its own way." This opening line from Tolstoy's *Anna Karenina* (1875) remains the best-known challenge to the happiness of well-feeling. Exactly what qualities Tolstoy thought were alike in happy families is certainly debatable. If one were attempting to specify those qualities, they would likely reside in the moral or spiritual attainment of personal character, one that keeps individuals firmly committed to ideals and immune to the passions and diversions that drag down Tolstoy's unhappy characters.[1] Here we are interested only in how the action of the novel exposes Anna's false claim to happiness and gradually reveals the misery that led to her suicide.

Tolstoy's portrayal of Anna's unhappiness presents a stronger case against subjective happiness than it does for any particular theory of happiness, including the author's own. Although literature lacks the cachet of science or immediate experience, it is in such books, nonetheless, that we can continue to encounter characters who teach us about virtue, vice, and all the ambiguities of the human in-between.[2] Taken at face value, the opening line of *Anna Karenina* states the issue that most concerns Anna, her husband Alexey, son Seryozha, lover Vronsky, brother Stephan, sister-in-law Dolly, and Dolly's sister Kitty and Kitty's husband Levin. As much as the novel is about infidelity, deceit, and the possibilities of genuine love, it is also about people pursuing happiness in a world entering modernity and awkwardly adjusting to the erosion of long-established and rigidly structured social relationships.

The topic of happiness emerges not only out of Anna's escape from the misery of a marriage to a man she does not love, but also out of the many subplots: Alexey's pietistic embrace of spiritualism in reaction to Anna's desertion; Levin's esteem for his peasants and his adjustment to married life; Kitty's recovery from being jilted by Vronsky through the mediation of Varenka; Dolly's repeated attempts to remain with her lecherous husband Stephan. The novel is as much about the many ways of finding unhappiness as it is about the possibility of knowing and possessing the happiness that is "alike." Consequently, the narrator must assume that, at least in some cases, true and false claims to happiness are distinguishable and that the reader knows how to recognize them.

What makes the case of Anna Karenina significant for a critique of subjective happiness is that Tolstoy's narrator relies on the willingness of the reader to see through Anna's false claims and her self-deception. In other words, if the contemporary reader, one hundred years after the publication of the novel, has completely accepted happiness as well-feeling, then he or she should be unable to understand the dramatic action of the novel. The reader who is unwilling to hear such claims to happiness described as fraudulent and self-deceiving will be left untouched and baffled by Anna's gradual discovery of her misery and her eventual suicide. The identification of happiness with well-feeling makes any reading of *Anna Karenina* almost incomprehensible and may even lead the reader to accuse both the narrator and some of the characters of being judgmental toward Anna.

In one of the central scenes of the novel (part 6, chapters 17-24), Dolly visits the country home of Anna and Vronsky, some years after Anna has left Moscow and deserted her husband and son. This visit ironically parallels the opening episodes of the novel, which depict the visit of Anna to Dolly's home in order to help heal a breach between her brother and Dolly. Dolly wishes now that she had not taken Anna's advice; she admires Anna for taking steps to put an end to her domestic misery with Alexey. "Anna did quite right, and certainly I shall never reproach her for it. She is happy, she makes another person happy, and she's not broken down as I am. . . " (651).[3] Dolly's arrival has been preceded by a long period of fantasizing about following in Anna's footsteps out of an unhappy marriage and into the bliss of romantic love.

The visit proves Dolly wrong; little by little the evidence mounts that Anna's life, rather than being enriched by her love affair, has become superficial. During their first chance to talk alone, Anna confirms Dolly's fantasy by reporting several times that she is "inexcusably happy" and commends at some length the joys of her life with Vronsky and their daughter Annie. As they enter the nursery and Dolly begins to question Anna about her child, she notices "that Anna, the two nurses, and the child had no common existence, and that the mother's visit was something exceptional. Anna wanted to get her baby her plaything, and could not find it." Embarrassed, she admits to her sister-in-law that she often feels "superfluous" in the nursery, to which Dolly replies, "I expected it the other way" (662).

Later in the day Dolly's romantic picture of Vronsky and Anna crumbles further as Dolly becomes irritated by the "fashionable tone" used by Anna and her circle. Then, as Vronsky takes Dolly aside, hoping that she can talk to Anna about obtaining a divorce, his strained demeanor, coupled with his complaints about being alienated from society, cause a "moment" of doubt to enter Dolly's mind concerning Anna's happiness (670). Yet, like Anna, Vronsky repeatedly insists on the happiness of their life together. Confused by the combination of Vronsky's insecurity about the future and his effusions about the present, Dolly agrees to talk to Anna while "she remembered that Anna drooped her eyelids just when the deeper questions of life were touched upon" (672).

Dolly has not found the adulterous couple sharing the romantic dream she had imagined for herself. She decides to return home the next morning, a day earlier than planned, but that evening, after dinner conversation that to Dolly appears alternately arrogant and supercilious, she returns to her room, finding herself drawn back to the very family responsibilities she had previously wanted to escape. The final revelation of Anna's actual state of mind occurs when she visits Dolly's room later that evening. The discussion turns to Anna's insistence on not having any more children.

> "What is reason given me for, if I am not to use it to avoid bringing unhappy beings into the world! . . . I should always feel I had wronged these unhappy children," she said. "If they are not, at any rate they are not unhappy; while if they are unhappy, I alone should be to blame for it." (683)

Although in these words Dolly recognizes her own thoughts about her marriage and her children, she no longer is persuaded by her former logic.

"How can one wrong creatures that don't exist?" she thought. And all
at once the idea struck her: could it possibly, under any circumstances,
have been better for her favorite Grisha, *if he had never existed?* And
this seemed to her so wild, so strange, that she shook her head to drive
away this tangle of whirling, mad ideas. "No, I don't know; it's not
right," was all she said, with an expression of disgust on her face. (683;
emphasis mine)

Then, as the two square off over the question of children and
Vronsky's desire for a divorce, Anna suddenly loses her veneer of
gaiety in the face of Dolly's mounting disapproval. An anguished
confession begins to pour out, in pathetic contrast to their earlier
conversation. As the layers of self-deception peel off, Anna recognizes she is forever torn between love for her son Seryozha and
her love for Vronsky. Only a few hours earlier she sat with Dolly,
who was clearly lost in admiration for her state, in the same guest
room bragging about her happiness with Vronsky. Now, drawn out
by the noticeable change in Dolly's attitude, she completes the reversal, saying, "Don't despise me, I don't deserve contempt. I'm
simply unhappy. If anyone is unhappy, I am" (685), and she retreats
to her room for her nightly draught of a morphine solution.

The scene illustrates the way our judgments about other people's happiness are often made. First, Dolly notices in Anna a self-
conscious vanity, reinforced by her new circle of friends, that was
previously not to be found in her speech or her behavior. Second,
the strong woman who was once able to manage Dolly's home in
time of crisis has assumed the role of an ornamental mistress barely engaged in any part of the home beyond dressing herself and
entertaining her guests. Third, the excessiveness of this self-con-
cern, as expressed in her attitude toward children, is finally revealed
as a disguise for despair, which is magnified by her repeated deni-
als. Dolly's thoughts are believable to the reader because like the
reader, she is part of a "public" that knows Anna well enough to
infer the painful inner division caused by her circumstances.

Judgments about happiness, except in extreme instances, call for
a degree of intimacy requisite to knowing how a person's life has
developed. Not everyone is able to see that Anna's superficial chat-
ter about being happy is among her habits of avoidance. Thus,
Dolly's judgment about Anna's happiness depends on her status as
an involved observer who knows Anna's previous habits of character and expressed values. Given her standpoint, Dolly can plausibly

judge her friend's behavior as out of character, which, therefore, places her integrity at risk.

Internal consistency or the maintenance of a stable character, of course, is not the only issue at stake in this happiness judgment. One could imagine someone picking up Anna's own defense of her actions as being for the better, arguing that this unhappiness stems from true love rather than domestic convention. Yes, Anna's character is changing, it might be argued, but she has succeeded in exercising greater freedom and autonomy over her circumstances. As Dolly sees it, however, Anna's choices have backfired: she now has less freedom, less personal authority, and less reason to live than she had in her unhappy marriage. Anna's decision to undergo sterilization, to wish no more fecundity to her love with Vronsky, sadly convinces Dolly that her friend's character and vision of life are now diminished.

The narration is made especially powerful by the fact that Dolly, initially biased by her own unhappiness, is very willing to believe Anna's claim, but Dolly quickly grows skeptical. The reader discovers through Dolly's eyes what was obliquely known, namely, that Anna and Vronsky's talk about happiness is escapist and self-deceiving. Dolly's appraisal of their happiness expresses a deeply felt concern for the fate of an old friend, while also serving as an avenue for becoming clear about her own future. Her judgment exemplifies how claims to happiness, whether they are those of the subject or of an observer, are often heard not only as reports but also as recommendations. As Gregory Vlastos puts it, among the Greek moralists the appeal to eudaimonia was always the "question stopper"; beyond this justification for an intention or an action one did not need to go.[4] Happiness as the proper end of life was taken for granted. The question was what this end consisted in, which demonstrates once again how the question of happiness, conceived eudaemonistically, directs us to the question of a common human nature. Thus, to speak in any eudaemonistic terms of a happy life was implicitly to recommend certain aspects of that life to others.

This scene is also an instance of how reports of happiness are complicated by mood, tactics of avoidance and denial, and changes in the angle of self-scrutiny. The validity of self-reported data, now commonly used in the social sciences, is only one of the many issues raised by the conflict between subjective and objective conceptions of happiness. To uphold subjective happiness one must limit oneself to description, withholding all third-person judgments, of a person's pleasure, enjoyment, or, most commonly, a satisfied state of mind. While satisfaction may itself be complicated by such questions as time, intensity, depth, objects, and range of appraisal, fundamentally being happy is a report about how one feels about oneself and the world.

The eudaemonistic meaning of happiness encompasses a wide range of possible content other than subjective satisfaction, although that is not excluded. Depending on the particular classical tradition being interpreted, any number of specific goods can be thought necessary for a happy life: traditionally, these goods are divided between goods of the soul, goods of the body, and external goods,[5] but regardless of differences in the exact configuration of goods, the presence of a stable moral character, constituted by moral virtue, was thought to be necessary for a happy life. St. Augustine writes while commenting on the theories of happiness in antiquity, that "virtue makes a good use both of itself and of all other goods in which lies man's happiness . . . no matter how many good things a man has, they are not his good, and consequently should not be called good things while they belong to one who makes them useless by using them badly."[6] Virtue may have been thought as a means to happiness, a constitutive part of it, or identical with it, but the conjunction of the two in moral discourse was considered a given.[7] To count someone happy was, at least in part, a judgment about a person's moral character which to some degree was open to public scrutiny.

Therefore, eudaemonistic versions of happiness have at least this in common: a subjective state is a necessary condition of being happy, and judgments about happiness must apply some moral criteria in order to understand the meaning of those states in the context of a whole life. When Socrates says in the *Gorgias* that judging whether a man is happy or not is one of the noblest things we do, he is concerned with more than honoring people who display positive attitudes.[8]

This is not to say that eudaemonistic theories exclude subjective satisfactions and their attendant attitudes.[9] Many of the ancient versions of eudaimonia, especially in the Stoic emphasis on freedom from disturbance (*ataraxia/tranquilitas*) recognize the necessity of a positive psychological state to the happy life, but not to the extent of leaving happy states of mind free from moral accountability. As Democritus says, the mental repose of an evil man was not thought to make him happy.[10] Even the internal good of satisfaction can be put to bad use. Dolly's willingness to look below the surface of Anna and Vronsky's "happy" sociability evinces just such a suspicion, and the fact that she overcomes the gullibility fueled by her own romantic expectations becomes crucial to clarifying the future of her own family and avoiding a similar calamity.

A defender of the subjectivist position might argue that this is nothing more than another instance of insincerity unmasked. The defender could point to Anna's eventual admission of the unhappiness she had previously concealed. The insincerity, then, would consist of Anna's attempt to conceal and mislead others about her state of mind.

Yet more is at stake in this final scene than a simple case of insincerity. Anna has entered into an active state of self-deception; she is attempting to conceal her misery not merely from others but from herself as well. Because subjectivists ignore the larger context of happiness, they cannot admit to the validity of seeing through self-deceptive claims to happiness, even those made by a fool.[11] Anna's momentary honesty with herself is made possible by the presence of a friend whose claim against her professed happiness does not even require direct utterance. With her friend's departure, Anna knows she will have to hide from herself once again: "It hurt her to stir up these feelings, but yet she knew that that was the best part of her soul, and that that part of her soul would quickly be smothered by the life she was leading" (686). Dolly's unspoken challenge, far from being motivated by envy or moralistic perversity, arises from her clear-eyed concern for a despairing friend whose conversation resounds with the very emptiness she struggles to deny. The presence of a friend who has known her well for many years subjects Anna's reported happiness to the light of a publicity test. In the context of the novel, this single day represents Anna's last chance to avoid her suicidal plunge beneath the train.

Some defenders of subjectivism argue that the concept of happiness differs logically from well-being because it is a hedonic state of affairs which comes and goes in time, having no causal connection with what is beneficial.[12] Issues of hedonic effect certainly have been central to theorists of happiness; thus, it would be a mistake to counter them simply by evoking the classical ideal of happiness that seriously debated whether a person could be called happy while under torture.[13] Any attempt to renew the linkage between happiness and ethics must take cognizance of enjoyment and satisfaction or risk losing touch with ordinary language and experience. At the same time, that linkage cannot identify happiness with satisfaction so that it fails to take into account the way suffering assumes its necessary place in the lives of people who seek well-being.

Given both the history and the usage of the concept, hard distinctions between happiness and pain cannot be drawn so neatly. This distinction simplifies a mixed concept like happiness for the sake of logical clarity, but such simplification comes at the cost of dissociating happiness even further from its eudaemonist past. This alternative is rejected even by a leading scientist of happiness who, while accepting the basic psychological meaning of happiness, is reluctant to talk about happy lives unless "life-as-a-whole" is taken into account.[14] Without even such a minimal condition added to the sole criterion of satisfaction, psychological happiness becomes so trivial as scarcely to require lengthy, serious attention from social scientists or philosophers.

The chasm between our uses of the term happiness and its family of concepts, that is, between usages that help to direct a person's life toward a specific end and those that mire someone further in the immediacy of feeling, is not a new problem in the history of the concept. Tolstoy's depiction of it in the life of Anna and Vronsky, though among the most powerful, is hardly unique. Yet much may be discovered in how contemporary readers react to Anna's reported happiness and, more significantly, whether or not they are willing, like Dolly, to scrutinize it. If readers find themselves less willing to question first-person claims to happiness, why should they be any more willing to join with the narrator and Dolly in their discovery of Anna's actual unhappiness?

Psychological happiness, sometimes called reported happiness, has become the consciously held norm. Consequently, moments in the narration when characters such as Anna, whose avowals of happiness serve to keep her more and more in the dark about herself, are revealed as false, must seem presumptuous and moralistic to readers who are disposed to give her the benefit of the doubt.

Eudaemonistic conceptions of happiness allow for the possibility of bringing judgment to bear on the lives of other people. Such judgments, which are admittedly tricky and often wrong, can also be used for purposes of control and manipulation. Despite these problems they are nonetheless important and necessary in our personal associations—the more personal the judgment, the more important. Though their validity may be denied in theory, these judgments are still made at significant times in our lives. The explicit belief that we can have knowledge of another's happiness, which he or she might not have, has been largely rejected. If happiness is psychological, then only each individual is in the position of knowing about it. The consequences of the privacy and inscrutability of claims to happiness are immense.

What is it that allows Dolly to invade Anna's privacy, so to speak? Obviously, it has to do not only with her privileged knowledge of Anna but also with some basic savvy about human nature. She can see that the changes wrought in Anna's character have made her less dependable, less concerned for others, and willing to fritter her life away amid superficial acquaintances while brooding over the future of a soured love affair. These disappointments come to a head in Dolly's recognition of Anna's indifference to her daughter—her behavior and her attitude, as opposed to her talk—indicate that she wishes not to have any more children, but a vestige of the old Anna rises to the surface later when we learn how much she misses her son.

Yet Anna's waffling back and forth in her attitude toward her circumstances seems only to scratch the surface of what Dolly rejects about Anna's claim to happiness. Dolly sees a woman in the process of becoming, in Kierkegaard's terms, an aesthete, dissociated from the daily responsibilities of life and increasingly occupied by vain displays and shallow conversation.[15] The bubble of romantic immediacy has burst, leaving Anna afraid of the life she herself has created and fearful that the future holds a choice between the two people she loves most—her son and her lover. Dolly is most horrified by the attitude toward children that emerges from the mixture of Anna's regret and guilt: "How can one harm children that don't exist?" (AK, 683). More than rejecting circumstances, Anna, who has lost her former vision of life, is now on the verge of losing hope.

Anna suffers from far more than a negative attitude toward her situation. In fact, the prospect of a positive or favorable attitude would serve only to prolong her deception and deepen her despair. The problem with the recommendation of positive thinking or a positive attitude is that it trivializes the meaning of being both happy and unhappy. What someone would remedy with a favorable attitude needs, in fact, a great deal more. For a person like Anna to regain hope requires more than a simple trick of the mind, such as visualization. Anna must see that good lies once more for her in the future. The loss of her son, her estrangement from her family and society, and her fear of losing Vronsky's love are realities posed as a consequence of her own choice. Without returning to her husband, she ensures herself a fragile future balanced only on the whims of a man whose very passion for her has proven to be destructive and unpredictable. Escape tactics become the only route to happiness for a person unwilling to reform his or her life for the sake of a viable future.

This is not to say that certain attitudes are not essential to happiness, but to suggest that attitudes themselves exist partially as products of character and fortune that should not be ignored. Anyone who has ever tried to change an attitude knows this: an attitude possesses the stubbornness of habit. What are the sources of this positive attitude? Cannot drug users and the self-deceived, as long as they possess a favorable attitude, all share in happiness?[16] Certainly a weakness of the positive-attitude account is that by not examining the various means people employ toward possessing this attitude, the theory fails in helping us pursue it. Thus positive thinkers provide an account in which the notion of attitude applies equally to an addict and to a nonaddict. On these terms, if a person like Anna were able to escape from her regret through morphine and vanity, she could validly claim to be happy. The effect of such trivialization is obvious. This chain of reasoning has carried us much farther from common usage than contemporary defenders of eudaimonia.

Several philosophers who have dissented against psychological happiness have noticed that our speech about happiness is far from uniform. Most of our peers would, if pushed to the wall, describe happiness as some sort of feeling-state, enjoyment, or sense of satisfaction. Yet, it is also true that the same people who would describe it in this way still persist in using "happiness" in other senses that involve the justification of personal, moral, political, and spiritual aims. The noun "happiness," the adjective "happy," and the adverb "happily" are used and heard often, despite common meaning, to recommend a way of life. In other words, people still use those words to evaluate life in global terms, not simply to express satisfaction with it.

To hear these words used in common speech, we must distinguish between the recommendation and the report. Obviously, to say "I want to marry you because we will have a happy life together" is to give plausible reasons to pursue such an end, but the comment "I want a divorce because we are so unhappy together" contains both a recommendation and a report. People will usually challenge the report but not the recommendation based on the report. The recommendation of divorce is made on the expectation that it will contribute to a happy life. The only way such reasoning can be challenged is by questioning the report, not the expressed desire for happiness. No doubt the two uses can become dangerously jumbled in these situations, but that does not obscure the basic intention of the speaker to provide some rational justification for an action that may deeply mark the direction of his or her future. Whatever our reasons for not challenging the report, they are fortified by the fact that in not questioning first-person claims to happiness we protect the unassailable character of our own.

As a mixed concept, it will not do to reduce happiness either in the direction of Stoic virtue or in the search for positive attitudes. Either of these alternatives makes it easier on the theorists while detracting from the historical richness of the concept. Theories of happiness that ignore either the element of hedonic effect or its justification stand out as peculiar. The complexity of happiness judgments has not gone unnoticed among recent commentators. One has suggested that we are inclined in these judgments not to accept claims based on the satisfaction of any set of desires, thus concurring with our comments that Dolly's judgments about Anna's happiness are self-involving. If we are averse to the set of desires being satisfied, such as those of an opium addict, we judge the addict to be unhappy.[17] On that basis, we can distinguish between calling people satisfied and calling them happy. Before we call someone happy, "we find it necessary to be sure, not only that his desires are satisfied, but also that the complete set of his desires is one which we are not very much averse to having ourselves."[18] We normally ascribe happiness to people who are, in some sense, whole and complete people.

This kind of judgment involves two kinds of criteria, one internal to an individual's life, the other external, as shared by Dolly and Anna. The experience of satisfaction may be much easier to come by for persons who have successfully narrowed the range of their desires to a few concerns, though they may have lost some perspective over themselves and their lives in the process. It is not the mere fact of Anna's new life that disturbs Dolly, but the realization that for the sake of her lover Anna has had to sacrifice the hope and the other habits of character that made her a valued friend in the first place. As we have seen, it is necessary, though not sufficient, that Dolly have a personal vantage point from which to view Anna's life. She must also be willing to think of Anna's life against a larger human standard. This is the standard that comes into play when Dolly decides that she cannot follow her friend into hopelessness.

The character of Anna Karenina aptly illustrates the problem of self-deception associated with well-feeling. It can be asked, though, whether considering Anna's status as a woman in a male-dominated society alters this characterization. In other words, given her lack of options as a married woman in nineteenth-century Russia, is it fair to focus on her ruin to illustrate a problem about happiness that infects a different kind of society, one in which people have too many choices rather than too few? The above characterization of Anna's self-deception should not be taken as indicating a lack of sympathy with her plight. Surely the route she chose was understandable in the general sense that people use that term. Of course, to say one understands the reasons why someone commits a self-destructive act is not to say that one would commend it.

Although Anna's tragic circumstances are exacerbated by her social limitations, they are not confined to her day and time. She had placed herself in the tragic situation of having to chose between two irreconcilable loves—still a common predicament—and even though the reader has deep sympathy for her, Anna's situation remains one of a false happiness bolstered by the excuses of self-deception. There is no question, however, that specific social situations encourage this sort of outcome.

Others might argue that such a reading of *Anna Karenina* suffers from the same gender bias found at the heart of the novel itself. By their very nature, such arguments tend to be irrefutable, since counterexamples are treated either as an exceptional example of a male writer overcoming his maleness or the more typical case of a female writer infected with the maleness of her education and upbringing. Although there are any number of novels about a woman's struggle for domestic happiness, there is one in particular, written by a woman, that serves as an unusually direct response to Tolstoy's *Anna Karenina*.

Images in a Mirror was written by the Norwegian novelist and 1926 Nobel Prize winner Sigrid Undset (1882-1949) in 1917.[19] Undset was an early feminist herself in the country that was the first in Europe to give women full voting rights (1913). Her early works portrayed the predicament of working-class women, both single and married, who worked outside the home and openly enjoyed their sexuality but still tried to accommodate themselves to the traditional roles of full-time mother and wife.[20]

Undset's Fru Hjelde, or Uni, as she is called, was a successful actress before she gave up the stage in order to marry and bear five children in ten years. Her marriage to Kristian has long since lost the brief erotic twinge that brought them together. Uni has little in common with her husband, a coarse, kind man who knows he falls short of fulfilling his wife's desire for companionship, much less her dreams of ongoing romantic love. The loss of a son has made her little remaining joy in her family seem fragile, even illusory. The opportunity for experiencing romantic love arrives unexpectedly when she meets Vegard, an old acquaintance, while on a month-long rest away from the family to recover from illness brought on by overwork. Vegard's intentions are clearly seductive as he flatters her with memories of her days on stage. She laughingly resists him but on returning home begins visiting him regularly in his apartment.

Like her counterpart Anna, Uni's affair has an immediate effect not merely on her treatment of her children, but on her attitude toward them. Also like Anna, Uni is given an opportunity, through the agency of a friend, to see the changes taking place in herself. That moment arrives on an afternoon when Uni, planning a rendezvous with Vegard, has just refused to go to the movies with her husband and children. Henriette, who for many years rented a room in her home, unexpectedly announces to Uni she must give up the room and enter the hospital. As Henriette begins to lay out her presents for the family, including savings allotted for each of the children, and talks about her love for them and her own fear of dying, Uni forgets her meeting with Vegard. Henriette's request that she sing at the piano suddenly makes Uni realize that the changes in her manner have been noticed:

> "Oh yes, you may be sure your music has been a delight to me, Fru Hjelde. You've hardly played at all lately—I've really felt the loss of it. When you used to sing to the children in the evening—But of course I can quite well understand you must get quite well sick of it. . . ."
> Uni sang all she knew.
> Kristian and the children came into the hall.
> "Oh, Mother's singing!" Nora burst in.
> "Oh, no, Mother, you musn't stop—do sing something for us too."

They swarmed around the piano. (187-88)

After singing well into the evening, she puts the children to bed,
only to be confronted by Kristian about her relationship with Vegard. Surprised by his boldness, Uni defends herself, saying they
ought to have more in common "besides just the children." "Do you
say "just the children'?" he said in a low voice (193). Growing
more defensive, she protests against the limitations of her domestic
circumstances and the burden of raising children: "If they are to
get nothing out of it but a new generation, in training which they
will wear themselves out, till these again go out in search of something which doesn't exist—" (194). At this moment, Uni is tempted
by the same cynicism, the loss of hope, the sense of absurdity that
weakened and destroyed Anna Karenina.

The argument ends, and the couple sits staring at each other. A
crisis has been reached, similar to that moment when Dolly con-
fronts Anna, as Uni realizes this is "the longed-for hour when a
human being has to decide the fate of his whole life, when a chance
word, forcing its way from a soul taken by surprise, can never be
unsaid" (196). Sensing this moment may not ever come again, Kristian presses his wife to reconsider the price of possessing her desires:

> "Yes, Uni. I'll tell you. What you mean by happiness that fills one
> to surfeit—you know you can never have that any more. Not at the
> price that—you could bring yourself to pay."
> Uni moved her lips without a sound. (197)

No longer able to blame her children, her domestic chores, and
her marriage to an unromantic man for her unhappiness, her sustaining vision is restored. She admits that Kristian is right that the
price of escaping with Vegard is far too great—the loss of her family and the sturdy joys of nurturing it. Kristian, thus, succeeds in a
way that Dolly failed: in helping Uni remember her deeper desires,
he helps her return to her former, better self. How rarely we come
on a moment like this in literature, a moment of genuine and realistic marital reconciliation. They lay down next to one another that
night:

> . . . it was only they two, husband and wife, who hurt each other and
> loved each other—as human beings hurt and love and know and do not
> know themselves. . . . They fell asleep cheek against cheek, with their

hands clasped in one another's, united in weariness and in the happy love it brings, driving a galled couple to seek each other in those hours when body and soul crave an assurance that there is a little life left, a little blood left, which their little greedy young have not yet sucked up. (203-4)

In the days that follow, Uni realizes that she has been drawn toward an "egoism" and a "thirst for sensation" that are incompatible with marriage and motherhood (206); she also regards the brief affair as having been urged on by her old aesthetic disposition, another trait bad for marriage—"it is more like a force that splits up and paralyzes one's capacity for living. It makes one fall in love with all that is contradictory in one and around one, attached to all the conflicting ways of life, or exasperated with them, but incapable of holding fast to any one line" (221-22).

By the time Uni meets Vegard for the last time her mind is clear. She wonders, "What if he had been able to make her believe that love and happiness were to be bought at a price a woman can pay when she has children who have a claim upon her heart. When she thought of what might have happened in that case, her feeling of shame and humiliation at her own stupidity almost equaled that of terror" (224).

Sitting up late that night trying to soothe one of her restless children, Uni tries to understand what led her to risk losing what she loved most in the world through choosing a man who, as she had realized that afternoon, cared so little for her:

"Happiness," she thought, "happiness—what was I doing, at my age, to go and believe in happiness—or doubt of happiness? The happiness that Kristian and I once shared. The happiness that is like a shooting star. In the brief instant that it shines one must think of one's heart's desire and wish; and in the brief space while caresses are new and thrilling, one is called to understand and determine one's life. I wonder how many there are who succeed.

"And happiness in one's children is so natural that one does not think of it. All the times when our heart gleams with joy—at the odd things they say, and their comical first steps, at their beginning to take notice, at their caresses and those we give them, at the fright which proved needless and an illness which did not turn out to be dangerous. It does not occur to us that this is happiness, all these thousand little gleams. And yet it's on them that we live. No one could live without being happy now and then, but we do not think of it when it is there. We are only truly conscious of ourselves when we are unhappy. So long

as I have my children I know that I can face life—cheerfully, in whatever way everything else may turn out." (225-26)

The desire to lose herself in the experience of romantic passion,
she recognizes, represents a narrowing of vision, not the expansion
falsely promised by its intensity. While blaming Kristian for his
insensitivity to her and the children, she sought only herself by turning her back on the source of a lasting happiness, the kind that is
enjoyed unawares, because it appears so close at hand, so natural.
What makes the thrill of romantic immediacy so hazardous is that
the unhappiness left in its wake leaves a self-consciousness even
hungrier for the source of its own unhappiness. The kind of social
orientation represented by children is lacking in romantic passion;
as seen in *Anna Karenina*, everything else but the lover is viewed
as an obstacle. Faced with similar circumstances and temptations,
Undset's heroine makes the choice to recover herself by choosing
a family over a lover.

Though some might view Undset's character of Uni as corrobo-
rating a defunct gender role, the intention of *Images in a Mirror*,
like much of Undset's fiction, is to draw our attention to possibilities of happiness that offer themselves through the very offices we
so often consider opposed to our own interests. As one scholar has
written, "Undset's work is ultimately a reflection on the strength
that surpasses autonomous self-expression, the strength embodied in
selfless forms of love."[21]

Psychological happiness, undoubtedly, risks being an impediment
to the dynamics of human growth in the context of communal life.
The sovereign unaccountability of satisfied states of mind destroys
in advance the field of discourse in which intimates can help one
another clarify their deepest aims and purposes. At the same time,
the real benefit of negative states goes unappreciated. What subjectivists consider an obstacle to happiness may well indicate, as the
figure of Anna shows, a period of self-examination that foreshadows a better life to come. To have seen mental and emotional satisfaction become the unacknowledged summum bonum of our age
is to have witnessed the tremendous encouragement of unhappiness
caused by consequent dissociations—from history, from community, from the self. Psychological happiness, as it has been said, de-
serves the kind of systematic refutation once afforded the catalogue
of false happinesses, such as is found in classical, medieval, and
Renaissance philosophy.

For the present, the idea of happiness lives a double life: on the one hand, it still claims the privilege of a human purpose that can justify any kind of individual and social effort; on the other hand, by being identified with mental satisfaction, it has been released from accessibility to public scrutiny. The common recognition of what happiness is and how it can be known plays too powerful a role in personal and public life for us to allow the psychological conception of happiness to discard all the benefits of eudaimonia.

Notes

1. Quotations are taken from Leo Tolstoy, *Anna Karenina*, trans. Constance Garnett (New York: Bobbs-Merrill, no date); page numbers to this edition are cited in the text.

2. For further discussion, see Algis Valiunas, "Tolstoy and the Pursuit of Happiness," *Commentary* 87: 6 (June 1988): 33-41.

3. In using Anna Karenina we are following philosopher Richard Hare's advice: "Anybody who thinks that to call a man happy is merely to report on his state of mind should read a little poetry and make a collection of the different circumstances in which people have been called happy" in *Freedom and Reason* (Oxford: Clarendon Press, 1963), 129. Two recent philosophical novels have dealt with the nature of happiness: Theodore Zeldin, *Happiness* (London: Collins Harvill, 1988), and Michael Frayn, *A Landing on the Sun* (New York: Viking Penguin, 1992); the latter is particularly interesting for its comic treatment of "quality of life" social programs.

4. The Russian word being translated here is *schástye*, which suggests a longer-lasting state than either *udácha*, good luck, or *naslazhdéniye*, short-term enjoyment. See Louis Segal, *New Complete English-Russian Dictionary* (New York: Beekman Publishers, 1958), 300 (enjoyment), 424 (happiness), 560 (luck), 728 (pleasure).

5. Gregory Vlastos, "Happiness and Virtue in Socrates' Moral Theory," *Proceedings of the Cambridge Philological Society* 30 (1984):183. It is important to note that prior to Socrates eudaimonia had a range of meanings more in line with its etymology; see C. de Heer, *Makar-Eudaimon-Olbios-Eutyches: A Study of the Semantic Field Denoting Happiness in Ancient Greek to the End of the 5th Century B.C.* (Amsterdam: Adolf M. Hakkert, 1969), 25-26, 38-44, 54, 59-67, 99-100.

6. *Nicomachean Ethics*, 1098 b 12-14 (19).

7. St. Augustine, *The City of God*, 19.1 (668).

8. St. Augustine, *The City of God*, 19.1 (669-70); also, Vlastos, 183; for further comment, see Donald Zeyl, "Socratic Virtue and Happiness," *Archiv für Geschichte der Philosophie* 64 (1982): 225-38.

9. Plato, *Gorgias*, 471c (35); page numbers in parentheses indicate the translation by W. C. Helmbold, which is used throughout (Indianapolis: Bobbs-Merrill, 1952).

10. See Richard Kraut and J. C. Dybiklowski, "Is Aristotelian Eudaimonia Happiness?" *Dialogue* 81 (1981): 185-200 for further comments and also an interesting application of an example of a wife's happiness that results from her husband's deception in a short story by Katherine Mansfield, "All Serene."

11. "The cheerful man *[euthemos]*, who is eager for just and lawful deeds, rejoices whether waking or sleeping and is strong and free from care; but him that cares nought for justice and does not the things that are right finds all such things joyless, when he remembers them, and is afraid and reproaches himself," in *The Presocratic Philosophers*, eds. G. S. Kirk and J. E. Raven (Cambridge: Cambridge University Press, 1969), 424. A counter-example can be found in Epictetus, who associates happiness with eurhoia or "good flow" and writes, "If one had to be deceived in order to learn that nothing external to us and outside our decision is anything to us, I would be ready to undergo this deception, from which I would live a well-flowing and undisturbed life" (*Discourses* 1.4. 27); see translation and comment by T. H. Irwin, "Stoic and Aristotelian Conceptions of Happiness," in *The Norms of Nature: Studies in Hellenistic Ethics*, eds. Malcolm Schofield and Gisela Striker (New York: Cambridge University Press, 1986), 224-28. As Irwin notes, this comment suggests that the later Stoics were at least aware of the ramifications of divorcing the content of happiness, which they identified with tranquility, from the requirement of virtue. Evidently the gestation period of a purely psychological happiness has been a long one with its roots in Epictetus. See chapter 4 for further comment.

12. G. B. von Wright, *The Varieties of Goodness*, 99.

13. G. B. von Wright, *The Varieties of Goodness*, 87.

14. The debate over happiness while under torture was common in classical Greece and Rome. Epicurus surprisingly argues its possibility while Aristotle accuses him of "just talking." For the broad outlines of the controversy see Cicero, *Tusculan Disputations*, trans. J. E. King (Cambridge: Harvard University Press, 1971), bks. 2-4.

15. Veenhoven, 38.

16. Kierkegaard's portraits of the aesthetic life are found in *Either/Or*, 2 vols., trans. David F. Swenson and Walter Lowrie (Princeton: Princeton University Press, 1944). A helpful discussion of "aesthetic" unhappiness is found in Louis Mackey, *Kierkegaard: A Kind of Poet* (Philadelphia: University of Pennsylvania Press, 1971).

17. Robin Barrow, *Happiness and Schooling* (New York: St. Martin's Press, 1980), 74.

18. Hare, 127.

19. Hare, 128.

20. *Images in a Mirror*, trans. Arthur G. Chater (New York: Alfred A. Knopf, 1938); page numbers to this edition are cited in the text. The Norwe-

gian title is *Fru Hjelde*, which was originally only one of the two novellas published under the title *Splinten av troldspeilet* ("*Splinter from the Troll's Looking-Glass*").

21. In 1907 she wrote *Mrs. Marte Oulie* with a startling opening line: "I have been unfaithful to my husband." A leading Undset scholar calls this "the most devastatingly honest view of women's lives since Ibsen's Nora had outraged Europe by slamming the door of her Doll House in their faces"; see Mitzi Brunsdale, *Sigrid Undset: Chronicler of Norway* (New York: Berg, 1988), 83. *Jenny*, written in 1911, is considered one of the greatest realistic novels of the period, about a young woman in an artistic circle in Rome who commits suicide; it explores every possible aspect of a woman's love. It shocked traditionalists in Norway with its gruesome descriptions of pregnancy and childbirth, and also enraged the feminists by saying that women cannot live by work or art alone.

22. Elisabeth Solbakklen, *Redefining Integrity: The Portrayal of Women in the Contemporary Novels of Sigrid Undset* (New York: Peter Lang, 1992), 204.

Chapter 3

The Rejection of Psychological Happiness

The proponents of psychological happiness have some good intentions. They are motivated, among other reasons, by a concern for putting highly valued human states—satisfaction, contentment, joy—within the reach of ordinary people, namely, those who are neither contemplatives in the manner of philosophers or ecstatics like many of the saints.

It is thus ironic that the emergence of the notion of well-feeling has prompted some commentators to reject happiness as a serious goal for human pursuit. For this minority party, as it were, the supporters of well-feeling have effectively posited a goal that is impossible to realize, have trivialized the historical legacy of the term, and have encouraged the dissociation of "happy" persons both from themselves and from their concrete surroundings.

These problems facing the ideal of psychological happiness have been well known for quite some time. Having been offered far in advance of the twentieth century, a critique of well-feeling has been available for many years, yet the warnings of the older critics have gone unheeded—the ideal of happiness as well-feeling flourishes in contemporary culture. Still there is a significant and perhaps growing minority opinion among those who, keeping alive centuries-old objections, consider simple well-feeling as—as we have already seen in the previous chapter—(1) an active cause of self-deception, but in addition, (2) an unworthy and demeaning human aim, (3) a tactic of social control, and (4) an inappropriate response to the state of an unhappy world.

This chapter contains a whole chorus of voices that have questioned the ascendancy of well-feeling. We will first sample some of the twentieth-century protests before returning to the earliest demurrals in the seventeenth century.

The most basic aspect of the rejection of happiness as a psychological state is the view that to pursue happiness is no longer a worthy purpose. In *The Tragic Sense of Life* (1913), Miguel de Unamuno pits love against happiness. If happiness is nothing else than self-satisfaction, then we have no business treating it as a final end. The happy man, he says, is "without substance" because his central achievement in life is the avoidance of love, a commitment to persons and ideals that inevitably involves suffering.

Since happy persons never have the occasion to harden their wills on the forge of dissatisfaction, they pass through life "without any inner meaning . . . the satisfied, the happy ones, do not love; they fall asleep in habit, near neighbor to annihilation."[1] Unamuno calls this choice "the terrible and tragic formula of the inner, spiritual life . . . either to obtain the most happiness with the least love or the most love with the least happiness."[2] Writing prior to World War I, he saw with prescience the kind of anesthetized individualism that would be encouraged by well-feeling, by the unwillingness to accept any threat to the bubble of self-satisfaction.

Perhaps Unamuno overreacts when he asks, "Is our happiness, perchance, the end-purpose of the Universe? Or do we not perhaps sustain some *alien* well-being with our suffering?"[3] Presumably, the irony of calling well-being "alien" is that it arrives without the benefit of being announced by some positive affect; it resides instead in the moral or spiritual fact of a person's character, for example, in the willingness to sacrifice. The trouble with such severity is that it deprives us of any but intellectual consolation in the course of our loves. Unamuno scrupulously gives all satisfaction away to the enemy, and what is left is an inevitable choice between love and happiness—a choice between altruism and egoism, absorption in self or commitment to others. Unamuno's protests against excessive concern for complacency and the encouragement of benign isolation set the tone for this century's rejection of happiness.

No less severe in his commentary on the fate of the West is Alexander Solzhenitsyn, who would find Naipal's earlier comment on happiness astonishing in the historical record it ignores. How could Naipal overlook the progressive weakening of the will, the vulnerability to tyranny, the self-absorbed and self-destructive tendencies in democratic societies? These are themes Solzhenitsyn explored in a novel written well before he left Russia. In *Cancer Ward* (1950) the character Shulubin calls happiness "an idol of the market" and, like Unamuno, insists on a distinction between the capacity for self-gratification, the essence of happiness, and love: "a wild animal gnawing at its prey is happy, but only humans can love, and it is the highest thing man can achieve." Shulubin denounces the social engineering that uses psychological happiness as its primary bait; answering his fellow patient's wish to die happy, he says:

> "Happiness is a mirage. . . . [f]or that happiness I burned books that contained truth. This applies even more to the so-called 'happiness of future generations.' Who can foresee it? Who has talked with these future generations, who knows what other idols they will yet bow down to? Ideas of happiness have changed too much down the centuries to foresee how to prepare it in advance. When we have white loaves to trample under our heels and we're choking on milk, it won't make us happy at all. But if we shared our meager portion, we could be happy right now! If we think only of 'happiness' and 'growth,' we shall fill up the earth senselessly and create a frightening society."[4]

Few passages better illustrate the interrelation of all the objections against well-feeling and, in particular, the way in which the egoism encouraged by well-feeling can be put into service of collectivist projects seeking to ensure the happiness of society. The state only has to devise some means of providing its citizens a palpable sense of self-satisfaction and they can be conditioned to accept their loss of freedom.

It is crucial in recognizing the limits of satisfaction that the social consequences of allegiance to well-feeling be grasped together with the personal side of self-deceiving happiness.

The conceptual issues underlying this connection have been addressed by the philosopher Alasdair MacIntyre. He has consistently criticized the use of happiness as a principle in moral judgment. His early comment that happiness is a "polymorphous" and "morally dangerous" concept remains unqualified, despite the fact that he has recently attempted to return ethics to a shared notion of the human good.[5]

Happiness, as MacIntyre argues, has been used as a label "to name whatever men aim at" and, as a consequence, has become useless in the evaluation of moral purposes—it cannot mediate the problem of competing desires. The concept of happiness, insofar as it has diminished since antiquity, lacks a normative content. It has evolved into a purely formal notion: anything can be placed into it by an association with pleasure and satisfaction. Once happiness came to be identified with forms of well-feeling in the seventeenth and eighteenth century, the door was opened to claiming that any personal or social state of affairs *causes* happiness, in the sense that it provides requisite satisfaction. Thus, as MacIntyre comments, when used at the political level, the concept of public or general happiness could conceivably justify the Holocaust or "license any enormity."[6]

MacIntyre's concern includes but surpasses the individual dilemmas of a deceived lover and, like that of Ghita Ionescu, addresses the ideological forces that have employed the concept of happiness as a promissory note for a perfect society. He sympathizes with Mill's attempt to repudiate Bentham's simple and univocal notion of happiness as units of pleasure that "cannot provide us with a criterion for making our key choices,"[7] but he criticizes Mill's shaping of Bentham's theory as an admission of defeat for the entire Enlightenment project: "To have understood the polymorphous character of pleasure and happiness is of course to have rendered those concepts useless for utilitarian purposes."[8]

MacIntyre, himself now something of a Thomist, has made no attempt to redefine happiness in eudaemonistic terms. For him the road back to *eudaimonia* is blocked not merely by the current disagreement over a shared human nature, but also by the incommensurability of real human goods. For him a summum bonum, a "summing happiness" in any formula, makes no sense because the internal and external goods constitutive of the activity of the happy life cannot be accommodated to one another. In other words, wisdom does not bestow wealth, and, in point of fact, the former may stand in the way of the latter. If one accepts the necessity of a *complete* possession of both moral and nonmoral goods for the happy life, his criticism stands.

The last objection—the inappropriateness of happiness in an unhappy world—raises the issue of what might be called the contemporary worry about worry. The extent to which people expect to enjoy states of well-feeling and become anxious when they are absent is spoofed by novelist Walker Percy. In *Lost in the Cosmos*, for example, he sees no reason to wonder why so many people are unhappy and depressed—"Any person, man, woman, or child, who is not depressed by the nuclear arms race, by the modern city, by family life in the exurb, suburb, apartment, villa, and later in a retirement home, is himself deranged."[9]

Percy's last novel explores the lengths to which people will go to avoid "feeling down." In *The Thanatos Syndrome* a group of physicians start dumping large amounts of sodium into the local drinking water to promote greater happiness and "quality of life."[10] The effect of the sodium on the brain suppresses the psychological disturbances that cause family conflict, crime, social unrest, and rebellion against authority. Dr. Thomas More, the novel's chief protagonist, has just returned after a two-year prison term to his home in Louisiana, in the aptly named parish of Feliciana, to discover that his former psychiatric patients have exchanged their symptoms of anxiety and dread for a combination of uncharacteristic sensuality and feats of mathematico-spatial memory. Dr. More, pondering the newly found contentment and erotic freedom of his former clients and friends, asks,

What's going on? What do they have in common? Are they better or worse? Well, better in the sense that they do not have the old symptoms, as we shrinks called them, the ancient anxiety, guilt, obsessions, rage repressed, sex suppressed. Happy is better than unhappy, right? But—But what? They're somehow—diminished. Diminished how? (85)

His suggestion that the absence of these symptoms may represent a loss to the patient's humanity rather than a gain is met with disbelief. People have a right not to suffer, he is told, because suffering ruins someone's chance "for a life of acceptable quality" (333). The "qualitarians" insist they are just interested in helping people; as one of them challenges Dr. More, *"You can't give me one good reason why what I am doing is wrong"* (347; italics in original). More's lack of a response is both discomforting and typical of an era when the lack of moral consensus deprives many people of their old articulateness.

Through the silence of his protagonist, Percy's novel replies indirectly. Dr. More repeatedly utters a cryptic "I see" to the explanations offered in support of the plan to force-feed happiness, as if to encourage the reader to pay close attention to what is happening. No one ever explains what is wrong with the sodium project, the implication being that one more explanation cannot help and may actually hurt the chances of recognition. Rather, the action of the novel discloses the possibilities of cruelty and unbridled power that lie concealed in the sentiment to "just help people." A commitment to greater happiness for all leads the qualitarians to imprison Dr. More as one who does not conform to their idea of acceptable life and personhood. It also encourages them to ignore evidence of sexual abuse against children, abuse brought about by the liberating effects of the sodium-laced water. Both are small prices to pay, they argue, for a better world. What if a few unenlightened souls have to lose their freedom? What if some innocent souls are introduced to sexual gratification before it is conventionally acceptable? The totalitarian logic is unmistakable. The alliance of biotechnology and happiness purveyors threatens to create a race of self-satisfied but dehumanized citizens, compliant to the law but socially dissociated and erotically dangerous. Dr. More is led finally to understand the meaning of an unsettling conversation with a seemingly mad priest who lives atop a fire tower. The priest asks More,

> "Do you know where tenderness always leads?"
> "No, where?" I ask, watching the stranger with curiosity.
> "To the gas chamber."
> "I see."
> "Tenderness is the first disguise of the murderer."
> "Right." (128)

It is a great irony that happiness and death can be associated. Freud makes the connection almost axiomatic, as we shall see in his discussion of the "thanatos syndrome." For Percy, though, the association rubs two ways. First of all, there is the danger hidden beneath the sentiment of those who seek to relieve our suffering—how far will they go? If suffering is seen as either intractable or unavoidable, will they move to destroy the life on which suffering depends for its accidental existence? Or, what if my life or the life of the part to which I belong is a permanent source of unhappiness to the whole? Does it not follow that my existence stands in jeopardy when the happiness of the whole is taken into account? Indeed, a society in which people are given a right not to suffer becomes a place where happiness and death necessarily entail one another.

Second, there is the more obvious way in which the personal pursuit of well-feeling can be viewed as an unconscious death wish. Given the constraints of reality, the expectation of an uninterrupted immediacy of either pleasure or satisfaction can be fulfilled only in a state of nonexistence, since it is only in the void that such a state is entirely free from the possibility of disturbance. No doubt the remark "tenderness leads to the gas chamber" appears initially preposterous until one follows this moral logic that has already led to genocidal holocaust. Twenty years earlier, the writer Flannery O'Connor employed an almost identical expression to identify an attitude toward those slowly dying from disease: "In this popular pity, we mark our gain in sensibility and our loss in vision."[11]

In spite of the relative popularity of works such as Ernest Becker's *The Denial of Death*,[12] it remains to be widely recognized how the pursuit of happiness in this century remains strangely entangled with death. This vision of the dissociating and destructive role that the idea of happiness plays in society has been lent support by a recent sociological study of American life. In *Habits of the Heart*, Robert Bellah and his coauthors offer portraits of those who are suffering severe psychic and political dislocation as a result of "The Pursuit of Happiness," the title of the first chapter. A Californian, Brian Palmer, has difficulty in expressing his present preference for the demands of family life as opposed to his earlier single-minded commitment to his career. This change in what makes Brian Palmer happy seems "arbitrary and unexamined" to him and has no place in the overall purpose of his life. "Brian sees himself as consistently pursuing a utilitarian calculus—devotion to his own self-interest—except that there has been an almost inexplicable change in his personal preferences."[13]

In Bellah's view Americans have lost their objective grounding for values; choices have become a simple matter of sheer preference. Personal satisfaction through material success may give way at a moment's notice to the delights of the family hearth without even the possibility of an explanation. The kind of fragmented, inarticulate self that ironically has come to take a dominant voice in American life leads to an increasing lack of involvement in public life and its issues of social justice.

It is significant, as these authors state, that Americans do not report being happy in pursuit of these satisfactions. Instead, they report feeling locked inside an isolated self of their own making. They desire connections to a large community but are stuck in an ambivalent posture of having to choose whether to refuse all social expectations or succumb to total conformity. In the face of this perceived choice the American disposition to individualism inevitably reasserts itself.

The most extreme case of this, and the most frightening, is that of Shelia Larsen. Shelia, a young nurse who has received a great

amount of therapy, was asked about her religious faith. She described it as "Sheliaism." As she explains: "I believe in God. I'm
not a religious fanatic. I can't remember the last time I went to
church. My faith has carried me a long way. It's Sheliaism. Just
my own little voice."[14] With the figure of Shelia, *Habits of the Heart*
heralds the culmination of the mind-cure tradition, the so-called
"New Age," before it became widely known through the media.

If Shelia Larsen is representative, this is an age in which happiness can mean anything anyone wants it to mean and thereby lend
justification to any kind of lie, any kind of behavior, any kind of
character, and nobody can claim the grounds to challenge the authority of someone else's "own little voice." Shelia could have ar-
rived at the same state by taking the advice of John Cowper Powys
or even Paul Kurtz.

Robert Bellah's concern is that the radical individualism that he
and his coauthors uncovered in American life has been encouraged
by

> modern psychological ideals . . . [that] to be free is not simply to be
> left alone by others; it is also somehow to be your own person in the
> sense that you have defined who you are, decided for yourself what
> you want out of life, free as much as possible from the demands of
> conformity to family, friends, or community. From this point of view,
> to be free psychologically is to succeed in separating oneself from the
> values imposed by one's past or by conformity to one's social milieu,
> so that one can discover what one really wants. . . .The difficulty, of
> course, is that this vision of freedom as freedom *from* the demands of
> others provides no vocabulary [with which] Americans can easily ad-
> dress common conceptions of the ends of a good life or ways to coor-
> dinate cooperative action with others.[15]

Like most other critics of happiness, Bellah and his coauthors
see the fate of happiness as tied closely to questions about the foundation of morality. They see, further, that Americans have failed to
develop a consistent moral vocabulary that would allow them to
connect their individual pursuits of satisfaction with the happiness
of others and that of their country as a whole. The popular notion
of success epitomizes this attitude, forcing the traditional ideal of
freedom into an egocentric posture: freedom *from* social restraint
and the concern for a common good.

For Bellah, the philosophical roots of these attitudes are found
in the history of the idea of happiness, specifically in a train of
thought beginning with Thomas Hobbes (1588-1679). Because of his

closeness to the eudaemonist tradition and his rejection of any fixed ends corresponding to the desires of human nature, Hobbes's definition of happiness stands as easily the most radical in the history of the concept and foreshadows contemporary opinion:

Continually to out-go the next before, is *felicity*.[16]

But for an *utmost* end, in which the ancient philosophers have placed *felicity*, and disputed much concerning the way thereto, there is no such thing in this world, nor way to it, more than to Utopia; for while we live, we have desires, and desire presupposeth a further end.[17]

Continual success in obtaining those things which a man from time to time desireth, that is to say, continual prospering, is that men call FE-LICITY; I mean the felicity of this life. For there is no such thing as perpetual tranquillity of mind, while we live here; because life itself is but motion, and can never be without desire, nor without fear, no more than without sense. What kind of felicity God hath ordained to them that devoutly honor him, a man shall no sooner know, than enjoy; being joyless, that now are as incomprehensible, as the word of School-men *beatifical vision* is unintelligible.[18]

Even outside of their context, these comments speak for themselves—happiness is not a state, it is a process of moving from one gratification to another. No single object of desire is better than another—desire, in fact, confers its own value on objects. The value we perceive in objects, their capacity to gratify us, is complicated by the need to surpass the gratifications of others. The pursuit of happiness, then, is fundamentally competitive and aggressive.

Hobbes's refusal to accept the classical ideal of the summum bonum and his identification of happiness with "prospering" or "continual success" in the "progress of desire" act as intellectual catalysts for the further developments in the idea of happiness. Some of these will be considered more closely in the next chapter. Hobbes's comments, if taken as they should be, as descriptions of human behavior rather than normative recommendations, are benign, but what if Hobbesian happiness were to be given political and social warrant? Then Bellah's final comment should not be considered exaggerated: "But we are beginning to see now that the race of which he [Hobbes] speaks has no winner, and if power is our only end, the death in question may not be merely personal, but civilizational."[19]

The figures just surveyed represent a minority party in the present age, those who have challenged the consensus sustaining the happiness of well-feeling. Their objections look backward to the day when to speak of another's "false happiness" was not to commit the high crime of offending their feelings. Rather, it was to make a judgment about those things that are stable, lasting, and beneficial to human company. The change in attitude toward happiness announced by Hobbes did not make these judgments offensive but nonsensical. To say that happiness was success in gratifying desire, whatever that desire is, removes any moral ground for third-person judgment. If persons say they are happy, they are. The only possible ground for judgment is to say that they are mistaken about their gratification. To follow the trail of this debate, as has been the case in contemporary philosophy, seems trivial compared to quarrels over happiness among the ancients. It is no wonder that the philosophy of happiness has become a kind of subgenre in philosophical psychology.

The consequence of the Hobbesian outlook—the trivialization of happiness—did not go unnoticed in the seventeenth century. One of Hobbes's more influential contemporaries, Blaise Pascal (1623-1662), is the prophetic figure who prefigures the later critiques of happiness by Samuel Johnson, Voltaire, and Kant, and the later discussion by Kierkegaard, Nietzsche, and Freud. Writing his *Pensées* at the dawn of the Enlightenment, Pascal adds a new twist to psychological happiness as it begins to take hold in the culture. Yes, happiness is sought in diversion, and the hunt rather than the capture satisfies the human mind but benumbs the spirit. The "progress of desire" was an excuse for ignoring, rather than addressing, questions of human mortality and ultimate destiny (133, 136).[20] Pascal was not attempting merely to produce a chuckle of recognition about the spectacle of life, but to issue a warning.

As a remedy, Pascal does not recommend a return to the contemplative ideal of classical eudaemonism. He recognizes people's penchant for avoiding themselves and the thoughts that arise unforseen in quiet solitude; he writes in a famous aphorism: "The sole cause of man's unhappiness is that he does not know how to stay quietly in his room" (136). The ancient philosophers who have recommended the life of leisurely contemplation as a means to happiness may have understood that true happiness consists in total rest, but they did not understand that even in this life human nature requires an infinite object to satisfy its aspirations. For Pascal, a religious thinker, such an object is not available to us in this life. All one needs to do is survey the happiness of the king who, in spite of having all the satisfactions and advantages of earthly life, is still restless for more (137).[21]

From Pascal's perspective Hobbes was simply placing us on another kind of happiness treadmill—"continual success" would also entail continual seeking after new enjoyments. This form of happiness encourages false consciousness and self-deception: "Imagination cannot make fools wise, but it makes them happy" (44). For Pascal the refusal to know oneself is the necessary condition of this illusory happiness (687).

In the century after Pascal's death, interest in the idea of happiness reached fever pitch. It was the period in which, as we have already noted, "happiness became a right, something to which we were entitled."[22] The 1775 American declaration of the inalienable right of "the pursuit of happiness" was followed in 1789 by the French Declaration of the Rights of Man (the words "and of the Citizen" were added a month later). The first line in the French declaration reads, "The goal of society is common happiness." The promise of public happiness became the key idea that fueled the revolutionary discourse of the French Revolution and its aftermath.[23] The now famous utterance of the Jacobin leader Armand St. Just— "Happiness [*le bonheur*] is a new idea in Europe"—was true in the sense that the idea of happiness had entered politics in a decisively new way. The age of the Enlightenment, inspired by the writing of Locke and the French *philosophes*, was beginning to formulate a moral and political philosophy based entirely on a happiness calculus, a project that would come to fruition in the utilitarianism of Jeremy Bentham and J. S. Mill.

The appearance in 1756 of Samuel Johnson's *Rasselas* and Voltaire's *Candide* are made all the more remarkable by the context of the Enlightenment obsession with defining the conditions and possibilities of obtaining happiness. They signal the coming of an exhausted cynicism about happiness. The age of optimism was showing signs of losing faith in one of its cardinal principles, even before the French Revolution began. Johnson and Voltaire, like Pascal earlier, detect in the common "pursuit of happiness" spreading confusion about the value of basic human endeavors—politics, commerce, religion, education, marriage, and, of course, pleasure.

For example, the perennially resilient and gullible Candide, committed to his belief in the "best of all possible worlds," ends up withdrawing from society altogether to the privacy of his backyard. Candide's travels are a survey, in classical fashion, of the various candidates for true happiness, all of which turn out to be false. Philosophers, emperors, the wealthy, and the pious all fail to achieve happiness. Even utopia fails him. Candide arrives in El Dorado, only to leave in search of his "earthly paradise," Cunegonde. Finally reunited with his childhood sweetheart, her beauty reduced to ugliness by suffering, Candide's decision to "cultivate one's own garden" in order to make life bearable is a striking example of lowered expectations in an age whose appetite was operating at full tilt.

Likewise, Samuel Johnson's *Rasselas* tests the Enlightenment assumption that the end toward which a human life aims is uninterrupted pleasure and satisfaction. Rasselas, a Prince of Abyssinia, is required to live his life in the Happy Valley where he is shielded from the toil and misery of the outside world and "every desire is satisfied." The Prince, growing bored, asks what distinguishes his pleasures from those of the animals who graze nearby and concludes with the complaint that since he wants for nothing he cannot experience happiness. He looks for a way of escape so that he can have a "choice of life."[24] Like Candide, Rasselas surveys the traditional options for securing happiness: the pleasure-seeking of youth, the pastoral life in the country, the enjoyment of wealth, the life of the hermit, the philosopher who extols nature, the might of the powerful, the delights of marriage and children. Observation reveals in each of them the lack of felt and constant satisfaction that Rasselas had thought happiness must be. The only exception to this is the figure of the astronomer, who is the only "happy" character he meets whose happiness is not immediately exposed as masking a deeper suffering. What his happiness is based on, we find out, is the belief that he controls the movements of the moon, the sun, the stars, and the tides. When his delusion ends so does his happiness.

Voltaire's book is similar in subject matter and overall outlook but very different in treatment. Pangloss, for example, never gives up his claim that this is the "best of all possible worlds," in spite of the loss of a number of important body parts. *Candide* satirizes while *Rasselas* calmly converses. Both show disdain for the philosophers' approach to happiness, as one of many false options. What each has in common is the pursuit of a completely satisfying *felt* happiness, one that puts an end to all sense of lack. Rasselas leaves the Happy Valley because he lacks free choice, Candide leaves El Dorado because he lacks Cundegonde, and each eventually returns to where they started: Rasselas back to the Happy Valley; and Candide back to the family he lost in Westphalia, much older and much disfigured, transplanted to Turkey, where they decide the wiser course is to "cultivate their own garden," rather than roam the world in search of the perfect world Pangloss promised. Both books seem to speak of the impossibility of any single activity providing happiness, but the issues they address more deeply are the nature of happiness itself and the futility of seeking perfect mental repose in a world vulnerable to misfortune and human weakness. They also testify to the human unwillingness to purchase happiness at the cost of gullibility or, even worse, of self-deception.

A few decades later, Immanuel Kant embraced the same skepticism toward happiness in his critical ethics. The fact that Kant takes no issue with the eighteenth-century conception of happiness itself as the "satisfaction of desire" all but fixed its meaning for subsequent philosophical reflection. So having accepted the trivialized meaning of happiness, he sets out to defuse what he sees as its disastrous implications for moral reasoning.[25] Kant's fundamental change is to remove happiness (*Glückseligkeit*) as a valid motive for moral judgment and action. His reasons for this shift stem from the empirical observation that attainment of moral virtue does not necessarily bear the happiness of satisfaction in its wake, at least in this life. The virtuous are often miserable while the wicked are satisfied. Because he is a hedonist on the question of happiness, Kant can argue against the eudaemonist tradition that no necessary connection exists between virtue and happiness. It is important to bear in mind that Kant is writing in the same generation as the American Founders, who, as discussed in the next chapter, find so much political promise in the idea of happiness.

At the basis of Kant's critique is the insistence that good ought to done for its own sake, that the natural desire for subjective satisfaction interferes with the freedom to act with a morally good will. He explains, "the contentment with one's condition which is called happiness, makes for pride and even arrogance if there is not a good will to correct its influence on the mind and on its principles of action so as to make it universally conformable to its end."[26] The principle of the categorical imperative, of course, is intended to guarantee the impartiality of judgment and action. Good moral actions are good regardless of their benefit to the moral agent.

Egoism inevitably arises when happiness becomes a first-order consideration in moral judgment. Happiness belongs to the domain of psychology, and, as such, "the concept of happiness is so indefinite . . . [and] empirical."[27] The morally good for Kant must be independent of our desires, of whether we want it or not. "When one's own happiness is made the determining ground of the will, the result is the direct opposite of the principle of morality."[28] Otherwise, morality loses its rational and binding character—being morally good would mean doing only what one wants, what one needs to satisfy his or her desires. There is no way of distinguishing between good and bad among the faculty of desires: in short, wants do not translate into oughts—"The principle of one's own happiness, however much reason and understanding may be used in it, contains no other determinants for the will than those which belong to the lower faculty of desire."[29] Thus, for Kant, the desire for happiness cannot provide a reliable guide or a good moral action, much less a good moral life or character. Kant's intention is to preserve the freedom and rationality of the moral agent and to protect ethics from being subsumed to a bastardized form of the final good.

This is not to say that Kant fails to recognize the universal desire for happiness. He does affirm it, as well as our duty to pursue it. Kant includes happiness in his account of the eternal summum bonum, where he distinguishes the two elements of moral virtue and happiness. Although natural desire and moral freedom should be kept distinct and although happiness cannot be considered a motive for moral action, God will reward morally good souls with the eternal happiness they deserve. Kant can safely relegate the concern for happiness to eternal life, where those who are morally worthy of happiness will be made perfectly happy by divine gift. In fact, Kant treats this happiness in heaven as a rational ideal that reason must prescribe to exist; otherwise, moral action would leave natural desire searching in vain for its fulfillment. Rejected as a guide to action, happiness becomes an object of moral faith. The promise of personal benefit bolsters our commitment to the impersonal dictates of the categorical imperative.

Like Kant, Sigmund Freud noticed that the natural desire for happiness, as it was defined by the Enlightenment, is a catch-22 of inescapable but unrealizable desire for immediate and lasting satisfaction. Freud, also like Kant, accepts without question the inherited paradigm of well-feeling. In his *Civilization and Its Discontents* (1930), originally entitled "Unhappiness in Culture," Freud identifies happiness (*Glück*) with satisfaction of instinctual drives.[30] His analysis starts from the assumption that given the "economics of the individual's libido," "every man must find out for himself in what particular fashion he can be saved. . . . It is a question of how much real satisfaction he can expect to get from the external world, how far he is led to make himself independent of it, and, finally, how much strength he feels he has for altering the world to suit his wishes."[31] The problem, as Freud points out, is that the world cannot be altered without serious consequences for both society and the renegade individual.

The universal human drive for instinctual gratification that Freud identifies with happiness is doomed to frustration. The external world not only fails to conform to our desires for uninterrupted immediacy, but the requirements of civilization also prohibit the very primal behavior such as incest, polygamy, and murder that would allow for gratification. Thus, regarding the desire for happiness, Freud writes, "there is no possibility of it being carried through. . . . One feels inclined to say that the intention that man should be 'happy' is not included in the plan of Creation."[32]

Civilization demands the restriction of genital gratification for the sake of a cohesive social existence, but within the very nature of happiness, epitomized for Freud by the sexual orgasm and the child being carried within the mother's womb, are dynamics that disallow sustained and long-term satisfaction. The sheer intensity of gratification in the experience of happiness stands in stark contrast with ordinary life. Regardless of the fact that the very dynamic of the pleasure principles limits happiness to momentary experience, Freud, holding fast to his biological paradigm of human nature, thinks the whole of life is still measured against it.

The object of psychoanalytic therapy, however, is not the happiness of the patient, but something less. Given the impossibility of its realization, Freud is led to the conclusion that the object of therapy is not happiness at all but "common unhappiness."[33] There may indeed be a certain wisdom in this remark, given his assumptions about the nature of happiness itself, but against the larger historical background of the concept one cannot help but notice the diminished value it ascribes to human life. The pursuit of happiness has become a problem that the analyst has to solve through lower, more realistic and socially beneficial expectations. But this may not take us far enough. The desire for happiness becomes for Freud the innate motive for mental and emotional pathology in some and for constant frustration in all. As a product of our instinctual drive for gratification, happiness does not belong to intellectual or psychic capacities, which themselves must mediate the inherent dispute between the pleasure principle and the reality principle in favor of renunciation, that is, common unhappiness.

It should not be surprising that later psychoanalysis makes use of Freud's theory of happiness to destroy the pretensions to continuous immediacy found in hedonism. This attitude, as will be seen, is less evident in empirically based psychologists and sociologists. For example, Isidor Silbermann takes Freud's notion of the compulsion to repeat, implicit in the pleasure principle, as the basis of his critique of happiness: "The perverted as well as the addicted would like to live in a state of unlimited narcissistic indulgence, to drift in a vast orgiastic ocean, disregarding reality and decrying its limitations. . . . [C]an we call the result feeling happiness?"[34] He comes close to bringing moral judgment on our claims to happiness but finally backs off to stay safely within the Freudian boundaries of beneficial social interaction: "Psychoanalysis strives to make people *contented* and adjusted to life. Once that goal has been reached, no attempt is made to reach the lofty and illusory goal of perpetual happiness."[35] One wonders, given the aim of "common unhappiness," whether Freud himself would have embraced even this goal, as modest as Silbermann makes it seem. Psychological goals such as contentment, it has been argued, contain their own temptations to illusory forms of immediacy, analogous to those of sensualists.

For Freud sexual gratification has become the paradigm and the touchstone of happiness—"genital love" is the prototype of all happiness—although he clearly points out the futility of pursuing it in this manner.[36] The greatest experiences of happiness are those satisfactions of sudden untamed instinctual impulses.[37] For Freud, as for Kant, the biological desire for happiness dominates human beings "from below"; it "dominates the mental apparatus."[38] Unlike the tradition of eudaemonism, the desire for happiness does not arise from human rationality and the appetite for knowledge, the distinguishing characteristic of the species; it arises instead from certain drives that humans have in common with other species as animals. Reason enters not in the pursuit of happiness, but in the renunciation of it. Our higher mental activities allow a redirection of these instinctual energies so that we may collectively profit from the benefits of an orderly society.[39] Since the very thing that human beings most deeply desire cannot be possessed, Freud recommends the path of "sublimations," release of these instinctual energies into higher activities such as art and work. It is this same desire to escape suffering from restrictions to the libido that leads to the strategies of obtaining happiness exhibited by the Stoic, the yoga, the hermit, the drunk, the aesthete. Indeed, the perennial struggle of mankind is between the individual's instinctual need for gratification and the needs of the group.

It is important that we notice in Freud the inversion of the classical tradition: the idea of happiness has become fundamentally at odds with what is most praiseworthy in human life. Hobbes stands as one of Freud's earlier precursors, identifying the pursuit of happiness with a generalized desire for gratification; Kant rejected happiness as a motive in ethics but retained it as a portion of the final end; and Freud banished it altogether. An unrestrained pursuit of happiness leads to violence; the victor can only hope to convince society of at least one "thou shalt not" prohibiting murder to avoid being killed himself.[40] As Philip Rieff has shown, Freud was a moralist who did not share the utilitarian confidence in measuring the goodness of morality and politics by aggregates of pleasure: the pleasure principle on its own leads to a destructive compulsion to repeat, while the reality principle restricts the enjoyment of pleasure to what can be socially beneficial.[41]

With Freud, however, what was once identified with the greatest good of human life has become the motive for aggression, war, and annihilation. George Steiner uses Freud's analysis of culture as a key to understanding the slaughters that characterize the history of modernity. In Freud we see that the "portrayal of the tensions which civilized manners impose on central, unfulfilled human instincts remains valid. As do hints . . . that there is in human interrelations an inescapable drive toward war, toward a supreme assertion of identity at the cost of mutual destruction."[42] From an ideal of personal and political human perfection to the primary motive and explanation of human destruction, the ideal of happiness has traveled a long way. The same satisfaction that Kant retained as a portion of the summum bonum Freud regards as an inexorable human motive toward socially destructive ends. The decision against happiness as a noble goal for living, as we have seen, was not inaugurated by the father of psychoanalysis. There were many precursors, including Kierkegaard and Nietzsche, who issued prophetic rejections and reformulations of their own kind. As a consequence of its growing association with psychological satisfaction, even the mention of the topic of happiness is met with disdain by some as unworthy of serious attention. Others react to talk about happiness as a veiled excuse for doing whatever you feel like doing, making happiness morally dangerous, in addition to being frivolous. Indeed, for some time a number of voices, some even considered prophetic, have warned contemporary society to abandon the pursuit of happiness, claiming not only that it trivializes more sober and earnest purposes of life, but also that it risks the introduction of unchecked self-centeredness into our moral judgment.

The reasons just surveyed for removing the idea of happiness from the heart of philosophical reflection provide significant reasons for doubting whether this modern faith in mental repose can ultimately prevail. The evolution toward psychological happiness was a long time in coming and is still not entirely complete. The reduction of happiness to reported satisfaction received, as has been shown, a serious critique in advance of its coming. The evidence indicates that the problems inherent in the overlapping traditions of happiness as the summum bonum and as psychological satisfaction have bequeathed an explosive conflict of meanings to the present age. What has become the unacknowledged greatest good in the public mind—subjective satisfaction—has been shown to be problematic since at least the last half of the eighteenth century.

How and when happiness slipped free of its ethical moorings in classical thought and became an "Ichthian act" of "personal power" is impossible to pinpoint, but it has not gone without comment that some kernel of the same ambiguity was built into the American character at its foundation. Howard Mumford Jones was worried about the effect of psychological happiness in the present age. He writes, "[H]appiness ceased to have supernatural sanctions and turned into something called 'adjustment,' as the social worker and eventually the psychiatrist replaced the minister as a guide to life."[43] Jefferson, he says, would have been horrified at the governmental bureaucracy that has been generated in order to cultivate this brand of happiness. The hedonism of the Enlightenment by itself, as Jones argues, is not to blame for the removal of happiness from its moral context. Rather, he attributes this dislodging to a confluence of other leitmotifs in American thought. His *Pursuit of Happiness*, written more than thirty-five years ago, warns against the growing tendency to use happiness for the justification of self-centered and self-absorbed lives—one more warning gone unheard.

Notes

1. Miguel de Unamuno, *The Tragic Sense of Life in Men and Nations*, trans. Anthony Kerrigan (Princeton: Princeton University Press, 1972), 255; hereafter cited as *TSL*.

2. *TSL*, 226.

3. *TSL*, 268; emphasis added.

4. Aleksandr I. Solzhenitsyn, *The Cancer Ward*, trans. Rebecca Frank (New York: Dell Publishing, 1968), 513.

5. Alasdair MacIntyre, *A Short History of Ethics* (New York: Macmillan Publishing, 1966), 237; also 167, 195, 207, 236-38.

6. MacIntyre, *A Short History of Ethics*, 238-40.

7. Alasdair MacIntyre, *After Virtue* (Notre Dame, Ind.: University of Notre Dame Press, 1984), 43, 63.

8. MacIntyre, *After Virtue*, 64.

9. Walker Percy, *Lost in the Cosmos: The Last Self-Help Book* (New York: Farrar, Straus, Giroux, 1983), 75.

10. Walker Percy, *The Thanatos Syndrome* (New York: Farrar, Straus, Giroux, 1987); page numbers in parentheses are taken from this edition. Peter D. Kramer has recently compared the use of heavy sodium in Percy's novel to the increasing use of antidepressant drugs; see his *Listening to Prozac* (New York: Viking, 1993), 250-300.

11. Percy is on record saying that he did not remember seeing it in O'Connor. See Flannery O'Connor's introduction to *A Memoir of Mary Ann* (New York: Farrar, Staus and Cudahy, 1961), 19. The specific audience for O'Connor's remarks are those who use the suffering of children to reject the goodness of God: "In this popular pity, we mark our gain in sensibility and our loss in vision. . . . In this absence of faith now, we govern by tenderness. It is a tenderness which, long since cut off from the person of Christ, is wrapped in theory. When tenderness is detached from the source of tenderness, its logical outcome is terror. It ends in forced labor camps and in the fumes of the gas chamber."

12. Ernest Becker, *The Denial of Death* (New York: The Free Press, 1973). Also relevant is his *Escape from Evil* (New York: The Free Press, 1975).

13. Robert N. Bellah, Richard Madsen, William M. Sullivan, Ann Swidler, and Stephen M. Tipton, *Habits of the Heart: Individualism and Commitment in American Life* (New York: Harper & Row, 1986), 6.

14. Bellah et al., 221.

15. Bellah et al., 23-24.

16. Thomas Hobbes, *Human Nature*, 7.7 quoted in D. D. Raphael, *British Moralists: 1650-1800*, 2 vols. (Oxford: Oxford University Press, 1969), 6.

17. Hobbes, 7.6.

18. Hobbes, *Leviathan* 1.6 (London: Oxford University Press, 1958), 48.

19. Bellah et al., 295.

20. Blaise Pascal, *Pensées*, trans. A. J. Krailsheimer (New York: Penguin Books, 1966); numbers in parenthesis indicate the aphorism in this edition.

21. Pascal's critique of the self-deception implicit in psychological happiness is grounded in a religious view that unhappiness itself bears witness to the Fall of creatures from union with the Creator (117). Cut off from its origin, human desire being by nature infinite can be satisfied by nothing short of God. From the moment desire possesses any object other than God, boredom ensues and new desires are born (687). True happiness is in God alone but this desire for God is perverted through the myriad ways of imagination.

22. Paul Hazard, *European Thought in the Eighteenth Century: From Montesquieu to Lessing* (London: Hollis & Carter, 1954), 24.

23. Ghita Ionescu, *Politics and the Pursuit of Happiness*, 79-80.

24. Samuel Johnson, *Rasselas* (New York: Barron's, 1963), 72.

25. Immanuel Kant defines happiness as a "a rational being's consciousness of the agreeableness of life which without interruption accompanies his whole existence" in *The Critique of Practical Reason*, trans. Lewis White Beck (Indianapolis: Bobbs-Merrill 1956), 20; hereafter cited as *PR*.

26. Immanuel Kant, *Foundations of the Metaphysics of Morals*, trans. Lewis White Beck (Indianapolis: Bobbs-Merril, 1959), 9; hereafter cited as *FM*.

27. *FM*, 25.

28. *PR*, 36.

29. *PR*, 23.

30. Sigmund Freud, *Civilization and Its Discontents*, trans. James Strachey (New York: W. & W. Norton, 1961), 25; hereafter cited as *CD*.

31. *CD*, 30.

32. *CD*, 23.

33. Sigmund Freud, *Studies in Hysteria*, 2.305 quoted in Philip Rieff, *Freud: The Mind of the Moralist* (New York: Doubleday, 1961), 358.

34. Isidor Silbermann, "On Happiness," *The Psychoanalytic Study of the Child* 40 (New Haven: Yale University Press, 1985), 461.

35. Silbermann, 46.

36. Silbermann, 48.

37. Silbermann, 26.

38. Silbermann, 23.

39. Silbermann, 40-41.

40. Sigmund Freud, *The Future of an Illusion*, trans. W. D. Robson-Scott (New York: Anchor Books, 1964), 19-20.

41. Philip Rieff, 355-57.

42. George Steiner, *Bluebeard's Castle: Some Notes toward the Redefinition of Culture* (New Haven: Yale University Press, 1971), 24; see also the comments of Paul Ricoeur on the implications of the death instinct for civilization, *Freud and Philosophy: An Essay in Interpretation*, trans. Denis Savage (New Haven: Yale University Press, 1971), 304.

43. Howard Mumford Jones, *The Pursuit of Happiness*, 104.

Part II

Assessments

Chapter 4

The Shadow of Eudaemonism

If objective judgments about happiness rely on the legacy of *eudaimonia*, as well as its Latin equivalents, *beatitudo* and *felicitas*, it is necessary to clarify what that legacy bequeathed to modernity. The space of a single chapter will not allow anything approaching a comprehensive view of classical eudaemonism, but it will allow an overview of its general features, in particular, those that are relevant to the critique of well-feeling.

Some would argue, however, that it is impossible to bring ancient eudaemonism to bear directly on modern happiness. For example, several classicists avoid translating *eudaimonia* as "happiness" since its meanings in English usage are normally associated with pleasure, enjoyment, or satisfaction. Instead, they render *eudaimonia* as "human flourishing" or "well-being" or simply leave it untranslated.[1]

These attempts to emphasize the difference between the ancient and modern concepts raise important questions about the continued use of the term *happiness*. From the perspective of classicism one might argue that any critique of contemporary views of happiness would be better served by a change of diction. To revise our thinking about happiness requires, perhaps, a totally new word or phrase, one closer to the meaning of the Greek and Latin terms.

There are, nonetheless, decisive reasons to stay with the word *happiness*. First of all, as has been pointed out, there are still too many traces of eudaemonism in our concept of happiness to disavow altogether its connections to *eudaimonia*. As one commentator has written, "I find that a theory of happiness that assigns non-hedonic evaluative criteria a role in the logic or grammar or meaning of happiness words better accounts for past *and present* thoughts about happiness."[2] Although one can agree that it would be futile to expect people to correct their linguistic habits in accord with philosophical demands, we can expect them to be honest about what they are already saying.

Therefore, expressions such as "human flourishing" and "well-being" offer variations of expression but fail to do justice to the echo of eudaemonism that still reverberates within modern usage. Furthermore, the new renderings appear also to distance themselves from the ancient Greek usage. Gregory Vlastos, in his defense of *eudaimonia* as happiness, argues that neither the modern nor ancient meaning is so easily characterized or differentiated. He also points to the continuing presence of an objective meaning of happiness, as witnessed in leading English dictionaries, and to the three primary meanings *eudaimonia* enjoyed between the fourth and fifth centuries B.C.—prosperity, pleasure, and moral attainment. "Thus if hedonism is a mistake, having *eudaimonia* as your word for 'happiness' won't save you from it."[3]

Though we might share the concern of those who want to distinguish *eudaimonia* from some of the ordinary connotations of happiness, there is no guarantee that a change of diction can keep us from associating flourishing or well-being with satisfaction and pleasure. Such a strategy seems doomed to only momentary success before it falls prey to the current summum bonum of subjective satisfaction, which can attach itself to whatever words are employed. The odd phrase "subjective well-being" is already in use among social scientists. Even terms that seem explicitly antagonistic to hedonic interpretation, such as *tranquillity* and *peace of mind*, can be construed in this way.

The attempt to substitute new words for happiness may enrich our philosophical vocabulary, but at the cost of further deadening everyday speech. Imagine the insertion of *well-being* or *human flourishing* into all the grammatical slots normally allotted to happiness, a difficult task since neither term has an adjectival or adverbial form. The case is similar to the use of words taken from the language of physics that have already taken hold in the language about love—*relationship* and *bonding* have become common parlance. These phrases have had their day and have helped to bolster a depleted vocabulary, but inevitably they will succumb to the pressures they were designed to withstand. Once we tire of "bonding" we will return, thankfully, to "love." This is true especially in the case of happiness, since both its evaluative and psychological usages lie too deeply embedded in our culture to be erased by linguistic fiat. One can predict that the growing usage of *well-being* in professional discussions will soon be embroiled in the same debates over the problem of subjectivity that plague happiness and produce instances in which the content of well-being is assumed to be well-feeling.[4]

The fact that classical eudaemonism held a so-called objective view of happiness does not mean that the psychological and affective side of happiness was ignored.[5] By asserting an objective view of happiness, all one is saying is that the claim to happiness is subject to third-person appraisal. At the very least, eudaemonism puts those judgments in the context of character and the success of one's life-as-a-whole in fulfilling basic human needs.

Psychological states, as will be seen, were usually a part of any judgment about a person's happiness. In fact, there is not a single version of classical eudaemonism that does not depict the happy person possessing some manner of desirable mental state, usually tranquillity or freedom from disturbance. The point to be made in this chapter is that, regardless of the importance ascribed to the psychological state, it is never considered solely constitutive of happiness, or even associated with it, unless it is the product of a morally good life.

In looking at the tradition of eudaemonism, however, we see that there were some serious disagreements about the nature of happiness. For example, in *The City of God* St. Augustine refers to a lost work by the Roman philosopher Varro that calculated 288 competing versions of happiness.[6] But as part of Augustine's rhetorical strategy to discredit pagan philosophy this number is misleading. These differing conceptions of happiness, extrapolated from the main philosophical traditions of Plato, Aristotle, Epicurus, and the Stoics, were also attempts at envisioning the summum bonum, the best and most desirable life for human beings.[7] This is the most distinctive aspect of eudaemonism, that judgments about and claims to happiness must be measured against a standard of an ideal life as measured by a final end. "The idea behind this notion [*eudaimonia*] is that he who is happy in this sense has what is *worth* desiring and worth having in life."[8] Since this worthwhile life was thought naturally to include the attainment of moral goodness, the happy life and the morally good life were considered necessary to one other, and even identical by some, such as the Stoics.

The fact is that the classical schools did not agree about the good for human life. They argued as if theories of happiness rested on a view of human nature, but their disagreements generated shared lists of formal criteria, not a consensus on the material content fulfilling those criteria.[9] Aristotle's list from *Nicomachean Ethics* is representative: *eudaimonia* must be (1) the final end, (2) complete, (3) self-sufficient, and (4) choiceworthy.[10] Bearing in mind that all of these criteria require a fixed view of human nature, they can be interpreted as follows: the happy life must (1) contain everything that is good for a human being; (2) be sought for its own sake and not for the sake of anything else; (3) possess all the good(s), lacking in nothing; and (4) be a life more desirable than all others.

Use of these criteria was not uniform among the different schools; it is the first, the completeness criterion, that was the most widely used.[11] As we will see later, the application of these formal conditions pushed classical philosophers to unfortunate extremes in framing the circumference of the happy life.

Still, even with the agreed moral imperatives there were significant differences whether happiness was a mixed or simple end—in other words, whether it included more than one good. For the Cynics, to be happy was simply to be virtuous; for the Stoics, it was to be virtuous and satisfied; and for still others, the Aristotelians, happiness meant that one was virtuous, satisfied, and fortunate. As noted in chapter two, however, the classical philosophers differed on the specific content of the best life; they agreed that these goods "exist in us in such sort that we must either desire virtue on their account, or them for the sake of virtue, or both for their own sake."[12] Virtue ensured that whatever goods made up the happy life, that life would be ordered toward its final end; its very composition ensured good use. As Cicero comments, "without virtue nothing is praiseworthy."[13]

This assurance applies as much to mental repose as to the other goods of a happy life. Virtue itself was for Augustine the only good that could not undermine a person's hold on happiness, since it virtually guaranteed beneficial use of anything and everything, whether pleasure seeking or confessed satisfaction with one's life. Tranquillity for Augustine, like the earlier classical philosophers, was not exempt from the concern for its use; it had not yet attained the status of an unqualified good. Augustine summarizes the basic attitude of eudaemonism when he says, "Thus no one is happy but the man who has everything he wants, and wants nothing wrongly."[14]

For these ancient philosophers, pagans as well as Christians, there was agreement that all the elements of a happy life should be morally governed, and that virtue ensured that those ends that are naturally desirable, such as pleasure and satisfaction, do not take complete command of a person's life. There were few exceptions to the rule that "only moral and rational behavior leads to happiness."[15]

Whether the primary characteristic of the summum bonum was thought to be enjoyment, some form of pleasure, or some level of emotional or psychological satisfaction, none of those qualities were by themselves considered a sufficient basis on which to judge a life a happy one. In lacking the stable dispositions of character and judgment, that is, the virtues, to protect oneself from the push and pull of these desirable states, an individual was vulnerable to their control and liable to the moral blindness that could follow. Virtue either as an end or as an instrumental means was considered indispensable to happiness.

The virtues ensure free and rational agency, an inner control over one's life and happiness, that not only distinguishes classical eudaemonism from psychological happiness, but also from that of the prephilosophical world of Homeric Greece. As Bruno Snell explains, prior to the advent of philosophy, the Greeks had little inkling of this "internal" happiness. The Socratic call to virtue implied a radically changed idea of happiness that distinguished it from a more ancient association with profit and plenty, the notion of *oblios*; *eudaimonia* meant exactly what is conveyed by its etymology: one who is happy has "by his side a good demon who helps him succeed in everything he undertakes."[16]

So in reinterpreting the received concept of *eudaimonia* the early philosophers took the cause of happiness away from the external forces of fate and the gods and placed it in the internal motions of soul or psyche. As a consequence, external success gave way to aspects of individual character as the content of a happy life.

The explicit connection between virtue and happiness is first made by Democritus whose account of happiness, surprisingly, looks very psychological. It is an exaggeration to assert that his account is "virtually identical with modern ideas,"[17] but no doubt it seems less strange to our ears than that of Socrates, who, like the Stoics who admired him, often identified happiness with virtue alone. Democritus's word for happiness, *euthumia*, literally means having one's emotional and appetitive self, or *thumos*, in a good state; *euthumia* can be translated as *joy, gladness, cheerfulness,* or *good-heartedness*. He also employed *euesto*, "well-being," and *eudaimonia* as synonyms for *euthumia* but clearly dissociated himself from the older tradition that identified either kind of happiness with good fortune. "Happiness does not reside in cattle or gold; the soul is the dwelling place of one's good or evil genius."[18] As such, happiness does not signify the gift of *oblios*—"Good and ill fortune reside in the self."

Thus, Democritus, a generation before Plato, can be seen as providing the context for many subsequent uses of the word *eudaimonia*. He was in fact the first person to attempt a systematic ethical theory.[19] Not only would he distinguish happiness from fortune and argue for its invulnerability to luck, but he would further specify its status as the final end of human life and action. The actual content of happiness, *euthumia*, a cheerful and satisfied state of mind, seems to the contemporary reading just another form of well-feeling, but the happiness recommended by Democritus is far from a fifth-century B.C. version of American positive thinking: the *euthemos*, "The cheerful man . . . is strong and free from care; but him that cares nought for justice and does not the things that are right finds all such things joyless, when he remembers them, and is afraid and reproaches himself."[20]

This and other similar fragments create a composite portrait of Democritian *euthumia* whose appeal to modern tastes in happiness would be partial. Democritus's happy person is at once ascetic, careful not to enjoy intense pleasure, and self-disciplined to limit his desires so as to enjoy the calm of self-sufficiency. "The right-minded man is he who is not grieved by what he has not, but enjoys what he has."[21] Nonetheless, it is clear that Democritus made the issue of psychological satisfaction a central issue in the history of happiness. Later developments would strongly challenge, though not overthrow, *euthumia* as the actual content of happiness, as opposed to its causes or effects. Aristotle and the Stoics would be particularly sympathetic to including desirable mental states as a necessary condition of *eudaimonia*. The question for all of them was how to include satisfaction in their accounts of happiness without sacrificing the foundation of a good life.

This issue was also at the center of the controversy over whether happiness was a mixed or a simple good. While there was strong consensus in antiquity supporting the necessity of moral goodness as a basis for happiness, much debate was focused on the importance of bodily and external goods, such as health, pleasure, wealth, power, honor, and fame. Followers of Socrates and Plato, who included the Stoics and Cynics, often regarded moral virtue as the only unqualified good and, therefore, as the only necessary ingredient of the happy life. Mental and emotional states such as *ataraxia* or *tranquilitas*, therefore, tended to appear among descriptions of happiness itself and of concomitant effects of possessing virtue. Aristotelians, on the other hand, considered this a ridiculous narrowing of *eudaimonia*, arguing that a happy life, to be complete and self-sufficient, must include at least moderate and fairly lasting portions of all the goods.

The tension between virtue and psychological satisfaction can be seen especially in Stoic ethics. Although renowned for their emphasis on virtue in the happy life, the Stoics, like Democritus, did not ignore the subjective side of happiness, which they described as either *ataraxia* (freedom from disturbance), *tranquilitas*, or *eurboia biou* (good flow of life). They are said to have identified virtue with happiness, but that is an oversimplification. The virtues are both a final and an instrumental good for the Stoics; they are worth seeking in themselves but they are also worthy for the state of mind they can bestow. "Therefore someone who desires happiness, in the Stoics' sense, must desire virtue *for its own sake* since the former consists in the latter."[22]

For the Stoics the close relation of virtue with the happiness of "good flow" guarantees both its fulfilling the criteria of self-sufficiency and its worth. Stoic virtue must be invulnerable to misfortune and have no need for the pleasure-motive of Epicurus. Virtue is sought for its own sake, and any benefits derived from it are considered only advantages. The Stoic may, in fact, get a sort of refined pleasure from virtue but it cannot be counted as a good alongside the good of virtue. Tranquillity, along with wealth, honor, power, and the rest, is to be regarded as an advantage to the virtuous agent. As a result, the Stoic view of happiness meets the criterion of completeness since nothing other than virtue and its concomitant state of mind is considered good. Virtue alone qualifies as good since nothing can be considered good that is subject to evil use or that can be taken away by misfortune.

Epicurus is another classical eudaemonist who seems to offer support for contemporary well-feeling. His identification of the final good with pleasure (*hedone*), however, illustrates what seems paradoxical to the modern reader about the classical ideal of happiness. Happiness for Epicurus, like Democritus, who influenced him, consisted not in the enjoyment of raw pleasures, but with the states called *ataraxia* and *aponia*, meaning freedom from disturbance or pain. These are pleasures that qualify as happiness: pleasures that are the direct consequence of living a virtuous life—not kinetic pleasures involving the active seeking of new pleasure, but static pleasures which minimize the tribulations usually associated with pleasure seeking. *Ataraxia* is both durable and dependable; it is neither transient nor unpredictable, like the immoderate pleasures that inevitably lead to the pain of their passing. Consequently, Epicurus, the father of hedonism, counsels us to continence: "There are times when we pass by pleasures if they are outweighed by the hardships that follow."[23]

The pleasure signified by *ataraxia* was valued by Epicurus not simply because it was enjoyable or because it was mental, but because it signified something more important than subjective satisfaction. *Ataraxia* could be used to characterize the state of an individual who functions in an unimpeded fashion.[24] In other words, pleasure of this kind reflects the well-being of the whole person, the kind of state that can be retained only by the maintenance of virtue. This explains why Epicurus was so confident that virtue, especially prudence, provides the instrumental means to happiness.

Ataxaria signifies a person functioning smoothly; it is not the cause, but the effect, of that ease. To seek that state directly would necessarily flounder, since this bypasses the actual cause. Virtue is so central to his account that, at times, Epicurus seems to make virtue actually constitutive of happiness rather than a means to it. Like the Stoic relationship between virtue and good flow, the relationship of Epicurean virtue to pleasure is not simply an instrumental means.

Yet, as has been said, nothing underscores the pivotal role of virtue in the classical eudaemonism more than the Cynic and Epicurean argument for the possibility of happiness under torture. The notion of happiness under torture became a kind of litmus test among later Stoics, Cynics, and Epicureans to distinguish themselves from the Aristotelians, who included nonmoral goods in their definition of happiness. This certainly sets contemporary psychological happiness in sharp relief.

Such an outrageous notion was not easily accepted, however, even by all classical philosophers with Stoic sympathies. Cicero, attempting to understand the misfortune of his own life, sets out to defend the Stoic sufficiency of virtue and, surprisingly, scoffs at the idea of happiness under torture. He is particularly dismissive of the contradiction in position of Epicurus, who holds that while pain is the greatest evil, there is happiness under torture. Annas makes good use of this debate by showing how such a counterintuitive suggestion can prompt reflection on the nature of our final end.[24]

That some of the ancients embraced such a notion challenges us to a more complex evaluation of happiness than the application of simple well-feeling. What we in modernity commonly regard as providing support for our self-determined identity and freedom actually results in limiting our options, especially in grappling with the onslaught of suffering and disappointment. Self-satisfaction becomes an obstacle to happiness not only but also, and more fundamentally, to the critical reflection on one's life.

Cicero's circumstances when he wrote his major work on happiness, the *Tusculan Disputations* (45 B.C.), are illustrative. Composed during the crumbling of the Roman republic and mounting personal crises, the disputations are dedicated to Caesar's eventual assassin— Brutus. Cicero, divorced from his first wife, alienated from his brother, and in terrible grief over the death of his daughter, had just divorced his second wife because she did not approve of his grieving. The debates of the classical schools over the nature of the good, the completeness of the happy life, the role of pleasure and pain, these all became questions that Cicero sought to answer for the sake of his own consolation. In these dialogues, set over five days, he discusses death, pain, emotional distress, psychic disorder, and the relation of virtue to happiness:

> Let him, if he likes, say the same inside the bull of Phalaris as he would have said, had he been in his own bed: I do not attribute wisdom such wonderful power against pain. It is enough for duty if the wise man is brave in endurance; I do not require him to rejoice; for pain is a melancholy condition beyond doubt, unpleasing, distasteful, repugnant to nature, difficult to submit to and bear.

For Cicero the only evil is moral baseness and disgrace, and pain comes as a teacher, providing an opportunity for growth in the virtues.[25] This is not to say that the wise person seeks out pain for its own sake, but rather greets it as an occasion for self-mastery. He uses the example of the person who undergoes surgery without being tied down: "Marius showed that the sting of pain was severe, for he did not offer his other leg; thus being a man he bore pain, being human he refused to bear greater pain without actual necessity."[26]

Though Cicero takes a more realistic view of pain he still displays the influence of his Epicurean training when he insists that the happiness of the wise overcomes all inner disturbances and expunges all passions. To be overcome and broken by suffering evinces a lack of virtue, since virtue makes bad fortune endurable. Cicero's eclectic eudaemonism reveals the perfectionist tendencies of all the schools: happiness, if it is to be complete and self-sufficient means that nothing can be wanting—"And yet no one can be happy except when good is secure and certain and lasting. . . . For our wish is that the happy man be safe, impregnable, fenced and fortified, and so made inaccessible not only to a little fear, but to any fear at all."[27] So complete is their control that happy persons never have need to repent of anything, no need for regret.[28]

Two questions arise: (1) Who possibly qualifies as happy? (2) Is this degree of invulnerability really desirable? Later chapters address these as possible weaknesses in the classical account. For now, it is enough to notice that this version of eudaemonism is not merely elitist but unrealistic. What appears to be driving this argument is an unnecessarily stringent application of completeness and self-sufficiency criteria.

Aristotle, who affirmed pleasure as a basic good, also dismissed the torture argument.[29] Yet his reasons for finding the idea of happiness under torture strange has less to do with the role of pain in securing virtue than in his view of external goods, that is, goods of fortune. Aristotle, like Cicero and Epicurus, sees virtue as a necessary condition of happiness and will allow that a happy life contains some resiliency against suffering and modest strokes of misfortune—but he draws the line at torture. A happy man can never be utterly miserable, although the morally good man certainly can be, and will act nobly under the most adverse circumstances, as in the case of Priam, the king of Troy.[30] The happy life for Aristotle is the most pleasant, partly because of the pleasure a happy person derives from his virtue, but also because his exercise of virtue is unimpeded by a lack of external goods. The absence of these goods, even when lost through misfortune, deprive a person of happiness, since without friends, wealth, or power an individual's range of virtuous activity, and pleasure, is severely restricted.[31]

Our contemporaries, however, laugh at the suggestion of happiness on the rack for different reasons, because at some point in our tradition a happy life became conceivable apart from a morally good life and inconceivable apart from well-feeling. The issue is no longer what it was for Aristotle—the limits of what virtue can withstand in the face of misfortune—but rather how a person can possess, regardless of the means, those states of mind and feeling associated with being happy. Consequently, the suggestion of happiness under torture, or even while suffering pain, appears preposterous to the modern mind.

Regardless of the different solutions to the problem of pain posed by these classical thinkers, eudaemonists agree that the summum bonum of happiness contains an objective measure. To predicate happiness of someone's character or life is in part a moral appraisal of his or her aims and success in meeting them. In this sense one of the central marks of eudaemonism is that it not provide a measure or justification for individual actions but rather for states of character or lives; it is not a moral theory per se, but an approach to the ordering of a human life in its totality—it addresses the question of how to live. Thus eudaemonism can be used for the sake of self-clarification and self-appraisal through the range of a person's states and activities. While happiness is to be pursued as the most desirable life to live, it is simultaneously the standard that governs the pursuit of all its goods, even mental satisfaction.

If happiness can belong only to the morally good person, it will undoubtedly be possessed by the few rather than by the many. That the classical philosophers knew this is obvious from their preoccupation with making third-person judgments about other people's happiness: "When can we call a person happy?" was the constant refrain introducing this line of questioning, but the very shape of their question manifests the great honor implicit in being judged happy.

To call a person happy was not simply a pronouncement about his or her feeling states, although it may have included that, or worldly success, although it may have included that, or relation to divinity, although it may have included even that. Rather, it was to designate this person as having reached the proper end specified by his or her nature as a human being. *Eudaimonia, beatitudo,* and *felicitas* each became identified with the summum bonum or greatest good of human life, the fulfillment of aims, appetites and purposes integral to the perfection of human nature and, by implication,

human communities. Given the difficulty of satisfying this criterion, one wonders how often that honor was actually bestowed.

It is safe to say, however, that among the classical philosophers
themselves the central problem of happiness was the everyday problem of cultivating and maintaining virtue in a world often inhospi-
table to such aspirations. This would apply to those schools of
thought that identified virtue as only a means to happiness, which
itself was identified with pleasure or tranquillity or contemplation
(or with those who identified happiness as a concomitant state to
virtue). With the coming of Christianity, however, and the occasional
collision and occasional synthesis of pagan and Christian wisdoms,
the possibility of attaining happiness on earth, as the final good,
was beset by a much greater difficulty than the challenge of moral
development.

It would be difficult to overestimate the impact of the rejection
of earthly happiness in the eudaemonist tradition. The Christian
identification of the object of happiness with a transcendent object,
God, as a final end, extrinsic rather than intrinsic to our humanity,
created an unbridgeable gap between the now provisional terrain of
this life and the ultimate finality of the next. For the first time,
though, eudaemonism would have a theoretical foundation, albeit
based on faith, that would do justice to its demands for total and
perfect completeness.

For the next seven centuries, until the time of Aquinas, happiness would be identified simply with eternal life, regardless of a
person's moral or spiritual attainments. The basic reason for this
rejection of the traditional view was the transposition of final ends
that traded an immanent end of human perfection for a transcendent end. From this religious standpoint, human beings can be perfected only insofar as they possess an object more than human, not
the angels as the Arab philosophers of the Middle Ages would teach,
but perfect being itself—God.

Boethius, like Cicero, wrote his *Consolation of Philosophy* (524
A.D.) under the most excruciating of personal circumstances. Imprisoned unjustly as a traitor and facing death by torture at the height
of his fame as a statesman and a scholar, he was forced to accept
the conclusions of Augustine's critique written a century earlier.
From the viewpoint of the formal criteria for happiness he inherited from Aristotle, the philosopher he knew better than anyone in
the sixth century, Boethius, after a lifetime of success in everything
he had pursued, was suddenly deprived of happiness against his will.

Having suffered the fate of Priam, Boethius saw no other option than to reject the possibility of happiness in this world. Instead of holding firm to the Aristotelian insistence of external goods, he looked away from this world for his final object of happiness.

Boethius continued to argue that human happiness is a perfect state, self-sufficient and lacking in nothing, but through the mouthpiece of Lady Philosophy he asserts that all the goods of life can be possessed together only in the presence of God.[32] Since nothing can be lacking, happiness must drive out all pain and all fear, even fear of any future loss. Since only the good of moral virtue is immune from the wheel of misfortune and the happy life requires the possession of all goods in unity, they may be enjoyed only in eternity where God, standing in judgment of our merit, will confer them.

The religiously inspired view that there is no earthly happiness stood firm until the revival of Aristotelianism in the twelfth century. At the summit of this revival Thomas Aquinas attempted to retrieve a notion of earthly happiness by distinguishing between the imperfect happiness of this life and the perfect happiness of the next. For Aquinas, happiness on earth was always an *imperfect happiness*.[33] Although earthly life may in fact be called happy, it remains a life with imperfection, potentiality, and vulnerability. Earthly happiness is invariably *in via*, or in-the-making.

It could have been predicted that in the later Middle Ages and Renaissance much of the speculation about happiness would address itself to the tension between the two happinesses—temporal and eternal. Dante's view of happiness, for example, reveals the trajectory of Renaissance and modern thought in removing the goal of earthly happiness from its subordination to eternal happiness with God.[34] Doing so frees temporal authorities and individual political conscience from obedience to pope and church in secular matters.

The separation of church from state remains a debated principle of modern government, but what gets less attention is how government can assume those religious offices. It was precisely the heaven of Christianity, according to Eric Voegelin, that inspired the Gnostic vision of a perfect society. Those he calls the gnostic "directors of being" attempt to remake society in the image of perfect happiness; these utopian reformers are obviously not much interested in the concept of *beatitudo imperfecta*. No doubt the notion of a *peregrinal* happiness, the happiness of the way as coined by Augustine, resists the fanaticism generated by an impatience for the ideal. This is seen in the utopian project of a perfect society leading to totalitarianism or in the pursuit of a perfect immediacy of pleasure that culminates in cultural narcissism. Both of these outcomes are opposed by the prophetic principle generated by the shift of eudaemonism toward an eternal object, one that clearly distinguishes between the idols of false ultimacy and the true summum bonum. This idol breaking was already seen at work in Pascal and many of the happiness rejectors who combated the incipient secularism and materialism of the modern age.

As will be discussed in the next chapter, when happiness was once again considered mainly terrestrial, the good of psychological satisfaction emerged as the content of happiness. The problem became, in part because of the established authority of the eudaemonist tradition, to find the ethical justification for satisfaction so it could be called happiness.

The search for a justified satisfaction is now under debate by philosophers. Finding it, of course, depends entirely on the possibility of gaining a new moral consensus, an outcome that appears more and more unlikely. For the time being, however, the argument can take us at least this far. We can affirm what the present age takes so seriously—the importance of positive affect in human life, what used to be called joy, delight, peace of mind, ease, and so forth. We can agree that a portrait of the most desirable life would be very hard to accept without including such states. After all, we could argue that to ignore the role of affectivity would be to forget the unity of mind and body in the human composite, a denial that would be loath to thinkers such as Augustine and Aquinas. If a happy life represents the perfecting *in via* of the whole person, then the affective life must be included.

Still, the pursuit of well-feeling by itself is not only ineffective for well-feeling but also inherently destructive for individuals and communities. It draws attention away from the cultivation of basic goods—that is, health, friendship, wisdom, justice, and citizenship—and also promotes opportunities for active self-deception. In the latter case, well-feeling becomes, in effect, an unconscious smoke screen for the pursuit of destructive ends. In order to correct this situation we have to put the cart back behind the horse. We can begin by questioning the assumption that we are beings whose final end is solely psychological satisfaction. Aquinas, following Aristotle, points out that the joy that belongs to the happy life comes as a consequence, a concomitant, of possessing the goods that are ordinate to human nature. The *frui* or joy of the beatific vision, *beatitudo perfecta*, is the consequence of knowing and loving God.[35] Thus, the feelings of a happy life descend on us, so to speak, or arise, as a kind of surprise or afterthought insofar as we are actively pursuing other ends. Pursue joy directly, averting attention from the activity that yields the enjoyment, and you either diminish joy or miss it altogether—the classic dilemma of the bored aesthete in bondage to the immediate.

Psychological satisfaction can be affirmed as integral to the happy life only with the proviso that it is not consciously sought or intended. Both the concomitant and transitory character of the affections demand that we remove them from center stage. What is left, then, to the happy life when it has been deprived of life's finality and perfection? A distinction has been made between the happy moment and the happy life. As a consequence, happiness has been dissociated from its purely psychological interpretations, and it has been emphasized that a realistic account of the happy life must embrace some forms of suffering.

The purpose of this argument thus far has been to advance distinctions allowing us to understand and to accept the indispensable role of virtue, both intellectual and moral, in the happy life. Virtues are precisely those habits of character that provide persons with their identity; virtues are the dispositions that constitute a self over a lifetime; virtues in a sense are the foundation of a life, as opposed to the moment, that may be called happy. Since virtues, or excellences of character, do not operate deterministically, human beings can misfire. We can and do make mistakes, or others can do us in. Suffering may be the result, but even if it dispels our tranquillity for a season, suffering need not be considered the "spirit who negates" a happy life. Finally, the very concept of virtue embraces temporality and incompleteness. As dispositions, virtues face the future while having been cultivated in the past. A virtue stands in readiness to act; it has no explicit set of guidelines, no tablet of laws hanging over it that antecedently set out courses of action for all times and circumstances. Virtues exist radically *in via* and enable us to retain through the passage of time our grip both on ourselves and on our final goal.

At this, a strict eudaemonist may point out that the content of the summum bonum remains to be specified. As Annas has argued, the concept of *eudaimonia* in ancient ethics was itself thin and flexible; it could accommodate itself to different conceptions of the final end while remaining firm on the necessity of virtue and reflective consideration of one's whole life. Obviously the encounter with the later religious traditions, as is seen in the Augustinian critique, led to a thicker account, but it is enough if at this point the argument answers the charges leveled at happiness by its critics by showing that the rejection of happiness as a goal for our lives is not the only alternative to the reign of well-feeling. This attempt to link happiness once again to normative criteria must begin with the critique of happiness in the present age but must return to rectify the shortcomings of classical eudaemonism itself.

Our best hope for recovering the legacy of classical and medieval eudaemonism will be discovered in untangling the modern confusion implicit in appeals to well-feeling, and also in admitting that the classical accounts, although helpful in getting discussion started, were themselves far too scrupulous to last. As will be argued in part three, we must take advantage of the fact that once the medievals transferred perfect happiness from this world to eternity, where it belongs, we were left with a better version of eudaemonism.

For now, however, it still remains for us to assess how much of the eudaemonistic legacy has passed into contemporary society. The minority report against well-feeling has already been heard. Three more aspects of this question will be investigated. First, we look at the ambiguous role that the happiness principle played in the American founding. Second, we discuss the way in which happiness is treated in the social sciences. Operating on entirely different premises, empirical research has uncovered support for a renewed eudaimonism. Finally, we review a critical survey of recent philosophical treatments of happiness, most of which appear to be mired in assumptions that have little to do with the ancient meanings.

Notes

1. See the comments of John M. Cooper, *Reason and Human Good in Aristotle* (Cambridge: Harvard University Press, 1975), 89, n.1; he follows the suggestion of G. E. M. Anscombe, "Modern Moral Philosophy," *Philosophy* 33 (1958) 1-19; also, A. H. Armstrong in Plotinus, *Enneads* 1 (Cambridge: Harvard University Press, 1968), 170, n. 1, who remarks, "Happiness, as we normally use the word, means *feeling* good; but *eudaimonia* means *being* in a good state"; and Martha Nussbaum for whom happiness "gives supreme value to psychological states rather than to activities," in *The Fragility of Goodness: Luck and Ethics in Greek Tragedy and Philosophy* (Cambridge: Cambridge University Press, 1986), 6n.

2. Irwin Goldstein, "Happiness: The Role of Non-Hedonic Criteria in Its Evaluation," *International Philosophical Quarterly* 13 (1973): 532; emphasis added.

3. Gregory Vlastos, "Happiness and Virtue in Socrates' Moral Theory," 182. The issue of translation is comprehensively treated by J. C. Dybikowski in "Is Aristotelian *Eudaimonia* Happiness?" *Dialogue* 81 (1981): 185-200, in which he concludes that *eudaimonia* has a "deep kinship with happiness" (198).

4. This has already occurred in works such as *Interpersonal Comparisons of Well-Being*, ed. Jon Elster and John E. Roemer (Cambridge: Cambridge University Press, 1991), especially the paper by Thomas M. Scanlon, "The Moral Basis of Interpersonal Comparisions," 17-44; and James Griffin, *Well-Being: Its Meaning and Measurement* (Oxford: Clarendon Press, 1986).

5. A recent survey of ancient ethics stresses this point; see Julia Annas, *The Morality of Happiness*, 4.

6. St. Augustine, *The City of God*, 19.1 (671).

7. "The words . . . clustering around *agathos* and *eudaimonia*, characterize the qualities which all at this period set before themselves as desirable, the ends which they proposed to themselves, and, more generally, the kind of life which they hoped to lead." Arthur W. H. Adkins, *Merit and Responsibility: A Study in Greek Values* (Chicago: University of Chicago Press, 1960), 254.

8. Elizabeth Telfer, *Happiness* (New York: St. Martin's Press, 1980), 37. Annas takes great pains to point out that the appeals to nature and final ends in classical ethics is conditioned by the ethical standpoints of the various ancient schools (219).

9. T. H. Irwin, "Stoic and Aristotelian Conceptions of Happiness," *The Norms of Nature*, ed. Malcolm Schofield and Gisela Striker (Cambridge: Cambridge University Press, 1986), 206-7.

10. Aristotle, *Nicomachean Ethics*, 1097 a 27-1097 b 21 (14-15).

11. Annas, 6.

12. St. Augustine, *The City of God*, 19.2 (673).

13. Cicero, *Tusculan Diputations*, 5.16 (475).

14. St. Augustine, *The Trinity*, 13.2; trans. Edmund Hill, O. P. (Brooklyn: New City Press, 1990), 349.

15. Wladyslaw Tatarkiewicz, *Analysis of Happiness*, 31. One of these exceptions is Aristuppus, the founder of the Cyrenaics, who valued happiness as a means to the intense enjoyments. When asked why he took the three courtesans offered to him by a wealthy friend, he answered, "Paris paid dearly for giving preference to one out of three"; see Diogenes Laertius, *Lives of Eminent Philosophers*, trans. R. D. Hicks, vol. 1 (Cambridge: Harvard University Press, 1972), 197; but even the Cyrenaics had prudential safeguards according to T. H. Irwin in "Aristippus against Happiness," *Monist* (January 1991): 55-82.

16. Bruno Snell, *The Discovery of Mind: The Greek Origins of European Thought*, trans. T. G. Rosenmeyer (New York: Harper & Row, 1960), 158.

17. Tatarkiewicz, 29; Jonathan Barnes agrees with Tatarkiewicz that (1) Democritus prepares the way for Bentham's felicific calculus and that (2) *euthumia* is not a moral goal but a recipe, in the modern sense, for contentment; *The Presocratic Philosophers*, vol. 2 (London: Routledge & Kegan, Paul, 1979), 231.

18. G. S. Kirk and J. E. Raven, *The Presocratic Philosophers* (Cambridge: Cambridge University Press, 1957), frag. #595; see report of Diogenes Laertius, "He said that the end is *euthumia*, which is not the same as pleasure, as some have mistakenly reported, but is that state in which the soul remains in calm and stability, not shaken by any fear or superstition or any other emotion"; see Diogenes Laertius, vol. 2, 455.

19. Tranlated in J. C. B. Gosling and C. C. W. Taylor, *The Greeks on Pleasure* (Oxford: Clarendon Press, 1982), 29.

20. Gosling and Taylor, 29.

21. Kirk and Raven, frag. #594.

22. Kathleen Freeman, *Ancilla to the Pre-Socratic Philosophers* (Cambridge: Harvard University Press, 1970), 112.

23. *The Hellenistic Philosophers*, vol. 1, trans. and comm. by A. A. Long and D. N. Sedley (Cambridge: Cambridge University Press), 63.

24. *Letter to Menoeceus*, 129b (56); page numbers in parentheses refer to Epicurus, *Letters, Principal Doctrines and Vatican Sayings*, trans. Russel M. Geer (Indianapolis: Bobbs-Merrill, 1964); this translation is used throughout.

25. Julia Annas, "Epicurus on Pleasure and Happiness, *Philosophical Topics* 15:2 (Fall 1987): 12; also Philip Mitsis, *Epicurus' Ethical Theory: The Pleasures of Invulnerability* (Ithaca: Cornell University Press, 1988), 8.

26. Julia Annas, *The Morality of Happiness*, 349-50.

27. Cicero, *Tusculan Disputations*, 2.7 (165).

28. Cicero, 2.7 (203).

29. Cicero, 2.7 (207).

30. Cicero, 5.8 (465-7).

31. Cicero, 5.18 (479). For helpful commentary on this point, see "Cicero in Grief: The Classical Soul Revealed," by Robert E. Proctor in *Education's Great Amnesia: Reconsidering the Humanities from Petrarch to Freud* (Bloomington: Indiana University Press, 1988), 59-75.

32. NE, 1153 b 19-20 (209).

33. NE, 1101 a 1-13 (26).

34. NE, 1099 a 32-1099b1 (21).

35. Boethius, *The Consolation of Philosophy*, 3.10 (277); page numbers in parentheses refer to translation by S. J. Tester (Cambridge: Harvard University Press, 1918), which is used throughout.

36. *Summa Theologiae*, 1-2.5.a.3.

37. See Etienne Gilson, *Dante and Philosophy*, trans. David Moore (Gloucester, Mass.: Peter Smith, 1968), 191-201.

38. ST, 1-2.4.a.2.

39. Annas, *The Morality of Happiness*, ch. 1.

Chapter 5

The Enigma of Jefferson's "Pursuit"

To what extent does Jefferson's idea of happiness fall within the eudaemonistic tradition? The answer to this question is crucial: it determines whether a retrieval of an ordinate view of happiness coincides with the Founders' intentions. Conversely, does the Declaration of Independence license the pursuit of well-feeling? If so, then the project of tracing the limits of satisfaction is more difficult and countercultural than first imagined.

With the coming of modernity, the medieval idea of an eternal happiness gradually gave way to an emergent confidence about the possibilities of happiness in this world. Thomas Aquinas, a key figure in the thirteenth century, anticipated this development in his discussion of a this-worldly happiness ordered toward eternity, but later Renaissance thinkers would be less and less concerned with measuring the differences between terrestrial and eternal life, between the intermediary ends of this life and the final end of a supernatural destiny. Although conceptions of happiness changed slowly during the fifteenth and sixteenth centuries, the trajectory is plain: individual freedom replaces God as the locus for understanding happiness—and with that, "happiness as a state of perfection and the acme of life, faded into insignificance."[1]

The tenets of eudaemonism, as we have seen, demand that we order our momentary enjoyments according to the canons of a rationally directed life. In this context, freedom is understood as ordinate action suitable to human fulfillment, that is, as the possession of the final end. The idea of freedom changed, however, when plea-

sure broke free from its natural orientation toward a final satisfaction. As a consequence, the bond between happiness and ethics began
to weaken, and the desire for pleasure was treated as the source of
a dynamic, as opposed to a static, view of human action. Reaching
a culminating state of existence became less important than enjoying the free expression of human aspiration.

Although the pursuit of pleasure provided the dynamic force for
this transformation of values, freedom itself eventually replaced
happiness as the supreme good in modern ethics. Growing interest
in aspects of everyday life—pleasure, enjoyment, interest, and self-
love—were pursued apart from any overarching notion of how these
ought to be ordered in a good human life. As a consequence, happiness became a subjective concept, the kind we are already familiar with in first-person reporting of well-feeling. From this
perspective there need be no "confusion," according to Agnes Heller,
"if by happiness different people mean quite different things, or if
the same person at different times and in different connections uses
the word in different senses."[2]

This observation, even if it telescopes a complicated development, is helpful in charting the general direction of postmedieval
views of happiness.[3] Yet, in her resolve to see freedom alone as the
mediating link between rational conduct and the experience of happiness, Heller ignores the fact that eudaemonism survived into modernity: "It is most short-sighted to describe the utility theory
or the theory of rational egoism as 'eudaemonic' simply because
their starting point in the real man is in his totality, and his aspirations. . . ."[4] If by this Heller means that the consensual view of
happiness in civilization had changed, she is undoubtedly right;
if Heller means that the legacy of eudaemonism ceased playing
a role in cultural development, she is overlooking its many
residual traces.

Heller's statement can be kept in mind, however, as a warning
about the problematic nature of interpreting the idea of happiness
in the Enlightenment generally and in the American Founders in particular. No single period in Western civilization has been so pre-
occupied with the issue of happiness. It was a time, as Paul
Hazard puts it, of *obsession* with happiness.[5] For the most part, the
Founder's language about happiness is familiar. Both the classical
conjunction of virtue and happiness and the Christian insistence on
the providence of God are seen throughout the hundreds of eighteenth-century treatises on the subject. One can just as easily meet
someone who writes in a Horacean or Epicurean mode about the

happiness of contemplating a garden as one can find discussions of the eternal bliss of heaven.[6]

Yet, taken as a whole, the eighteenth century went well beyond its Renaissance precursors in bringing happiness back to earth—the religious sensibility of the medievals is effectively reversed. Obviously, the Italian Renaissance concern for the "everydayness" of happiness, which Heller underscores, was being pushed toward its logical outcome. It has already been suggested that the happiness of well-feeling was the candidate of choice in a society increasingly committed to happiness for all, and by gradually eschewing the moral requirements of eudaemonism, happiness becomes with every step more accessible to everyone.

Nevertheless, even in its seventeenth- and eighteenth-century versions, the happiness being proposed was still encased in the classical language of virtue and was recommended oftentimes with a view to pleasing God and earning the delights of heaven.[7] The eudaemonistic import of these formulas are blunted, however; they fail to convey unambiguously the honorific status of happiness known in classical antiquity. Individual freedom was in the process of becoming so important that its value superseded all else; it was the motive force overthrowing king and church, and it was threatening to overthrow the restraints of a summum bonum. Hobbes had clearly seen this development a century earlier, describing happiness as continual success in gratifying individual desires.

Thus there were other new elements in the eighteenth-century view of happiness—social pressures, for example, that threatened to undo what was left of eudaemonism itself. There had been too many centuries of Christian influence for an exact return to the classical model of perfection. As Carl Becker writes,

> [no] pale imitations of Greek pessimism would suffice for a society that had been so long and so well taught to look forward to another and better world to come. Without a new heaven to replace the old, a new way of salvation, of attaining perfection, the religion of humanity would appeal in vain to the common run of men. The new heaven had to be located somewhere within the confines of earthly life. . . . [8]

Just as Christianity had fueled medieval apocalypticism, it infused the legacy of happiness with an almost revolutionary expectancy, one that far outstripped the moral requirements of the Stoic and Epicurean sages and most certainly those of the medieval Christians born into a feudal system. Indeed, since heaven represented the communal happiness of the elect, the prime instance of the common good, what better warrant could be found for revolutionary appeals to happiness, especially in France, where it would include highly inflated political promises?[8] The political happiness of the Enlightenment was thus giddy with impatience for the revolutionary overturning of the old injustices and the ushering in of a golden age of happiness for all.

As a political concept, happiness can provide either the principle for maximizing the role of government or exactly the opposite. On the one hand, a government can take the attitude that it must actively cooperate in bringing about the well-being of its citizens, or it can discharge that task, allowing, or enabling, its citizens the right to pursue happiness on their own terms, even if it includes Mill's pig-happiness. Governmental involvement in the pursuit of happiness can take the form, say, of providing a minimum standard of living to all its citizens or even inculcating certain virtues. Or, it can mean ensuring that citizens can pursue happiness without interference from others, including the government. These options and their respective justifications inform the differing interpretations of Jefferson's intent in the Declaration. Suffice it to say, at this point, that understanding the significance of these alternatives is crucial to finding out whether a critique of contemporary well-feeling has any American political warrant.

In addition to social and political changes, the other main element that gave eighteenth-century happiness its explosive appeal was the continued renewal of hedonism. Pleasure and pain had emerged, in a way influentially articulated by Hobbes and Locke, as the principal motivating factors in human action. Between the Hobbesian happiness of "continual prospering" and Locke's definition of happiness as "the utmost pleasure we are capable of" the parameters of the discussion were set.[9]

Locke, unlike Hobbes, did not detach his conception of happiness from either a moral requirement or a final good. Heaven, for Locke, was the "greatest absent good," which humanity seeks to possess in the place of "nearer satisfactions." Locke seems confident in our prudential responses: "Change but a Man's view of these things; let him see, that Virtue and Religion are necessary to his Happiness; let him look into the future State of Bliss or misery, and see there God the righteous Judge, ready to render to every Man according to his Deeds. . . ."[10] Such arguments, based on the natural desire to fulfill the human appetite for complete satisfaction, were to become commonplace in the eighteenth century among writers such as Samuel Clarke, Abraham Tucker, William Paley, and David Hartley, who cast their hedonism in the mold of traditional religious beliefs.

Locke's conception of human nature, coupled with his Calvinist faith, resulted in a theological utilitarianism that appealed to what Locke considered the foundation of human action. Obviously, if the enjoyment of heaven was still a final end, he was attempting to condone cross, sensual pleasures. Locke's happiness was basically a state of psychological satisfaction: "So that happiness and misery seem to me wholly to consist in the pleasure and pain of the mind."[11] It is obvious that his hedonism derives from the tradition of Epicurus, learned in France from the work of Pierre Gassendi, rather than the materialism of Hobbes.[12] Locke found in Gassendi's version of Epicurus a way of treating the affections as the ground for all human activity in general and all moral action in particular. The moral life operates by virtue of a pleasure/pain mechanism. The human will is determined not by an intellectual appetite, but by the "uneasiness of desire" that is the "want of happiness" that directs the will toward "some absent good, either negative, as indolency to one in pain; or positive, as enjoyment of pleasure."[13]

What is essential to note is that once happiness was divested of all other content, pleasure itself became the criterion of good and evil; it also became capable of being measurable, and of being treated as an object of empirical science. The possibilities of a science of happiness would be explored in Great Britain and Europe by philosophers with very different sensibilities, from Francis Hutcheson, who believed that human beings have an innate moral sense of benevolence, to Helvetius, who viewed the pleasure/pain axis as fundamentally egotistic and in need of modification by education and government. These differing views of human nature, and of the role of feeling in directing human action, have resulted in radically differing conceptions of government. For those, such as Hutcheson and the other Scottish philosophers who see human feeling as basically sociocentric, governmental intrusion should be minimized so that it does not create barriers to our natural benevolent impulse toward others. For others, such as Helvetius and Jeremy Bentham, since the impulse toward pleasure is basically egocentric, the offices of government must be maximized in order to reorder action into a socially beneficial pattern.[14]

It seems apparent that the legacy of eudaemonism persists more visibly in the interpretations of happiness coming from Locke through Hutcheson and the Scottish thinkers than in French *philosophes* like Helvetius, who, starting with a radically empirical view of human behavior, prescind from the issue of human nature beyond the pleasure drive it has in common with other animals. This distinction provides the key to why the debate over the influences on Jefferson's notion of "the pursuit of happiness" is so important. Not only does it provide a clue to one of the basic principles informing the American founding, but it also reveals that the problem of interpreting happiness is not simply a twentieth-century problem but one lying at the heart of modernity itself: does a happy life represent sensual self-absorption, or does it represent the best life of a morally good citizen? As we have seen, the first alternative is not only repellant prima facie but also hazardous for the opportunity it provides to the would-be utopian reformers. A more difficult question to answer about political happiness is whether the good citizen pursues Lockean self-interest in a rational way or puts the interests of others on a par with his or her own, led by Hutcheson's natural sentiment of benevolence.[15] This question harkens back to the choice between a state actively involved in providing happiness for its citizens and one that enables them to pursue it for themselves.

With these issues in mind one can see that the attempt of Helvetius to conceive a "natureless" human being—one moved to action and aversion by pleasure and pain but not defined by a "nature"—represents the most progressive wing of the modernist temperament and, consequently, the one most destructive to the foundations of eudaemonism.[16] The pleasure drive allows human beings to be shaped and manipulated by anyone with the vision of a better society and the means to implement it. This is not a view that Locke, Jefferson, or any of the other American Founders share. Jefferson, in fact, explicitly rejects the position Helvetius represented. The desire for happiness is seen by Jefferson as implanted in human beings naturally either by "Nature or Nature's God" and is, therefore, integral to the dignity of the human condition: "We hold these truths to be self-evident, that all men are created equal, that they are endowed by their Creator with certain inalienable rights, that among these are Life, Liberty, and the Pursuit of Happiness."

There has been a long-standing and strongly worded debate concerning the influences on Jefferson's language in the Declaration of Independence.[17] It should be clear by now that this debate is not simply of historical interest. To be clear on what Jefferson had in mind when he talked about happiness enables us to engage the issue of political warrant with those who use it to justify the extreme pursuit of well-feeling. Simply put, none of the influences on Jefferson's thinking, regardless of which one is cited as foremost, will support the radicalism underlying this extremism. Whether the chief influence was John Locke, as most scholars still seem to think, or Frances Hutcheson, as a few have argued, or Hutcheson's Swiss disciple Jean Jacques Burlamaqui, none of these positions cuts the pursuit of happiness from its ethical and political moorings.[18]

For example, Morton White has shown how the logical substructure of Jefferson's language can be located in the natural law philosophy of Burlamaqui.[19] A simplified version of his point of view would run as follows: since God gave human beings their existence and implanted in human beings a nature distinguished both by its reason and by its desire for happiness, it is the duty of human beings to exercise their reason both in seeking to preserve the life given to them and in securing the happiness they naturally desire. Jefferson's "inalienable rights" then are derived from these more basic duties, which are founded on God's will as expressed in making human natures.

In other words, if God gave us the desire for happiness, we have the duty to pursue it, and in order to do so in the context of a governed society we must have the right to it. Jefferson's reasoning, therefore, does not have a utilitarian basis; happiness is not being used as the primary unit of value—it belongs to the natural order. "The crucial point is that he held that this duty [the pursuit of happiness] followed from the essence of man and therefore defended the principle by appealing to intuition . . . based upon the fact that God made the pursuit of happiness an end of man by incorporating a desire for happiness in man's essence."[20]

It is important to reiterate that since the arguments over Jefferson's view of happiness are basically arguments in support of various primary influences, whether those of Locke, Hutcheson, or Burlamaqui, any of these alternatives keeps Jefferson's view of happiness within an eighteenth-century version of eudaemonism, a morally directed pursuit of happiness construed as a unit of pleasure and conducted within the scope of a fixed human nature. Locke's epistemology, as it has been joined, generates a skeptical

attitude toward grasping the species of any nature, including human nature, but these darker implications of the "esoteric Locke"
are not to be seen operating among the Founders.[21]

The relevant difference between the traditional Lockean reading
of Jefferson and the Hutchesonian reading affects the issue of how
this pursuit is morally directed—whether this desire for happiness
is motivated by an innate sense of benevolence, the "sociocentric"
impulse (Hutcheson), or by the pursuit of self-interested pleasures
such as those enjoyed in the acquisition of property (Locke). This
standard reading of Locke, remembering his passages contrasting
the "nearer satisfactions" with "the greatest absent good," is something of a caricature that ignores the moral sections of the *Essay*. It
also ignores the fact that the commonsense philosophers were car-
rying on the tradition of Locke—they were not self-consciously
rejecting any egotism in Locke,[22] but a basic point of emphasis
between Locke and Hutcheson remains. As Jefferson writes:

> These good acts give us pleasure, but how happens it that they give us
> pleasure? Because nature hath implanted in our breasts a love of oth-
> ers, a sense of duty to them, a moral instinct, in short, which prompts
> us irresistibly to feel and to succor their distresses, and protects us
> against the language of Helvetius, "what other motive than self-interest
> could determine a man to generous action? It is as impossible for him
> to love what is good for the sake of good, as to love evil for the sake
> of evil." The Creator would have indeed been a bungling artist had he
> intended man for a social animal, without planting in him social dispo-
> sitions.[23]

Regardless of what one thinks about the Scottish commonsense
view of human benevolence, about its degree of influence on Jefferson, it is clear that Jefferson had great confidence in the pursuit
of happiness precisely because this innate moral sense was going
to guide it. God designed the pleasures of happiness to corroborate
actions and habits that arose from this natural reservoir of human
goodness. The unit of pleasure is not the key to value as it is among
the utilitarians: "Thus, where Bentham would argue that an action
is moral because it produces happiness, Jefferson argued that an
action produces happiness because it is moral."[24]

It has been said that both Hutcheson and Helvetius, in spite of
their differing moral viewpoints, thought that happiness could be
measured, that a science of happiness was possible.[25] Such an assertion seems strange not for a pure hedonist, but for someone who

insists on a moral foundation for the pursuit of happiness. This thought did not deter Hutcheson, who, in the second edition of *Inquiry into the Origin of Our Ideas of Beauty and Virtue* (1726), actually concocted an algebraic formula to measure morality itself. Garry Wills traces this project from its roots in Hutcheson through figures such as Pietro Verri and Cesare Beccaria to William Wollaston and the Marquis de Chastelleux and concludes, "when Jefferson spoke of pursuing happiness, he had nothing vague or private in mind. He meant a public happiness which is measurable."[26] As support for this position, Wills cites a number of instances in Jefferson's writings where he appears to appeal to Chastelleux's "indexes of happiness," factors such as population and agriculture, to argue that one state of affairs is, or will be, happier than another.

To include such external goods within Jefferson's pursuit is not unreasonable. It takes into account the fact that it was not just ideas that influenced his mind but the very presence of a new land, the boundaries of which were hardly known and that was rich in natural resources; and of a new people, many of whom had fled oppression and who were on the verge of an exciting experiment in democratic self-government as well as an opportunity to seek greater affluence.[27] The United States of America presented the very embodiment of Aristotelian good fortune necessary to happiness. As Howard Mumford Jones puts it:

> In one sense it is scarcely necessary to look for the philosophical antecedents of the right to happiness. The right to pursue happiness in America had, as it were, grown up in a fit of absence of mind; but if you doubted the validity of the idea, you had merely to look at the happiness around you to infer that any government which would destroy such felicity was unrighteous. *Post hoc ergo propter hoc* was as good as *quod est demonstrandum* in 1776. Such was the plain common sense of the matter.[28]

So it is not preposterous to assume, as Wills does, that Jefferson thought the condition of happiness had a quantitative dimension.[29] It was Jefferson, after all, who would later engineer the Louisiana Purchase, which ensured enough land for anyone who exerted the effort to acquire it.

The strict sense of a quantifiable happiness, however, like that found in the present century—which will be investigated in the next chapter—is at odds with eudaemonism because it diminishes, if not disallows, the role of moral scrutiny. Jefferson, convinced of both a moral sense—if not to the degree that Wills suggests—and the providential ordering of pleasures and pains, has far from a value-neutral attitude. Thus, we can conclude that neither Jefferson's hedonism nor his concern for material goods evinces a problem of well-feeling in his view of happiness or that of the Declaration.[30]

The meaning ascribed to the founding documents arises not from Jefferson's mind, but from a developing contrast between private and public happiness in American society. As Hannah Arendt has pointed out, the idea of public happiness was part of an eighteenth-century political vocabulary committed to the involvement of citizenry in self-governance:

> The very fact that the word 'happiness' was chosen in laying claim to a share in public power indicates strongly that there existed in the country, prior to the revolution, such a thing as 'public happiness', and that men knew that they could not be altogether happy if their happiness was located and enjoyed only in private life.[31]

In spite of Jefferson's intentions, the words of the Declaration undoubtedly bore a twofold meaning to its readers. It was important for the Founders, however, who had just succeeded in extracting themselves from a tyrannical power, to maintain this spirit of seeking the common good, which required foremost the maintenance of virtue above the private happiness. In Arendt's view the words of the Declaration "almost immediately" collapsed toward the side of private satisfaction and—in analysis that foreshadows the findings of *Habits of the Heart* in describing the gradual diminution of political involvement, that is, public happiness—toward the withdrawal of the individual to the "inward domain of consciousness" and the pitting of individual satisfactions, especially the avoidance of poverty, against the demands of common good.[32] In other words, the Founders' desire to uphold the common good was unintentionally thwarted by the language of the Declaration. The criterion of private satisfaction threatens not only the moral requirement of eudaemonism, but also its precept that a happy life be considered as a whole.

This development had nothing to do, of course, with Jefferson's intention but resulted from the continuing shift in consensual values reflecting the understanding of happiness itself. The change in conception has become so radical that the goal of happiness hardly seems worthy enough for our common pursuit: "It may even be that in announcing our goal as happiness we are selling ourselves short, and denying something that runs very deep in human life. . . . Willingness to sacrifice happiness and pleasure for other things seems at least as basic to human life as does the pursuit of happiness."[33] Such an opinion rests on the assumption that there is no way of recovering the moral meaning of happiness. If the assumption were correct then the conclusion would undoubtedly follow.

Jefferson's idea of the pursuit of happiness is undoubtedly linked to morality, but what about its relation to politics? It looks to be at odds with both extremes of the contemporary view: that it is the duty of government to maximize the happiness of its citizens and that it is the duty of the government only to protect the rights of its citizens to pursue happiness on their own. As Morton White remarks, the difference between a government that aids our pursuit of happiness and a government that protects our right to pursue it is a crucial distinction for political philosophy.[34] The decisiveness of this distinction can be seen in development among those who seek to maximize happiness. One of the leading spokespersons of postwar liberalism argues, "by recognizing a right to the pursuit of happiness, the state is committed to aiding its citizens in the constructive task of obtaining their desires, *whatever* they may be (emphasis added)."[35] If this is the case, then a perspective that was obviously eudaemonistic at its origin in Jefferson has lost its moral character. Such an outcome represents an invidious combination of the alternatives posed earlier in this chapter: the government no longer cooperates in seeking the eudaemonistic happiness of its citizens but in protecting their well-feeling. The subjective happiness that once demanded protection from governmental interference now becomes an object of its entitlement programs.

It is hard to treat this interpretation seriously since it ignores such obvious limitations placed on the satisfaction of desires, such as the restraint of civil law. More obviously, it assumes that the power of government can satisfy the most individual desires of its citizens, and, of course, it contradicts the intentions of the author of the Declaration himself, who thought that the conjunction of virtue with happiness marked the limits of a justified satisfaction. Jefferson's self-proclaimed Epicureanism, rather than weakening this contention, strengthens it, since he interpreted Epicurus as teaching moral happiness.[36]

At the other extreme are those who minimize government's role in the pursuit of happiness as that of protecting the rights of individuals to determine the path to their own earthly and heavenly salvation as they alone see fit. Governments may infringe this right only at the peril of violating the social contract on which their legitimacy ultimately rests. This appears to be the only interpretation consistent with Jefferson's views respecting individual autonomy within the structure and language of the Declaration. The Declaration does not proclaim that the end of government is the maximization of happiness, as Wills suggests, in either the sense of well-being or well-feeling, nor does it legitimate government on the basis of whether its citizens are happy, but on whether the rights of its citizens are respected. In the document the right to pursue happiness stands logically prior to the establishment of government, and the function of government is clearly to secure this right, not to see that most people attain what they pursue.[37]

The minimizers insist that the right to pursue happiness belongs to the individual by nature, not to the government. Therefore, the authority given to the government is one only of protection or non-interference, not of active copursuit. This position can elicit the same objections as its counterpart. In the former, it is the government that is called on to pursue a happiness without moral limits; in the latter, it is the individual.

The argument between these points of view is often couched in debate between Locke and Hutcheson. Jefferson himself never revealed the main influence on his thinking, because he did not know. As he wrote to Henry Lee in 1825 about the Declaration: "All its authority rests then on the harmonizing sentiments of the day, whether expressed in conversation, in letters, printed essays, or in the elementary books of public right, as Aristotle, Cicero, Locke, Sidney, &c." He goes on in the same letter to refer to his position as "the common sense of the subject"—"Neither aiming at originality of principle or sentiment, nor yet copied from any particular and previous writing, it was intended to be an expression of the American mind and to give that expression the proper tone and spirit called for by the occasion."[38]

Since Jefferson did not feel himself torn between the alternatives of Lockean egoism, which was bent on protecting the right to private property, and Hutchesonian benevolence, which was confident in the natural human disposition toward sharing its wealth and kindness with others, perhaps this can be taken as a clue in interpreting the Declaration. We have seen that he explicitly rejected the view of self-interest that Helvetius represented and that he affirmed an optimistic view of human nature both from a theological perspective and from a belief in the moral sense. Where does that leave Locke? If Jefferson had read Locke as supporting only self-interestedness, then he would have treated him as he did Helvetius. Perhaps the key to this tangle is that Jefferson read Locke as having close affinities with the moral-sense perspective that, to him, represented the "common sense of the subject."

Finally, there is another dimension of this debate that brings us back to the question about freedom itself, raised by Agnes Heller. It has already been observed that happiness can be identified with any human good and that, as shared valuations change, so have popular meanings of happiness. Perhaps another way out of the impasse is to see happiness as belonging not so much to the possession of some goal, but to the unfettered ability to pursue the goal. As James Harris, one of the many sources of Jefferson's "harmonizing sentiments," wrote, "Suppose we were to fix our Happiness *not in the actual attainment* of that Health, that Perfection of a Social State . . . but solely fix it *in the mere Doing of whatever is correspondent to such an end"* (emphasis mine).[39]

One doubts whether Harris, who had a firm idea of basic human goods, was indifferent to actually possessing those goods. His remark brings to the fore an aspect of self-conscious satisfaction that belongs to people in an age and to a country attempting for the first time to provide access both to governance and to prosperity for each individual regardless of birthright. To know one is free in both these respects, to participate in government and to own property, is certainly a mental state in keeping with eudaemonism by heightening a sense of individual agency. Problems arise, however, when satisfaction is taken in the exercise of freedom that ignores altogether the received understanding of human nature and human good, the relation between the potentialities of human essence and the realization of human character.

At the moment, the right to the "pursuit of happiness" has in fact become a license to the pursuit of well-feeling. The only restraint placed on it is the wide boundaries of civil law—character and moral disposition have become irrelevant. There is little doubt, therefore, that Jefferson and the Founders believed in ends as well as beginnings—they did not intend to license any and all pursuits of happiness. One wonders, however, what the future holds for law and public policy when the ethical consensus that can specify the limits on satisfaction is lacking. Forty years ago Howard Mumford Jones demonstrated that the happiness right had been used in jurisprudence to encourage free-market competition, and he predicted, "If the American people decide that the theory of happiness as [psychological] adjustment is paramount, they may profoundly alter constitutional theory and legal practise."[40] The alteration along the lines of well-feeling is under way. Charles Murray has already fired a warning shot in the direction of those bureaucracies that are attempting to bring about public happiness through social programs. The crucial issue, he argues, is that "people need to be self-determining, accountable, and absorbed in their capacities."[41] In other words, they need to be involved in the activity of happiness, not simply become the passive recipients of well-feeling. To avoid mistakes in public policy, the pursuit of happiness and satisfaction must be based on realistic assumptions about human nature and society. Allied with the happiness of well-feeling, freedom as an end in itself has proved to be a snake that swallowed its own tail.

Notes

1. Agnes Heller, *Renaissance Man*, trans. Richard E. Allen (New York: Schocken Books, 1981), 283.

2. Heller, 286.

3. A more conventional interpretation of Renaissance views of happiness can be found in C. E. Trinkaus, *Adversity's Noblemen: The Italian Humanists on Happiness* (New York: Columbia University Press, 1940).

4. Heller, 285.

5. Paul Hazard, *European Thought in the Eighteenth Century: From Montesquieu to Lessing* (London: Hollis & Carter, 1954), 17.

6. For examples, see Maren-Sofie Rostvig, *The Happy Man: Studies in the Metamorphoses of a Classical Ideal*, vol. 1, rev. ed (Oslo: University of Oslo, 1962) and Paul Hazard, ch. 2.

7. Even the delights of heaven undergo a transformation. Arthur Lovejoy offers the example of Bishop Edmund Law, who was assuming that a hedonic happiness was unable to imagine eternal life as a fixed state of perfection, which would lead to "indolence and insensibility . . . which nothing but alteration and variety can cure." See *The Great Chain of Being: A Study in the History of An Idea* (New York: Harper Torchbook, 1960), 249.

8. Carl L. Becker, *The Heavenly City of the Eighteenth-Century Philosophers* (New Haven: Yale University Press, 1932), 129.

9. This can be seen in the treatment of *bonheur* in Diderot's *Encyclopedie*; for comment, see James F. Jones, Jr., "Prolegomena to a History of Happiness in the Eighteenth Century," *French-American Review* 6 (1982): 286: "It was not by mere chance that the eighteenth century was the classical age of Utopian promise. . . . The Utopian ideal was intricately related at this time to the sociological growth of the bourgeoise and to the dreams and aspirations of this new class, dreams and aspirations which were intimately linked themselves within the eighteenth-century *Zeitgeist* to the issue of happiness." See also, Paul Hazard, *The European Mind, 1680-1715* (New York: World Publishing, 1963), 293-303.

10. John Locke, *An Essay On Human Understanding*, 2.21 (258). For Hobbes, see ch. 3, n.11 *supra*; to compare their views of happiness, human nature, and human action, see Andrzey Rapaczynski, *Nature and Politics: Liberalism in the Philosophies of Hobbes, Locke and Rousseau* (Ithaca: Cornell University Press, 1987).

11. Locke, 2.21.60 (273).

12. Quoted in Edward A. Driscoll, "The Influence of Gassendt on Locke's Hedonism," *International Philosophical Quarterly* 12 (March 1961): 99.

13. Driscoll, 88.

14. Robert G. Weyant, "Helvetius and Jefferson: Studies of Human Nature and Government in the Eighteenth Century," *Journal of the History of Behavioral Sciences* 9 (1973): 29-41.

15. Hutcheson writes, "This powerful Determination even to a limited Benevolence, and other moral sentiments, is observ'd to give strong Bias to our Minds towards a universal Goodness, Tenderness, Humanity, Generosity, and Contempt of private Good in whole conduct. . . . As soon as a Heart, before hard and obdurate, is soften'd in this Flame, we shall observe, arising along with it, a Love of Poetry, Music, the Beauty of nature in rural scenes, a Contempt of other selfish Pleasures of the external senses and a neat Dress, a human deportment, a Delight in, and Emulation of, every thing which is gallant, generous, and friendly." *An Inquiry into the Original of Our Ideas of Beauty and Virtue*, 4th ed. (London: 1738), 2.6.5.

16. See Eric Voegelin, *From Enlightenment to Revolution* (Chapel Hill: Duke University Press, 1975), chs. 2-3.   .

17. Among all the reactions to Will's *Inventing America*, the most provocative is that of Harry V. Jaffa, "Inventing the Past: Garry Will's *Inventing America* and the Pathology of Ideological Scholarship," *American Conservatism and the American Founding* (Durham, N.C.: Carolina Academic Press, 1984), 76-109. See also Jeffrey D. Wallin, "John Locke and the American Founding," *Natural Right and Political Right: Essays in Honor of Harry Jaffa,* ed. Thomas B. Siver and Peter W. Schramm (Durham, N.C.: Carolina Academic Press, 1984), 143-67.

18. Locke is proposed by Carl Becker, *The Declaration of Independence: A Study in the History of Political Ideas* (New York: Vintage Books, 1922); Hutcheson's influence is supported by Garry Wills, *Inventing America: Jefferson's Declaration of Indepedence* (Garden City, N.Y.: Doubleday, 1978);

and Burlamaqui by Morton White, *The Philosophy of the American Revolution* (New York: Oxford University Press, 1978); while the relation of the virtue tradition to happiness in Jefferson's thought is stressed by Caroline Robbins, *The Pursuit of Happiness* (Washingon D.C.: American Enterprise Institute, 1974).

19. White, 160ff.

20. White, 233.

21. Wallin, 154-55.

22. Jaffa, 106.

23. Letter to Thomas Law, 13 June 1814; quoted in Weyant, 37.

24. Weyant, 37.

25 See treatment in Wills, ch. 10.

26. Wills, 164.

27. Jack P. Greene, *Pursuits of Happiness: The Social Development of Early Modern British Colonies and the Formation of American Culture* (Chapel Hill: University of North Carolina Press, 1989), 193-197.

28. Howard Mumford Jones, *The Pursuit of Happiness*, 92.

29. For a discussion of the greatest happiness principle, see Robert Shackleton, "The Greatest Happiness of the Greatest Number: The History of Bentham's Phrase," *Studies on Voltaire and the 18th Century* 90 (1972): 1461-82.

30. In response to Wills, Jaffa doubts that Jefferson ever spoke about a measureable happiness; see Jaffa, 108.

31. Hannah Arendt, *On Revolution* (New York: Penguin Books, 1963), 127.

32. Arendt, 140.

33. Schaar, 26.

34. Schaar, 8.

35. Charles M. Wiltse, *The Jeffersonian Tradition in American Democracy* (Chapel Hill: University of North Carolina Press, 1937), 70-71. See also Arthur M. Schlesinger, "The Lost Meaning of the 'Pursuit of Happiness,'" *The William and Mary Quarterly* 3d series 21 (1964): 325-7; he argues that pursuit means practising rather than questing; therefore, happiness is provided by government to its citizens according to natural right (326).

36. Robbins, 17. She emphasizes that Jefferson considered the role of virtue indispensable in the maintainance of public happiness (18-19).

37. Ronald Hamowy, "Jefferson and the Scottish Enlightenment: A Critique of Garry Will's *Inventing America: Jefferson's Declaration of Independence*," *The William and Mary Quarterly* (1979): 519; his view has much support: "The whole thrust of [Jefferson's] thought leads, not to the conclusion that men pursue happiness in the political realm, but that political action is unfortunately necessary from time to time in order to arrange the public affairs so that it will be possible for individuals to pursue happiness in the private realm." John H. Schaar, ". . . And the Pursuit of Happiness," *The Virginia Quarterly Review* 46:1 (Winter 1970) 16; Schaar traces the four meanings of happiness in eighteenth-century Amerca: (1) prosperity and piety of the Puritans; (2) the materialist Whig view, which made property the

foundation and means of happiness; (3) the fulfillment of fraternal needs as seen in Paine and Thoreau; and (4) the socially virtuous and useful life exemplified by Franklin and Jefferson. Schaar contrasts these with three contemporary conceptions—bountiful consumption, having fun, and self-realization.

38. *The Writings of Jefferson*, ed. Paul L. Ford (Washington D.C.: The Thomas Jefferson Memorial Association, 1904), 16.118, letter dated 8 May 1825. One scholar, who also cites this letter, remarks, "we could not be blamed for wishing a fuller expression of his political philosophy"; see Robbins, 16.

39. Quoted in James F. Jones, Jr., 290.

40. Mumford Jones, 193; see ch. 2, "As by an Invisible Hand," for comments on the court decisions invoking the happiness right to protect property and investment.

41. Charles Murray, *In Pursuit of Happiness and Good Government* (New York: Simon and Schuster, 1988), 296.

Chapter 6

The Science of Happiness and Its Results

With the decline of eudaemonism and the emergence of the Enlightenment hedonism, the idea of happiness was welcomed into the world of the social sciences. Psychological happiness, the avowed happiness of first-person reporting or well-feeling, has become an important subject of empirical research in both psychology and sociology. The extent of this research indicates how thoroughly the idea of happiness has been recast. The uses of psychological happiness often resemble the approaches outlined earlier in popular literature, as if the call to create one's own happiness was taken up in the name of science. Whereas objections addressed to self-help authors are unlikely to be taken to heart, however, those who investigate happiness scientifically are looking at the notion of well-feeling more critically.

The gradual emergence of psychological happiness perfectly suited the needs of social science research. Scholars can embrace the new conception of happiness largely because it excludes the normative and objective character of *eudaimonia*. Needing reliable empirical data from which to generate quantifiable conclusions, social scientists have the most to gain from the identification of happiness with positive subjective experiences. Classical notions of happiness that originated in larger theories of human nature and goodness create a problem of hybridity, a notion of happiness comprising well-feeling and well-being, which compromises the purely experiential basis of reported happiness. With the moral criteria of classical happiness put aside, happiness can belong to the domain of the scientist rather than that of the philosopher.

Social scientists correctly point out that philosophers themselves have never agreed on the objective conditions of happiness, making the employment of objective standards in their investigation seem arbitrary. Empirical scientists simply rely on the reliability of first-person reports: if someone says he is happy, he is. The imposition of value systems has no place in empirical research; thus, judgments about real and illusory happiness are banished.

It comes as no surprise that the scientists who study happiness show little interest in philosophical reflection on the subject. Psychologists of happiness make remarks to the effect that little progress has been made in understanding happiness since the Greeks. Even the humanistic and existential psychologists, whose theories are indebted to the earlier traditions, show little interest in their philosophical precursors on happiness.[1]

One exception to this situation is Ruut Veenhoven, whose literature survey is the most comprehensive to date.[2] His research pays close critical attention to the conceptual presuppositions and the semantic consistency of happiness research. He lists many of the vague and contradictory terms employed by researchers. Part of the problem, as he shows, is that social scientists have differing practical aims: some are interested in individual clinical results; others are concerned with advancing education or the productivity of the workplace. Some social psychologists amass social indicators of happiness that enable them to compare the quality of life between different classes, ages, genders, cities, and even nations, but a lack of conceptual consistency, Veenhoven admits, plagues attempts to collate the rising mountain of research.

Although the social scientists who study happiness have found it necessary to reject any objective conditions, many of them have failed to follow any consistent or coherent definition of happiness. The description of happiness used by psychologist Jonathan Freedman is characteristic: happiness "is a positive, enduring state that consists of positive feelings about the self and the world and that includes both peace of mind and active pleasures and joy."[3] Such rambling attempts at defining happiness stumble over the ambiguity of words such as *feeling*. One may ask whether Freedman intends to include any kind of emotion as long as it is viewed as positive. What does positive mean? Does he mean to say that happy people never countenance negative or, presumably, critical feelings, that is, that they never disapprove of themselves or their world? (It is *attitude* rather than *feelings* that actually fits his definition.)

Finally, why does Freedman need to specify "peace of mind," "active pleasures," and "joy?" Except for the notion of an "active" pleasure, his definition seems arbitrary, given the long list of qualifiers that could be subsumed under his rubric of "positive feelings."

In spite of vague and contradictory theoretical constructs, happiness research is booming. Veenhoven collected more than two thousand studies conducted between 1912 and 1976, and other recent surveys by Argyle and Deiner suggest that the number of studies by social scientists is multiplying at an astonishing rate.[4] Taken together, these research surveys provide an overview of the work on happiness in the social sciences.

The tools of the happiness researchers are interviews and questionnaires. The actual measuring instruments vary greatly from study to study. Approaches range from direct and indirect questions, interviews, peer ratings, pictorial face scales (reactions to drawings of happy and sad faces), and Rorschach inkblots. Nearly all of the studies, with the exception of a few, rely entirely on first-person reports of happiness, satisfaction, contentment, and so forth. A data base of happiness is mounting quickly, with the correlates, conditions, and indicators of happiness being quantified as a result. Scales to measure these data have been developed; some purport to measure only specific items such as mood or positive and negative affect, while others aim more broadly at measuring subjective well-being or satisfaction with life. Some of the better known of the scales are Bradburn's Affect Balance Scale (1969), Andrews and Withey's Semantic Differential Happiness Scales (1976), Larsen's Affective Intensity Measure (1983), the Fordyce Happiness Measure (1972), and Kammaan and Flett's Affectometer (1983).

Studies have targeted such disparate items as mood, life satisfaction, peak experiences, well-being, quality of life, morale, mental state, adjustment, contentment, hedonic level, evaluation of life, elation, and positive attitudes toward life. Veenhoven admits that these differing methodologies make it very difficult to compare findings between the studies. Out of the two thousand abstracts of research Veenhoven could accept only 156 as containing acceptable indicators of happiness. His stringent requirements stem from an attempt to organize a definition of happiness as satisfaction with life-as-a-whole. It is notable that Veenhoven wants to go beyond measuring momentary satisfactions by factoring in Aristotle's ancient insistence that a life could be judged happy only if taken as a whole.

Of course, given that Veenhoven still relies on an individual's report of his or her life, there is a significant difference, as he admits, between Aristotle's insistence on necessity of virtue and a justified satisfaction. The classical tradition of *eudaimonia* was less concerned with an individual's claim to happiness than with the bestowing of that laurel on another person. Aristotle, like other philosophers on happiness, listened closely to the various claims about happiness while remaining skeptical about them. Although all claims express varying kinds of satisfaction, Aristotle left himself room to verify them. His central question about happiness is couched in the form, "When can we call a person happy?" The attribution of happiness was a matter of honor.

Most social scientists, and even some modern philosophers, base their rejection of third-person judgments on the assumption that a person's own report about his or her happiness is privileged. Each individual person is in the best, if not the only, position to know the facts of the case. Such information can be gathered only from the inside, so to speak; thus, our only access to information about happiness is to listen to what people say about themselves. For these defenders of psychological happiness, judging another person happy is no longer part of the general estimation of character demanded by social existence. Such appraisals of character are commonly found to be a part of making choices about people who will become significant in our lives. In fact, it can be observed that the theorists of psychological happiness deny in their theories a kind of judgment that is a daily part of social life, regardless of how tricky and inaccurate these judgments may be.

It has been asked whether this reliance on reported happiness will prove problematic in supporting the social indicators for quality of life studies.[5] Researchers admit to a number of unresolved questions about the possible bias of their findings. Beyond the obvious concern about fluctuation of mood and its effect on self-reporting are some serious issues. First, there is the semantic problem already mentioned: when someone is asked whether they are either satisfied, somewhat satisfied, or very satisfied in their life, how is the researcher to know what the person being interviewed takes as satisfaction or the degrees of it being sought? Second, there is a tendency to exaggerate claims to happiness when it is held to be socially desirable. Veenhoven remarks that anonymity in interviews encourages more honest reporting. Third, the entire setting of the interview and the relationship between interviewer and respondent can strongly influence what is said. For example, how much time were people given to think about their answers? Are respondents uniformly at a good time in their lives to answer questions about satisfaction? Last, and perhaps most problematic, can people be counted on to give accurate accounts of their feelings, their emotions, and their satisfactions? Are we not disposed, especially in hard times, toward distortion, denial, defensiveness, and repression?

Diener mentions a number of factors that concern researchers who rely on self-reporting: unhappy people tend to report being happy when they are not, especially when they live in a society where happiness is considered normative. Also, there is evidence that people are influenced by their moods: they tend to recall past events consonant with current affect. For Diener, however, none of these factors presents a major problem. Studies show, surprisingly, that happiness is not socially desirable to the extent that self-reporting would be compromised. Furthermore, studies employing self-reporting are found to correlate substantially with external criteria such as personality measures, demographic variables, facial coding such as smiling and laughing, and peer reports. Yet, Diener comments, more substantiation of self-reporting by external criteria is needed.

These problems, though recognized by some eudologists, do not stymie their research or their confidence in their conclusions. In *The Psychology of Happiness* Michael Argyle expresses confidence both in research based on self-reporting and in the conclusions he draws from it. He dismisses summarily the problems of self-reporting: "if someone says they are very satisfied with, say, their mud hut on stilts, then we must assume they *are*."[6] This laissez-faire view of happiness, as we will see, is not without philosophical support and political import.

Argyle investigates both the happiness of global satisfaction and the happiness of transient positive emotions, organizing his data, unlike Veenhoven, with both ends in view. His conclusions are optimistic: it is possible to increase the happiness of oneself and of others. The first of his seven suggestions is as follows:

> Short-term increases in positive mood can be induced by thinking about recent pleasant events, watching funny films or TV, listening to cheerful music, and to some extent by reciting positive self-statements, by smiles, jokes, small presents and hypnosis. The effects tend to be rather brief, but these activities can be engaged in regularly. The only drug which seems to be successful is alcohol, but in doses which are not too large.[7]

It must give some readers pause that after the study and collation of more than three hundred studies the author advises us to watch "funny films or TV."

If this advice is given to help short-term mood, the rest of his seven suggestions for long-term satisfaction fail to extend our knowledge past what seems to be good common sense. Argyle suggests that we can increase happiness by making a log of our most intense pleasures, which presumably would remind us to repeat them more often, by working at having good relationships, by enjoying our work and leisure, and by looking at things more positively. Given the promise of surpassing the Greeks, one can ask only how such conclusions surpass, or even approach, what the Greeks knew in the fifth century B.C. Given that a science of happiness is being promised, should one expect new insights or the testing of old ones?

Veenhoven's and Diener's aggregate of correlations to happiness are both more serious and a better indication of the contribution being made by researchers. Among Veenhoven's findings are the conclusions that factors such as gender, income, education, intelligence, social rank, unemployment, ascetic living, and being an only-child do not affect happiness. His correlations also debunk what he calls the myth about the prevalence of unhappiness in Western society, which has been thought to result from the increasing pressures of industrialization, urbanization, and pace of life. He recognizes that such conclusions have tremendous political significance and offers careful and repeated disclaimers about both the quality of the data and the possibility of generating lawlike generalizations from those data. Nonetheless, he firmly declares that his purpose is the promotion of happiness through the application of social science.

Diener organizes the research under the rubric of subjective well-being. His concern is with discovering the cognitive and affective factors influencing people who experience their lives in positive ways. Subjective well-being, as the phrase suggests, resides within the experience of the individual and relies on the standards of the respondent to determine the good life. It involves a global assessment of one's life with both positive and negative measures. Like Veenhoven, Diener's happiness occupies a middle ground between normative and positive affect theories.

The bulk of contemporary happiness research began in the 1960s when one of the first cumulative studies portrayed the happy person as a "young, healthy, well-educated, well-paid, extroverted, optimistic, worry-free, religious, married person, with high self-esteem, high job morale, modest aspirations, of either sex and of a wide range of intelligence."[8] Many of these correlations, as Diener says, have not held up under later scientific scrutiny. On the other hand, Norman Bradburn's early research into the independent relation of positive and negative affect has become a kind of cornerstone in the scientific understanding of happiness. Bradburn developed a scale to measure emotional well-being: happiness is really a global judgment people make by comparing their negative affect with their positive affect. His Affect Balance Scale works by subtracting the sum of negative items from the sum of positive ones, meaning that the absence of negative affect is not equivalent to the presence of positive affect. Thus, to enhance life, one must go beyond the removal of life's irritations and supply causes of positive enjoyment.

Perhaps the most important contribution of this research is its exploration of the causes of happiness. Diener distinguishes between objective conditions and subjective conditions and raises important overall questions concerning the direction of causality. For example, among subjective factors, self-esteem or self-satisfaction consistently receives the highest correlation with reports of happiness. Does this mean that self-esteem contributes to happiness or vice versa? The same is true of objective factors: do they cause happiness or does a happy person regard these factors in different ways than does an unhappy person?

This same problem of causality can be couched in terms of top-down versus bottom-up theories of happiness. A top-down view regards happiness as a trait rather than a state, something like an attitude that a person has toward himself and the world, like seeing the proverbial glass half-full rather than half-empty. Diener describes this as a disposition to experience things in a positive way, which, in turn, colors a person's reading of life, its fortunes and misfortunes. The bottom-up theory treats happiness a state of summed pleasures, an accumulation of happy moments. "In the bottom-up approach, a person should develop a sunny disposition and sanguine outlook as positive experiences accumulate in the person's life."[9] The issue raised by the contrast between the two positions is a crucial one for happiness, since it raises both the classical problem of objective success and the modern confidence in the power of mind over circumstance.

Among objective factors, the relation between income and hap-

piness appears to be much more significant at the extreme of poverty, while the happiness of the wealthy is closely tied to their concomitant access to status and power. There is no clear correlation
between age and happiness, except slightly more satisfaction among
the old and positive affect among the young. Women are not happier than men but women report greater enjoyment. African Americans report more unhappiness than whites, but these data are difficult
to separate from other factors, such as wealth and health. Interest-
ingly, since the political advances of the late 1960s, African Americans have reported even less happiness. Unemployment definitely
harvests unhappiness, while education has little direct impact. Religious people report more positive moods, especially if they are
young. Married people are happier unless they have children.

Extroverts are happier than introverts, possibly because they enjoy
more social contact—love, friendship, and play—which is important for reported happiness. Gerontologists have long argued that
active and involved people will be happier, but findings now show
that this depends on the kind of activities and individual personalities, but, again, Diener cautions that influence may be bidirection-
al. Good and bad events in life have a moderate effect on
self-reporting. This may be because of the importance of internality to the happy person, that is, the inclination toward taking responsibility for what happens in one's life, rather than blaming external
factors. The degree to which internality can affect happiness will
be qualified by one's perceived control of one's life. Seen in terms
of personalities, high self-esteem is one of the strongest indicators:
self-esteem drops during periods of unhappiness. Intelligence does
not yet seem as strongly correlated to happiness as, say, health,
especially one's satisfaction with one's health, but with health, as
with many of these factors, the issue must be raised concerning the
direction of causality: does health affect happiness or happiness
health? This is especially germane since it is satisfaction with one's
health, not actual objective health, that affects self-reporting.

His survey of the research leads Diener to conclude that subjective well-being will not be accounted for by a small number of
variables—too many factors influence it. One interesting example
of its complexity are the data regarding the intimate relation of
pleasure and pain. Studies show that seeking a permanent state of
fulfillment proves to be counterproductive. We are made happier by
the cyclical fulfillment of deprivation-based need than by unremit-
ting joy. Thus related, life's enjoyments and distresses point the way

toward a more profound notion of the happy life, one that eschews the desire for pure immediacy and appreciates the role of suffering in reaching worthwhile aims.

Diener's findings suggest that avowed happiness actually may bear a eudaemonistic reading. Alan S. Waterman attempts to measure what he calls the experience of "personal expressiveness" implicit in the classical notion of *eudaimonia*.[10] Like other psychologists, he measures patterns and levels of reported satisfaction, but Waterman distinguishes between satisfaction taken in mundane activities, offering momentary pleasures and satisfactions, and those that contribute to an overall sense of well-being and identity. His research confirms that greater satisfaction is taken in personally expressive activities, those activities in which individuals actualize their highest potentials.

To experience an activity as personally expressive, that is, as eudaemonistic, the activity must give "rise to feelings . . . in which an individual experiences self-realization through the fulfillment of personal potentials in the form of the development of one's skills and talents, the advancement of one's purposes in living, or both."[11] Activities are experienced as personally expressive to the extent that they are recognized as the means for progressing toward goals that represent the most desirable kind of life. Waterman's suggestion that all such activities should be enjoyed is reminiscent of Aristotle's view that the happiest life is also the most pleasant one.

The question that naturally occurs is whether the enjoyment of any kind of goals or purposes that render a person personally expressive also renders a person happy in the classical sense. Waterman admits that he is not dealing with the normative questions of moral limits. He also acknowledges that working out of the tradition of *eudaimonia* entails greater problems in the use of self-reporting. Whereas persons can hardly be said to be wrong about reports of their own hedonic state, persons' appraisal of their own deepest potentials, as well as the activities that appear to realize them, complicate this research.

As in some of the contemporary philosophers who seek to revive eudaemonism, certain aspects of the classical picture are employed while others are ignored. Personal ideals, human excellence, and individual responsibility are all implied by Aristotle's happy life in accordance with virtue. Waterman's contribution to research on happiness is to suggest that the subjective component of *eudaimonia* cannot be divorced from specific kinds of activities—they cannot be trivialized without loss. Greater satisfaction is found in the experiences that result from efforts to live well according to one's own goals.

Another significant contribution toward a more eudaemonistic understanding of happiness is Mihaly Csikszentmihalyi's study of the phenomenon called *flow*.[12] The original data were taken from a study of rock climbers who exemplify the experience of being so engrossed in a difficult but delightful activity that they lose consciousness of themselves. The sense of self reemerges more strongly when the activity is finished; thus, the experience of flow enhances both the activity and the person. Csikszentmihalyi's findings reinforce a eudaemonistic reading of happiness because flow activities are *autotelic*, that is, done for their own sake. Any thought of utility, or a payoff, must be absent. The delight one derives from flow comes as a kind of afterthought, which once again confirms Aristotle's analysis of pleasure: pleasure is the concomitant result of activities. Aim at pleasure directly and you miss it; trust that it will arise out of skillful exertions and it will.

To experience the optimal experience of flow, the activity must be one that we can complete; it must fall within our skill range while not being too easy for us. We must be able to concentrate on the activity and to block out the anxieties of daily life. We must experience ourselves as being in control of our actions and seeking determinate goals that promise immediate feedback. Out of his analysis several recommendations are generated, such as setting rational goals, cultivating concentrated attention, and seeking the ability "to control inner experience which in turn enables us to determine the quality of life."[13]

Some caution must be exercised in using research such as this. As we saw with the self-help literature, when a single factor becomes reductively identified with the secret to a happy life, distortion can result. This is especially true where the concept of happiness is called on to serve double duty. On the one hand, it is identified with a desirable psychological state (and once again there is no denying that it is desirable), but on the other hand, that state takes on cardinal status as, in the case of flow, signifying the quality of life. As Csikszentmihalyi cautions, the flow experiences of great figures, such as Napoleon and Mother Teresa, are essentially the same: to say that flow is good for us is not to say that it is morally good for us.[14] Social scientists stop short of tackling the moral question, but many of their findings lead back toward eudaemonism. The new science of happiness is slowly tracing its way back to the past. Some of the factors that were once eliminated from *eudaimonia* in order to allow for the emergence of a purely psychological happiness are reappearing and rising to the top in research. The well-feeling of satisfaction, we are finding, points outwardly toward the consideration of overall human excellence.

This development also can be seen in one of the recent uses of the research data on happiness. Starting with a definition of happiness as *justified satisfaction*, Charles Murray plots a course through much of the same empirical research treated by Veenhoven and Diener and formulates some recommendations for a public policy that will better support our "pursuit of happiness." His concern is with describing the conditions that enable persons to pursue their happiness with the least amount of obstruction. Taking the minimalist view, Murray argues that governments cannot guarantee that our pursuits will be successful but they can remove unnecessary obstructions, especially those that were mistakenly put in place in the name of happiness. He attempts such an explanation by moving backward, as it were, from the data toward recovering a philosophy of human nature.

Much of Murray's argument amounts to the encouragement of growth in small communities—"little platoons." Good social policy consists in recognizing that people need to pursue the basic goods of life by themselves; what they need is to be freed from paternalistic interference by others. Among the obstacles to social interaction are lawlessness and the growing lack of public civility. To provide for the need of safety governments must overcome the rule symbolized by the Miranda decision that makes law enforcement appear overly complicated and inefficient. Lacking the perception that government, police, and the courts have the power to enforce community standards of public civility, the citizen's need for safety is unsatisfied and the bonds of community are inevitably weakened as people live in irritation and sometimes outright fear.

Another problem, Murray argues, is the established public policy of providing the basic material needs of the poor before addressing the conditions affecting their happiness. The data about happiness do not support this approach. Given the basic nutrients of happiness, the way in which the basic material resources are provided must be considered: "The ways in which people go about achieving safety, self-respect, and self-fulfillment in their lives are inextricably bound up with each other and with the way in which people go about providing for their material well-being. We do not have the option of doing one good thing at a time."[15]

Murray uses much of the data to rethink the aims and justification of social assistance programs. If self-esteem, internality, and work are strong correlates of reported happiness, public policy must seek ways of encouraging citizens to take individual responsibility for their lives and their possession of material goods. Murray recasts the notion of self-esteem into self-respect since the former is so often promoted without relation to any discernable excellence in character or success in life. Unrestrained self-esteem breeds sheer narcissism. Self-respect is gained by actual achievement—we cannot have too much of it. Long-term welfare recipients may suffer a loss of self-respect because they lack a range of basic achievements crucial to being satisfied with their lives. The appeal to self-esteem, in this context, becomes a pretext, resulting in loss of self-respect and enjoyment of life.

As the data on happiness indicate, particularly the studies of flow, personal enjoyment itself is greater when it is the product of a challenge to an individual's skills. People enjoy overcoming obstacles, just as they enjoy finding self-respect in providing for the material needs of themselves and their families. For Murray, social-policy makers who support the present welfare system are misled by their view of human nature. His view of the happiness research, added to that of Diener, Veenhoven, Waterman, and Csikszentmihalyi, corroborates Aristotle's dictum that happiness is an activity requiring the effort of every individual who wants to possess it. What looks like a human preference for life-long dependence, for blaming circumstances for personal failure, for passive and easy enjoyments, is only apparent. Human beings are more satisfied by challenge, autonomy, and skillful performance than by any of the social devices that seek to save them from such exertions.

Murray's interpretation of the research data has been challenged on the basis that it ignores scholarship that would undermine his confidence in rational self-interest, in the nurturing community, and in the native ability of every person to gain access to economic opportunity.[16] Undoubtedly, the issue of a level playing field raises serious questions for any social theorist who wants to dwell on the need for individual responsibility. There is also the political responsibility of making sure that access to the material goods of happiness are available to anyone who makes a reasonable effort to obtain them. As suggested in the previous chapter, this is the chief concern of the maximizing view of government's role in the pursuit of happiness. The argument between minimizers and maximizers is not whether external goods are necessary to happiness but how the government should be involved in obtaining them.

Regardless of what should be done about restrictive social structures, both sides can agree that on the basis of happiness research the pursuit of well-feeling subverts lasting happiness or *eudaimonia*. The science of happiness may be undercutting the very happiness of well-feeling that gave it birth.

Notes

1. For a treatment of Maslow and other self-realization theorists, see V. J. McGill, *The Idea of Happiness* (New York: Frederick A. Praeger, 1967), ch. 11. It remains one of the best studies of happiness in English.

2. Ruut Veenhoven, *Conditions of Happiness* (Dordrecht: D. Riedel, 1984).

3. Jonathan Freedman, *Happy People: What Happiness Is, Who Has It, and Why* (New York: Harcourt, Brace Jovanovich, 1978), 35.

4. Ed Diener, "Subjective Well-Being," *Psychological Bulletin* 95 (1984): 542-75; Michael Argyle, *The Psychology of Happiness* (New York: Methuen, 1987). Another major source of research is a journal founded in 1974: *Social Indicators Research: An International Journal for the Study of the Indicators of Well-Being.*

5. Michael Freund, "Towards a Critical Theory of Happiness: Philosophical Background and Methodological Significance," *New Ideas in Psychology* 3 (1985): 3-12.

6. Argyle, 3.

7. Argyle, 216.

8. Diener, 542.

9. Diener, 565.

10. Alan S. Waterman, "Personal Expressiveness: Philosophical and Psychological Foundations," *Journal of Mind and Behavior* 11 (Winter 1990): 47-74.

11. Alan S. Waterman, "Two Conceptions of Happiness: Contrasts of Personal Expressiveness (*Eudaimonia*) and Hedonic Enjoyment," *Journal of Personality and Social Psychology* 64:4 (1993): 679.

12. Mihaly Csikszentmihalyi, *Flow: The Psychology of Optimum Experience* (New York: Harper & Row, 1990). There is historical warrant for this usage: *eurhoia*, or good flow, was often used by the Stoic Epictetus to describe happiness (*Discourses* 2.19.24).

13. Csikszentmihalyi, 2.

14. Csikszentmihalyi, 216.

15. Charles Murray, *The Pursuit of Happiness and Good Government* (New York: Simon and Schuster, 1988), 85.

16. See William Julius Wilson, "The Charge of the Little Platoons," *The New York Times Review of Books*, 23 October 1988, 12. Diener's survey of the research, however, supports much of Murray's argument as does the more recent popular survey by David G. Myers, *The Pursuit of Happiness: Who Is Happy—and Why* (New York: William Morrow, 1992), 105-25.

Chapter 7

Recent Philosophical Views

Most contemporary philosophers assume the primacy of psychological satisfaction in happiness. Locke and Mill, not Aristotle and Aquinas, set the parameters of the discussion. Rather than beginning with the question of the best life and then proceeding to the concomitant satisfaction that accompanies it, philosophers begin with satisfaction and then inquire about its possible justification. Some do not think that a justified satisfaction is necessary. Others provide reasonable criteria for evaluating happiness claims.

Contemporary philosophies of happiness can be organized into four groups—extreme subjectivism, subjectivism, moderate objectivism, and objectivism. Sorting out the issues between the poles of subjectivism and objectivism helps to focus attention on the contrast of well-feeling with eudaemonism and the search for a justified happiness.

Before beginning the survey it is helpful to review briefly the general characteristics of eudaemonism, so that the actual proximity of the modern accounts to the classical can be accurately gauged.[1] Happiness is a global consideration, that is, whole lives rather than momentary states can be called happy. Happiness is also a moral consideration, since happy lives are measured by a single standard, the summum bonum. One's commitment to a final or greatest good implies that it applies equally to everyone, based on the sharing of human nature. That standard, however, is somewhat flexible: a person's individual capabilities, taste, luck, and social circumstances are relevant to judgments about happiness.

For the eudaemonist, final ends can be dominant or inclusive; they can specify one end, for example, contemplation, or an aggregate of goods to be pursued in life. Either way, the moral and intellectual virtues are necessary to achieving the final end, either as instrumental to it or as constitutive of it. The requirement of virtue makes happiness a matter of character and personal responsibility—not accident, technique, or magic.

States of well-feeling, such as pleasure and satisfaction, belong to happy lives, but only as they are mediated by virtuous dispositions. What is true of pleasure is also true of the other basic goods: wealth, honor, work, and so on. The presence of virtue ensures that they will not be abused. The possession of any good, regardless of how highly prized, does not automatically bestow happiness. Judgments about happiness involve evaluations of character and circumstances in accordance with a norm provided by human nature.

It is precisely this appeal to human nature that makes many contemporary philosophers nervous. The universal view of human nature is now increasingly under attack. Postmoderns reject it as a hierarchical and essentialist perspective in service of powerful and oppressive interests. Aristotle's application of his intelligence principle to devise the natural slave and inferior woman exemplifies their concern. The postmodern view, of course, tends to be extremely localized—factors of gender, race, sexuality, wealth, and class create rationality, thus denying even the possibility of a correspondence of the mind with reality. As postmodernist Richard Rorty argues, "there is nothing deep down inside us except what we have put there ourselves, no criterion that we have not created in the course of creating a practice, no standard of rationality that is not an appeal to a such a criterion, no rigorous argumentation that is not obedience to our own conventions."[2] Rorty and other practitioners of postmodernism, such as Jacques Derrida and Michel Foucault, bring the legacy of radical existentialism and its monadic individualism to its logical conclusion. In its most extreme version a localized human nature is the sovereign individual, considered the source of all meaning and value.

Yet the call from Nietzsche to create oneself is only one part of the postmodern's inspiration. The other derives from another familiar source—the Marxist critique of ideas as masking economic interests. What is tricky about coming to grips with the postmodern views of human nature is the combination of these influences: while they purport to free human beings from any common teleology, they do so in the name of justice and service to the oppressed.

Whereas once upon a time it would have been considered axiomatic that an acknowledged common good grounded in the basic facts about human nature was considered necessary to have a conception of justice at all, this assumption is now viewed as one more temptation to exclude and to oppress in the name of a societal good as defined by those who benefit from that conception.

Jacques Derrida, for example, finds the roots of Martin Heidegger's attachment to Nazism in his attempt to portray the dignity of human existence vis-à-vis an overarching or totalizing account of being. Derrida regards Heidegger's retrieval of metaphysics as the clue to understanding his attraction to fascism—the case of Heidegger reveals the will-to-domination behind all hierarchical systems of reality. One commentator on this charge suggests that "the predicament in which we find ourselves at the end of the twentieth century is [whether] it is possible to have any theory of human nature that does not become an intolerable chain on human freedom. In short, do all metaphysics and humanisms inevitably lead to what we may call for shorthand totalitarianism?"[3] Once again we are reminded of how important it is to understand the quarrel between ancients and moderns, specifically over whether or not human beings are free to create their own final end, without delusion.

In spite of the more radical claims of the postmoderns, the following typology of recent thinking about happiness reveals a general move toward reaffirming common human nature as a ground for a justified happiness.

Extreme Subjectivism

Extreme subjective theorists are at the other end of the spectrum relative to eudaemonism. While relying on purely introspective criteria, whether pleasure, enjoyment, or a satisfied state of mind, they insist on the descriptive character of claims to happiness. The inner states that constitute happiness may be complicated by such questions as time, intensity, depth, and objects, but being happy is ultimately a report about how one views oneself in the world. As G. H. von Wright puts it, such happiness is fundamentally an attitude. Consequently, third-person judgments are dismissed as either "an expression of envy" or "a disguise for our own evaluation."[4] The sole criterion for knowing whether someone is happy is his or her own report of it.

Some of the larger implications of extreme subjectivism are evident in the work of Robin Barrow, who develops a theory along the lines suggested by von Wright. He argues against any specific material or objective conditions that might be considered necessary to the happy life. "A man might be poor, yet happy; he might be sick, yet happy; he might be friendless, yet happy; he might be unpleasant, yet happy; he might even be retired to bed to pass dried peas from one saucepan to another, yet be happy."[5] Barrow dismisses the classical linkage of virtue with happiness by arguing, for instance, that there is no contradiction in the idea of a selfish person who is also happy. Furthermore, he defends the avowed happiness of the drug-induced high as well as that of the habitually self-deceived, saying that in both cases the delusion creates the happiness. Even the Orwellian specter of mass indoctrination holds the promise of genuine happiness,[6] and just so as not to leave doubt in anyone's mind about his rejection of all moral limits to happiness, he refuses to rule out the idea that Hitler may have been happy. We cannot deny a person's happiness simply because their good state of mind was caused by something we find repulsive.

Since happiness is a certain state of mind, it belongs more to the study of psychology than to that of philosophy. For Barrow, as for von Wright, the only reliable source for finding out about an individual's happiness is his or her own report of it. Barrow's argument supports the contention of social scientists that happiness can be understood only through the study of states of satisfaction and feeling to which each individual holds privileged access; the researcher has to take the subject's word for it.

Barrow's discussion, however, is helpful in clarifying the extreme subjectivist position: beyond an attitude happiness can also be termed a sense of enmeshment with the world. Enmeshment signifies harmony. While enmeshed, a person will either not seek to withdraw from the world, nor seek relief from it, nor care to reform it. One's sense of enmeshment can rest on any rationale or belief, even those that are false or delusional, and be the product of any state of affairs. Thus, claims to happiness are limited only by the requirement that they be intelligible as reports of inner states, nothing more.

Given that happiness is the sense of enmeshment, two logical features of the concept emerge that would hold true in every instance: (1) only creatures with self-consciousness can be happy, and (2) being happy is fundamentally incompatible with certain negative states such as loneliness, nervousness, depression, self-doubt, low self-esteem, guilt, and remorse. In other words, being happy in the psychological sense requires self-conscious awareness of being pleased with one's state. To be in a state where one wishes that circumstances would change is incompatible with a report of being happy. Happiness reports are intelligible to the extent that they express a favorable attitude toward one's situation in the world. To be happy means that a person does not wish the world to be any different than it is. The inclination to reject one's circumstances is the only infallible symptom of unhappiness.

Subjectivism

The subjectivist argues that claims to happiness require something more than a psychological or hedonic state. Philosophers who propose subjective theories of happiness agree that individuals claiming happiness employ some criteria of self-evaluation. This stress on internality places subjectivism a step closer to eudaemonism. However, theorists agree that all the criteria for happiness remain in the province of personal preference.

Reasons for rejecting extreme subjectivism are given by Irwin Goldstein in his analysis of phrases such as "true happiness, "real happiness," and "deep happiness." Those who insist that happiness is entirely a hedonic notion fail to recognize that people commonly employ nonhedonic criteria in talking about their happiness and that of others. "There seems to be enough reason to say that while being hedonic, happiness words are also non-hedonically evaluative."[7] One reason for this lies in the long-standing utopian character of happiness concepts, that is, the attempt in the classical and medieval traditions to recommend an ideal life along with their notions of happiness. Goldstein points out numerous ways in which our talk about happiness remains evaluative, not just descriptive, of inner satisfaction. Before we call a man happy we require that his desires be both good and commendable.

For Goldstein, philosophers who derive an extreme subjectivist theory from ordinary language actually ignore the complexity in everyday usage for the sake of simplified, uncontroversial explanation. Conversation is replete with examples that do not conform to the paradigm of inscrutable well-feeling. Claims about happiness, then, cannot be as one-dimensional as the extreme subjectivist believes them to be. Simply because people commonly express themselves as being happy about trivial things, such as a cool day's relief from a hot summer, does not imply that all happiness usage should be understood in hedonic ways.

It has been argued, for example, that the word *friendship* is used in a similar way, without the same consequences. The fact that we use *friend* to describe recent acquaintances does not preclude our reasonably applying it to our oldest and closest friends.[8] *Happiness* has an analogous latitude. Usage does not support its reduction to a mere description of a certain prized hedonic state, whether maximized pleasure, lasting satisfaction, or peace of mind. Our talk about happiness is a complex of related factors: how one came to possess happiness, one's prospects for keeping it, and its effect on our lives. Such considerations serve both to justify actual claims to happiness and to govern its pursuit. Goldstein's analysis of ordinary language offers support to the position that in both usage and reflection the idea of happiness recommends a way of life.

The subjectivist stops short of recommending any external criteria in weighing claims to happiness. In what is the most widely discussed contemporary philosophical treatment of happiness, Richard Kraut rejects the extreme subjectivist position, arguing that happiness claims inevitably involve more than a report or description of a psychological state: to call oneself happy involves an *appraisal* of one's life in terms of one's standards and goals. We do in fact expect reports of happiness to arise out of some set of standards and goals, but we have no way of criticizing those standards themselves.

In other words, reports of feeling satisfied are contextual, as it were, in the amalgam of intentions and purposes persons have chosen for their lives. "When a person is asked what his idea of happiness is, he quite naturally answers by describing the kind of life he would like to lead."[9] Thus an inquiry into a person's claim to happiness is tantamount to asking what aims and purposes guide his life. To claim that one is satisfied implies that one is satisfied in having reached some goal or another.

For Kraut, persons are happy if they truly perceive that their major desires in life are being satisfied. Two aspects of this definition go beyond the extreme subjectivist position. First, the self-deceived are not happy—real achievement is a necessary condition. Second, he distinguishes between first-order desires for individual objects and second-order desires underlying whole sets of first-order desires. Only the satisfaction of second-order desires touches the heart of personal happiness—they express our self-identity and chosen purposes—but neither set of desires needs to be justified by an external standard. Kraut cannot accept the traditional appeals to human nature or social convention, while admitting that his relativism provides little direction in how to live our lives. Subjectivists tell us only that we should seek to possess what we value; they cannot tell us what is objectively worthwhile to value.

Kraut, like Goldstein, is sensitive to linguistic usage and offers an interesting example to support the subjectivist position. He notes the difference between our wishing happiness for a newborn baby and our judgments about their happiness when he or she is grown. Our wishes for children are filled with hopes for objective goods and success, that is, actual attainments as opposed to mere well-feeling. When they are grown we tend to become subjective in our judgments: if they are satisfied with their lives, regardless of their success, then it is enough for us to believe that they are happy. Kraut does not speculate on the reasons to lower the standards for our older children. An explanation, say, along the lines of parental denial would probably lead into objectivist territory where he does not want to go. Still, he recognizes the dangers of resisting the objectivist's demand for common standards. When we agree with a person's claim to happiness, Kraut admits, we may be encouraging him to remain in some basic error. Beyond the criterion of actual satisfaction, however, there are no grounds on which to raise objections.

Moderate Objectivism

The issue that drives the discussion toward a moderate objective theory is the justification for calling personal satisfaction happiness. Are there standards for the happy life that exceed the internal limits espoused by subjectivists? A number of writers have offered accounts that seek to define certain external standards for judging claims to happiness. These accounts differ, however, in the specific goods and values necessary to a happy life and in the standards of personhood and rationality necessary to an acceptable lifeplan. The philosophical mainstream presently lies somewhere between this position and that of the subjectivist. Moderate objectivists seek a justified happiness, but they distinguish themselves from objectivists by repudiating any final good by which all lives can be measured. They often refer to themselves as offering minimalist theories of happiness and evince discomfort with the kind of specificity about ideal lives that a maximal account would require, but they agree that something more than an individual, subjective standard is required.

For instance, the subjectivist cannot account for the complexity of our judgments about happiness. We are disinclined to accept claims based on the satisfaction of abhorrent desires. If we despise the set of desires being satisfied, such as those of an opium addict, we do not judge the addict to be happy. On that basis Richard Hare distinguishes between calling a person satisfied and calling him happy. Before we call someone happy, "we find it necessary to be sure, not only that *his* desires are satisfied, but also that the complete set of his desires is one which we are not very much averse to having ourselves."[10] We are in the habit of ascribing happiness to people who are, in some sense, whole and complete. For Hare, such judgments involve two kinds of criteria, one internal to another's life and the other internal to our own, yet shared with others.

Some moderate objectivists, in seeking to specify these shared criteria, are more minimal than others. Richard Warner, for example, emphasizes that happiness requires a certain type of appraisal, specifically, the satisfaction of a special class of E-desires. Like second-order desires, these desires are integral to the realization of one's self-concept; they have objects to which we are self-consciously and freely committed. The importance of personhood informs Warner's argument for the relation of freedom to desire: one must seek to satisfy E-desires often, believe that they are being satisfied, enjoy their satisfaction, and find these desires worthy of being desired.[11]

These criteria provide Warner with grounds for rejecting the claims to happiness of those people who seek to satisfy thoughtless and random desires, but his emphasis on self-concept as a necessary condition of happiness does not allow him to reject the claims of someone who, for example, devotes himself to counting blades of grass. For Warner, it is not necessary that the values implicit in the realization of a person's self-concept be truly valuable: "Misspent lives need not be unhappy ones."[12] The Counter, as Warner calls him, by virtue of his freely chosen commitment to his self-concept is justified in claiming happiness. Warner admits that although he would like to criticize the Counter, he cannot do so given the breadth of his criteria: self-concepts cover a great deal of ground.

The Counter has a freely chosen self-concept, knows what he wants, and finds it satisfying.

Other moderate objectivists maintain somewhat higher standards. Lynne McFall also applies the notion of personhood to happiness, but she finds that lives like that of the Counter are unhappy. Her overall project aims at renewing J. S. Mill's denial of "pig-happiness." She objects to Kraut's subjectivism because it cannot support his rejection of self-deception in happiness and because it avoids making explicit his objective standards. A consistent subjectivist would notice that many people in fact are willing to call happy someone who is both satisfied and deluded about having met his or her aims in life—"What if one prefers to be deceived?"[13]

McFall distinguishes between three conceptions of long-term happiness: satisfaction, affirmation, and justified affirmation or evaluative happiness. Satisfaction is common to each of these conceptions, but only evaluative happiness can provide an appropriate standard for judging a person's life. McFall, like other moderate objectivists, wants to provide an answer to the question that subjectivists cannot answer—"What *ought* we to care about?" A minimum objective ideal of happy lives is proposed by employing a standard of rationality as it bears on the meaning of personhood and value-constituted goods. McFall argues that it is always rational for persons to maximize value: as persons our values must meet this requirement of maximizing value, or we can be said to have fallen short. This is not proposed as a standard that stands independently of person's lives, but rather as one that derives its force from the fact that it is important to us.

Seven minimal conditions are considered necessary for the happiness of rational affirmation: logical consistency, conformity of behavior with value, motivation by reason, conscious awareness of values, absence of regret, belief in justified values, and affirmation of one's whole life. Beliefs do not have to be true for happiness, but they must be well-grounded. Truth sets too high a standard of justification and knowledge, one that we do not have, but, McFall adds, rational affirmation requires that one must be able to overcome the experience of learning that one's beliefs were false without sliding into dissatisfaction.

Yet as a moderate objectivist McFall does not mean that claims to happiness go unchallenged: her reliance on the standard of rational affirmation allows her to reject some claims as irrational. For instance, someone who has made bottle cap collecting a final end has no internal ideal, no place in his or her life for evaluating character. Thus, the goal of bottle cap collecting, like counting blades of grass, does not qualify as a rational goal for a person to seek.

The successful immoralist, such as Thrasymacus of the *Republic*, also breaks one of the canons of rational affirmation. His flouting of conventional standards of justice subverts the likelihood that he will complete his life free from regret, and he thereby lacks the disposition to affirm his life as a whole. Thus the pursuit of injustice is clearly not in anyone's rational interest. Justice does not guarantee such a disposition, but since observation teaches that one's satisfaction is put at risk by injustice there is little reason for doing it.

Like other minimal theorists, McFall stops short of a more radical objectivism. The positing of values completely independent of actual beliefs is, she argues, both impossible and incoherent: "What is important *is* what is important to us. Our standards could have no further support."[14]

In spite of their rejection of happiness as an ideal final end, moderate objectivists often refer to themselves as eudaemonists. This appellation is at least partly justified, not only by their bringing moral concerns of the good life to bear upon claims to a happy life, but also by their emphasizing human excellence in general. John Kekes, for example, prefers to speak of eudaemonism rather than happiness since many of the heroes and saints we admire and emulate deliberately eschewed the contentment we now identify with happiness, but his eudaemonism steers clear of a final good that gives human life the instrumental character of serving a predetermined end.[15] He considers the diversity in conceptions of good lives evidence enough for rejecting such a theory. Respect for pluralism requires that we affirm a eudaemonism that balances between morality and human individuality. The philosophical weight once allotted to human nature has shifted to the historical tradition. Many good lives are possible within the broad canvas of tradition, making it impossible to specify all their necessary conditions.

The general test of good lives is the lasting possession of external and internal goods and a satisfaction in these goods that is greater than any suffering. The subjectivist would agree and insist that individuals must seek what goods are valuable to them, but Kekes argues that beliefs about values can be incorrect. We can make third-person objective judgments by appealing to minimal moral standards for good lives. These standards are minimal in the sense that they are both incomplete and insufficient, but they are objective in that they apply to everyone regardless of what they believe. These conditions are not infallible guides to good lives, although we can use them with certainty to predict which lives will fail.

For Kekes the difference between his minimal objectivism and the ontological objectivism he disowns is the appeal to human nature. Human nature does provide some basic facts, the starting point for all of us, about the body, self, and social life which go into the making of eudaemonistic judgments, but ontological objectivists overestimate the intelligible aspects of eudaemonistic lives. What we can know, and what we can demand of such lives, is that they (1) at least minimally satisfy the wants of the body, self, and social life, (2) basically conform to the prevailing conventions of social morality, that is, exhibit decency, and (3) include the justifiable belief that the life we lead is a good one. Unless all these conditions are fulfilled, a person may be judged as lacking a good life by eudaemonistic standards. Three additional tests may be applied to these judgments: successful self-direction, the wish that life would go on without essential changes, and the explanation that we possess the internal and external goods we seek.

Like Kekes, James Griffin also rejects both subjectivist accounts of happiness but stops well short of a perfectionist theory of happiness: there is no single ideal life by which we measure how close each of us is to happiness. Such an ideal blatantly disregards the individual variations of the human excellences that make up well-being. In its place, Griffin offers the most elaborate of moderate objectivist accounts. He declares his break with the utilitarian tradition by following the trail of informed desire as opposed to actual desires. As seen in the habits of consumerism, actual desires can be faulty—people sometimes want things that harm their well-being. Moreover, accounts of actual desire cannot explain why we desire some things over positive states of mind. When a father wishes happiness for his children, "what he wants, what is valuable to him, is a state of the world, not a state of mind; merely to delude him into thinking that his children flourish, therefore, does not give him what he values."[16] The fulfillment of human desire cannot be understood in just a psychological way: a desire is fulfilled when what is desired comes about.

Griffin's informed-desire account places happiness once again in the public arena. Happiness no longer depends entirely on the make-up of individual desires; some values are values for everyone, even while they might be in conflict in the lives of certain individuals. He develops a minimum list of objective prudential values, prudence meaning the factors that bear on a person's self-interest. The global realization of these fundamental values holds the best chance for a happiness that is at once sensitive to the differences between individuals but at the same time rejects pig-happiness. These values, which "contribute to making a normal human life go well," provide Griffin with more determinate content than other moderate theories of happiness: accomplishment; the components of human existence—autonomy, health, liberty, and so on; understanding; enjoyment; and deep personal relations.[17] His argument in support of these values is consensual, meaning that almost everybody would be willing to affirm them.

While individuals will agree on these values in theory, they will realize them in differing ways. Thus, like the other moderate objectivists, Griffin cannot tell us specifically what purpose in life one ought to pursue, yet he is optimistic about individual inclinations: persons who *want* to fulfill these basic prudential aims will find that they *ought* to follow some moral standards. Prudential values and moral values to a large extent coincide. "Part of having a life of point and substance is having a life in which moral reasons take their place, along with other practical reasons, in motivation."[18] Griffin, like other moderates, can go no further than this; he is bound by his rejection of the perfectionist position to keep the moral content of his theory at the level of a formal necessity.

Objectivism

An objectivist theory of happiness can embrace the content but not the rationale of other theories. It can acknowledge the necessity of subjective satisfaction without regarding it as the only content of happiness. An objectivist can affirm the importance of freely choosing personal goals and of being committed to personal values without a relativist accent on the personal. An objectivist could no doubt stress the importance of employing a rational approach to weighing and measuring important choices within the context of an overall lifeplan that embraces what are regarded consensually as the basic goods of life—as long as the weighing and measuring is done with a universal and determinate goal in mind.

The problem that arises for the objectivist when he surveys his minimalist counterpart is the question of how those basic goods are ordered and how the lifeplan is chosen. Does not some single factor have to outweigh the others? Do not both practical deliberation and action require a final end without which these basic goods simply square off in incommensurable confusion? And most of all, is not the idea of happiness inextricably wed to facts about human nature and not to the results of individual deliberation? Or are we back to square one, that of personal preference?

Among contemporary philosophers, Thomists have most consistently addressed the issue of happiness in line with the tradition of eudaemonism, but their philosophical work, especially in the area of ethics, is complicated by the fact that the existence and the content of the summum bonum is anchored by Christian belief. Because of this, Jacques Maritain, a leading modern Thomist, caused some controversy fifty years ago when he proposed an outright subordination of moral philosophy to moral theology. Moral philosophy, he argued, could not provide an adequate account of our ordination to God—it needs theology to provide its revealed data.

Few Thomistic philosophers have been willing to adopt explicitly this strategy. Nonetheless, the topic of human happiness has immediate theological implications for Thomists and reminds them of the limits of their philosophical enterprise. While some Thomists continue to recognize that the immortality of the soul and the existence of God can be established by rational means, personal encounter with God cannot. The final object of our happiness, from this perspective, outstrips any philosophy based on unaided human reason. This places philosophers in the tradition of St. Thomas Aquinas, and those working in other religious traditions, in a peculiar position. On one hand, as philosophers they are charged with seeking the truth while, on the other, they are expected, as philosophers, not to exceed the natural and rational means put at their disposal. But the fact that Thomists work in a tradition that, at least implicitly, relies on revelation is most likely responsible for their continued support of an objectivist position when many Aristotelians have retreated to weaker claims.[19]

This is not to say that Thomistic work bears no resemblance to the mainstream of the philosophical world. Apart from the obvious issue of the relationship between happiness and morality, modern Thomists have been concerned with the problem of Aristotelian intellectualism, inclusive versus dominant end theory, practical reasoning and canons of rationality, politics and happiness, and the role of affectivity. Yet for modern Thomists, the most important issue remains the relation of intermediate to final ends, the happiness we seek in this world and the happiness of the next. Thomists have understandably been concerned with defending the veracity of the latter while, it must be admitted, doing very little to fill out the picture of the former.

The most recent and highly visible treatment of the subject among more recent Thomists is metaphysically undecided just at the point where more well-known Thomists of a generation ago were the most insistent—the grounding of earthly happiness directly on the final end of the beatific vision. Germain Grisez, Joseph Boyle, and John Finnis have collaborated on a minimalistic version of Thomistic ethics and happiness founded on eight basic goods and integral human fulfillment. They spurn the intellectualist and dominant-end theory of happiness as an outmoded Thomism that depreciates the complexity of the basic needs of the human person.[20]

Finnis, for example, affirms Aristotle's eudaemonism formally while rejecting its content—the contemplative life. First, the desire for happiness, he argues, is for the individual's free integration of the basic goods. These basic goods, not God, provide our reasons for acting; they answer our natural need for fulfillment.[21] Actions are rational when they are motivated by these goods. God cannot be the ultimate reason for our actions because, first, human happiness must be actualized by human action. "The hearts of human persons, considered precisely according to their human nature, are not made for God; rather they are made for human fulfillment."[22] Second, human actions cannot instantiate divine goodness; that is, what is a gift from God cannot be claimed through human action. These distinctions serve the purposes of preserving both the strictly philosophical approach to ethics as well as the distinctive character of a theology of grace and the sacraments.

The Aristotelian-Thomistic ideal of contemplation has been dominated by empiricist images of knowing, making human fulfillment entirely too simple, too isolated, and too passive. Earthly or imperfect happiness, in this view, is a manifold of goods each of which is a good in itself but not a final good; happiness is the unifying of these goods in a lifeplan by practical reasoning.

Similarly, perfect or eternal happiness, which we know about only through faith, has been misunderstood by traditional Thomists who are too literal in their understanding of the beatific vision. To know and to love God redeems and fulfills the image of God: it "would be an imitation not of the Aristotelian divine contemplative, but of the fully practical (as well as contemplative) intelligence and will of the true God, creator of irreducibly many forms of good."[23] Eternal happiness, like earthly happiness, should be thought of not as something to be possessed, but as a participation in both the common good of the heavenly city and, ultimately, the divine goodness. Happiness, it is said, is less like the thought of spending a holiday in Miami than the prospect of performing a symphony one has studied for many years.

More traditional Thomists have been quick to object to a life-plan approach. Stephen Theron objects that this type of deliberated moderation for the sake of quantified satisfaction makes no room for passion or sacrifice for one great aim: "to fall in love, what havoc that would work with this plan of life!"[24] This discovery of passion, as will be argued in the last chapter, rather than performing a symphony, better suits the trajectory of Aquinas's account. His happiness is not the gathering together of various goods but that of a lover pursuing the vision of his beloved. When we love, we quit calculating, we want nothing less than to reach and hold the person we desire, even if the search requires suffering. All joking aside, it usually does.

In this way, Theron defends a dominant-end theory of happiness. The object of happiness, for better or worse, is a transcendent one. This can be shown by Aquinas's account of human desire, willing, and action. What we naturally desire as a final end is not chosen; it does not fall within the scope of our freedom. Happiness stills all desire, but there is no willing in this life that results in lasting satisfaction. Experience teaches us that even the greatest of joys can be lost. Time and change always frustrate desire. To be happy, as Boethius said, one must be confident in the security of one's happiness. Thus, temporal life is a chain of events, a means to an end. Only the hope of happiness, not beatitude itself, is possible in this life; patience, not calculation, is preparation for what is to come.

Human desire is infinite; nothing finite can quench it. The happiness we desire must be outside of time, where we can possess all we desire without possibility of losing it. This is not a selfish desire; it is also an aspiration toward the love shared in a community. Since all that is presently enjoyed can be lost, happiness is not compatible with anything transitory. Regardless of a person's self-understanding, a nontemporal aim is what is being sought. For Theron, those who reject the traditional conception of the summum bonum have ignored this inherent grammar in their pursuit of happiness. Instead, by recreating the final end out of the self-satisfied consciousness, they risk a happiness of subjective stupidity, a state of mind that cannot be checked against its object.

Theron's kind of straightforward affirmation of Aquinas's theological intellectualism was almost standard among the last generations' Thomists. Etienne Gilson, for example, insists on the primacy of the contemplative act, rooted philosophically in the Aristotelian view of human nature and theologically in the goal of the Beatific Vision. The natural aspirations of a rational nature can be met only by an act of the intellect, since neither the motions of the will nor those of the sensitive appetites are capable of possessing an object of knowledge. Happiness requires that all human desire be brought to rest and satisfaction be complete; this occurs only when the highest human faculty grasps its highest possible object—God.[25]

As Gilson's historical work shows, this contemplative and theological account did not pass through the Renaissance unscathed. Dante, who is so often mentioned in the same breath with Aquinas, is partly responsible for the most dramatic challenge to the Thomistic view. Aquinas had allowed for the possibility of an imperfect happiness on earth but kept the notion of a final end reserved for God alone. Dante posited two final ends of happiness, one belonging to the order of the natural world, the other to the order of grace and eternity. Although it was Dante's antipapal politics that encouraged his formulation, his two final ends made it possible to pursue a happy life outside of theological jurisdiction, so to speak. Although Dante considered these happinesses compatible with one another, his distinction between them signals further developments in the Italian Renaissance that would eventually make eternity irrelevant to the consideration of happiness at all.[26]

Joseph Pieper, however, attempts to make Aquinas's view more plausible by writing an apologetics for contemplation itself. He maintains that the notion of contemplation is misunderstood as an arid and elitist kind of scholarly endeavor. The cognitive activity of contemplation, rather, is the indispensable premise of love and joy in everyday life. Pieper makes the point, often underemphasized by Thomists, that human beings, differentiated from other animals by their rationality, are also differentiated by this factor in all of their actions, including their emotional life. In other words, to assume that the call to contemplation somehow excludes the passions of the soul completely misses the role of the intellect in producing these affections. "Only the presence of what is loved makes us happy, but that presence is actualized by the power of cognition."[27] Human happiness is founded on the possibility of seeing what is *other* than us and possessing what we love through an act of knowledge. Our mistake is overlooking the unique rational power underlying and informing the human gaze.

Other Thomists seek to do justice to the rational character of happiness but without seeking to revive the priority of contemplation. Yves R. Simon regards accounts such as those of Gilson and Pieper as discounting the importance of the active life and, especially, the role of meaningful work. He interprets the intellectualism of Thomas Aquinas in terms of the overall rationality and aim of the happy life. True happiness is the end of voluntary action and involves the real achievement in satisfying the tendencies, desires, and inclinations of the whole person for the good.

What Simon regards as crucial in this pattern of satisfactions is the teleological relation in practical judgment of intermediate ends to the final end. Happiness in this life is complicated by a multiplicity of real goods that must be given their due while being ordered toward God. The dynamic character of practical reasoning ensures that some good will serve as the last end in deliberation, but it will not necessarily be God. "Within the same day of the same man the last end may be placed first in God, then in some good—say, pleasure—then in another created good—say, honor—and in God again."[28] Simon is not denying the Thomistic principle that the will unconditionally desires the *bonum universale*; but here he accounts for the manner in which God becomes the object of deliberation and choice among other real and apparent goods. Even though human beings possess a determined will, choice remains free. This allows God, who is the final end, to take the character of a means and become an object of our free choice, yet at the same time that we are choosing God, He remains the formal cause of our choice.

Jacques Maritain concurs with both Simon and Gilson that at the heart of any Thomistic account of earthly happiness is the proper ordering of this life to the next. The central issue is not just contemplation, but where we direct our attention and our love. Do we seek only an immanent human end or an infravalent earthly end stretching toward a transcendent end? This contrast represents the essential difference between the Aristotelian and Thomistic accounts of happiness: for Aristotle happiness consists in realizing a human ideal, while for Aquinas, human beings must possess God before they can be fully perfected in themselves. "It is impossible for Aristotelian ethics to escape from the embrace of the self. . . . And yet in the end it is just such a deliverance that we long for."[29]

This ordering of the self and society toward eternity does not have the expected result, however, of making Maritain's philosophy otherworldly. Quite the contrary, the necessity of turning outward textures his discussion of happiness with a deep appreciation of its psychological and affective aspects. The suffering and self-giving required of a temporal happiness extending beyond itself exposes the core of human subjectivity. It is here that Maritain finds an anguish in our pursuit of happiness, a painful longing that underlies our search through the finite goods of this life for an object that satisfies our infinite desire.

Maritain contends with the ideologies that sought to exploit this vulnerability for their own collectivist and totalitarian purposes.[30] He proposed an integral humanism that would seek to revivify temporal institutions by reordering them toward a spiritual end, one that would ensure that the dignity of the individual would never be destroyed by a perverted notion of the common good. Governments should not interfere with a person's destiny beyond this world, least of all deprive him or her of basic rights in the name of a just or happy society. Indeed, for Maritain it was this recognition of persons as having an eternal destiny that gave the political sphere its decisive importance for human happiness. The perfecting of the human person, the preparation for eternity, takes place in society. Not to recognize this fact is another symptom of the Cartesian angelism that Maritain diagnosed as being at the heart of modern thought. Descartes thought he had direct intuitive access to clear and distinct ideas; he rejected the evidence of the senses and the necessary reliance of the mind's operation on the working of the body. Similarly, Maritain would have said that we do not pursue happiness in isolation from our bodies, whether individual and corporate.

Finally, it must be said that no contemporary writer has paid greater attention to the civic importance of happiness than Mortimer J. Adler. According to him, happiness, properly understood, provides a criterion by which a just or unjust society can be recognized. The Hobbesian portrayal of happiness as a mad scramble over the bodies of others to the top of the pile may describe our age, but it distorts the philosophical tradition by trading on the old news that human beings are corruptible. Adler, like Aristotle, cannot conceive of an individual's happiness apart from the happiness of the city. Individuals aim at their happiness as citizens guided by the virtue of justice, which serves the happiness of others. Whereas we are disposed by justice to consider the happiness of our friends and acquaintances, the state is mandated to serve the happiness of all, but again, if happiness is misunderstood as well-feeling, those who govern are left without a clear picture of how to serve the common good.

Adler has consistently sought to promulgate an objective, Aristotelian view of happiness. Nothing has come to pass, he argues, since the fifth century B.C. that requires any basic changes to the happiness presented in the *Nicomachean Ethics*. For Adler, to call an idea unpopular is not a judgment on its truth. Yes, social life has changed, but human nature and its moral problems remain the same. Human happiness is objectively grounded in the perennial, fundamental needs of human beings for basic goods—health, wealth, pleasure, the goods of self-improvement (leisure, friendship, knowledge, and so on), and the goods of fortune, and it consists in possessing those goods over the course of a person's lifetime. Happiness is, therefore, better described as the *totum* bonum, the whole good, than as the summum bonum, the highest good. The latter suggests an identification of happiness with moral perfection, whereas happiness embraces both goods of choice and goods of fortune. By seeking the possession of all the basic goods of life over one's lifetime a person does justice to the array of human needs and avoids the top-heavy quality of detached intellectualism. The notion of contemplation itself is subsumed under leisure which is a need of everyone.

If happiness is the possession of basic goods over a lifetime, it can never be experienced or enjoyed in the manner of well-feeling. For example, one could enjoy a friend at a given time, but happiness evades direct experience since it spans the whole of a person's life. Adler has repeatedly argued against psychological happiness. His favorite example is that of the contented miser whose contentment demonstrates that such a happiness is available to both the morally good and the morally bad.[31] Such a view of happiness not only diminishes personal life, but also makes it impossible for a government to rule with an eye to promoting happiness, because such an aim becomes hopelessly conditioned by individual preferences. His analysis of apparent goods, real goods, needs and wants anticipates the current distinctions between informed and actual desires and between first and second-order desires.

Adler refers to himself as an Aristotelian rather than as a Thomist, but in his treatment of the problem of ends he is an objectivist who leaves the door open for a supernatural version of the final end. In this world, Adler explains, the happy life is dynamic; if we are happy, it can be rightly said that we are continually "becoming happy."[32] There is no state of culminating perfection because the goods of fortune can always be lost. Like Priam, we can be visited at any time by a traumatic misfortune that strips us of our happiness.

Though temporal happiness is never perfect, Adler rejects the inference, made by John Dewey, that happiness cannot be a final end. Here Adler distinguishes between a terminal end, which can be possessed, and a normative end, which, while always being somehow beyond possession, nonetheless retains the character of finality, as that purpose that one strives to fulfill. This is perfectly compatible with Aquinas's rationale for the difference between the imperfect happiness of this world and the perfect happiness of eternity. Adler's defense of normative ends upholds the plausibility of a final end beyond this world.

If there were such an eternal happiness, he maintained in an early work, it would be the only situation in which satisfaction could be considered the sole criterion for happiness.[33] Yet, as we have seen, this conception of happiness has been seriously entertained for nearly a century. Philosophers such as Mortimer Adler and his Thomist friend, Jacques Maritain, never succumbed to the spirit of the age. Perhaps they knew that we would soon be getting over what the historian Carl L. Becker described as the legacy of the eighteenth century to modernity: the project of transposing the Kingdom of Heaven, with its complete and unending satisfaction, into a kingdom on earth.[34] The philosophical evidence suggests that the eighteenth-century dream of sublime self-satisfaction is close to being exhausted.

Notes

1. This overview is not intended to represent any particular classical school. Theories of *eudaimonia* in the Greek world, as we have seen in chap. 4, were varied. Stoics, Epicureans, Cynics, Aristotelians, and Platonists each contributed to its meaning.

2. Richard Rorty, *Consequences of Pragmaticism* (Minneapolis: University of Minnesota Press, 1982), xiii.

3. Robert Royal, "Human Nature and Unnatural Humanisms" in *From Twilight to Dawn: The Cultural Vision of Jacques Maritain*, ed. Peter A. Redpath (Notre Dame: University of Notre Dame Press, 1990), 175.

4. G. H. von Wright, *Varieties of Goodness*, 98-99.

5. Robin Barrow, *Happiness and Schooling* (New York: St. Martin's Press, 1980), 69.

6. Another implication of Barrow's position is seen in his defense of Plato against Karl Popper. Barrow argues that in the kind of state proposed in the *Republic* there is much more likelihood that its citizens will report happiness, given the fact that its leaders will have the power to change both the expectations of every individual as well as the actual circumstances in which he or she lives. The open society as proposed by Popper with its liberal values of freedom and equality will lead inevitably to greater reported unhappiness because of the instability of personal expectation in relation to actual attainment. There could be no clearer example of the political consequences of our theories of happiness. Robin Barrow, *Plato, Utilitarianism, and Education* (Boston: Routledge & Kegan Paul, 1975), 65-74.

7. Irwin Goldstein, "Happiness: The Role of Non-Hedonic Criteria in Its Evaluation," 530; emphases removed.

8. Douglas den Uyl and Tibor Machan, "Recent Work on the Concept of Happiness," *American Philosophical Quarterly* 20 (April 1983): 131. This is a helpful survey of the contemporary philosophical literature.

9. Richard Kraut, "Two Conceptions of Happiness," 178.

10. Richard Hare, *Freedom and Reason* (Oxford: Clarendon Press, 1980), 128.

11. Richard Warner, *Freedom, Enjoyment, and Happiness: An Essay on Moral Psychology* (Ithaca: Cornell University Press, 1987), 172-73.

12. Warner, 174.

13. Lynne McFall, *Happiness* (New York: Peter Lang, 1989), 30.

14. McFall, 117.

15. John Kekes, *Moral Tradition and Individuality* (Princeton, N.J.: Princeton University Press, 1989), 115.

16. James Griffin, *Well Being: Its Meaning, Measurement, and Moral Importance* (Oxford: Clarendon Press, 1986), 13.

17. Griffin, 131.

18. Griffin, 134.

19. One notable exception is Henry Veatch; see *Human Rights: Fact or Fancy?* (Baton Rouge: Louisiana State University Press, 1985), 49-112.

20. Germain Grisez, Joseph Boyle, and John Finnis, "Practical Principles, Moral Truth, and Ultimate Ends," *American Journal of Jurisprudence* 32 (1987): 99-151.

21. John Finnis, "Practical Reasoning, Human Goods, and the End of Man," *Proceedings of the American Catholic Philosophical Association* 58 (1985): 23-36. His basic goods are life, knowledge, play, aesthetic experience, sociability, practical reasonableness, and religion.

22. Grisez et al., 134.

23. Grisez et al., 32.

24. Stephen Theron, "Happiness and Transcendent Happiness," *Religious Studies* 21 (September 1985): 349-67.

25. Etienne Gilson, *The Christian Philosophy of St. Thomas Aquinas*, trans. L. K. Shook, C. S. B. (New York: Random House, 1956), 353.

26. Etienne Gilson, *Dante and Philosophy*, trans. David Moore (New York: Random House, 1956), 191-201.

27. Joseph Pieper, *Happiness and Contemplation*, trans. Richard and Clara Winston (New York: Pantheon Press, 1958), 17.

28. Yves R. Simon, *Freedom of Choice*, trans. Peter Wolff (New York: Fordham University Press, 1969), 48.

29. Jacques Maritain, *Moral Philosophy* (London: Geoffrey Bles, 1964), 49.

30. Jacques Maritain, *Integral Humanism*, trans. Joseph W. Evans (New York: Charles Scribner's Sons, 1986), 35-94.

31. Mortimer J. Adler, *Ten Philosophical Mistakes* (New York: Macmillan, 1985), 122.

32. Mortimer J. Adler, *The Time of Our Lives: The Ethics of Common Sense* (New York: Holt, Rinehart and Winston, 1970), 62.

33. Mortimer J. Adler, *The Dialectic of Morals: Towards the Foundations of Political Philosophy* (New York: Frederick Ungar, 1941), 50.

34. Carol L. Becker, *The Heavenly City of the Eighteenth-Century Philosophers* (New York: Yale University Press, 1932), 49, 129.

Part III

Reconsiderations

Chapter 8

Happiness and Pain

It has been said that unhappiness is more easily described than happiness. Try to write about happiness, says French novelist Henri de Montherland, and it "writes white." As we have seen, it was family unhappiness that provided Tolstoy with his story to tell. Unhappiness has the advantage of fastening our attention quickly; we identify easily with characters who suffer and struggle toward the light, while the stories of happy people can seem remote and boring, except in the hands of an exceptional writer. The world of literature thrives in this purgatory of conflict and surprise—how many readers of the Dante's *Commedia* are interested enough in the serenity of the beatified to enter Paradise?

The ancient and medieval philosophers felt at home in discussing happiness as the final end of human life. Speculative treatises on happiness remained commonplace until the middle of the nineteenth century, one of the last belonging to Herbert Spencer, a neo-Darwinian.[1] Since then, however, as we have seen, there has been a noticeable decline of attention, until very recently. In the interim, philosophers such as the Existentialists have adopted the attitude of poets and novelists in finding it more rewarding to consider the multiplicity of human unhappiness in its doubt, despair, and alienation. The change in focus is significant. For centuries philosophers treated happiness as the pivotal issue in determining the ideal shape of human life and society. The summum bonum of happiness specified the basic elements of a morally good life, offered directives to statesmen who wished to rule wisely, and guided clerics whose job was the care of souls on their journey to the beatific vision.

Eudaemonism, however, has not held its own against the chal-

lenge of more psychologically based views of happiness. Some of
the reasons for this can be traced to certain weaknesses in the account itself—they contain extreme forms of optimism, perfection-
ism, and intellectualism. A revival of the eudaemonistic tradition
cannot succeed without dealing directly with some of the problematic assumptions that led to its demise. Eudaemonism has definite
advantages, such as its basis in virtue, but we cannot be blind to
the shortcomings in its treatment of pain, perfection, and passion.
Thus in the remaining chapters we reconsider these themes in eudaemonism in the hope of strengthening those areas in which it was
found lacking over the course of historical development.

Existentialist writers such as Camus, Sartre, Kafka, Nietzsche,
and Dostoevsky offer an important corrective to the optimism of
classical eudaemonism and, as will be argued shortly, offer also a
clue to its reinterpretation. They pay attention to the dark side of
the human pursuit of happiness, to the pain that may come with the
frustration of our desires and the even more surprising pain that
often arrives with their fulfillment. Whether it stems from an unwillingness, an indifference, or an inability, the lack of attention to
the relation of happiness to suffering is one of the reasons that eudaemonism presently carries little philosophical weight, a situation
that is unfortunate but deserved. This missing link in the
understanding of well-being has forced us toward embracing well-
feeling and making private and inscrutable one of the most important goods of human life. It goes without saying that the pursuit of
happiness does not end because philosophers hold it in less esteem;
as it has been argued, our implicit ideas of happiness continue to
underlie our knowledge of what we are and our intentions about
what we want to become.

It may sound paradoxical to state that the failure to appreciate
the role of pain and suffering in the formation and maintenance of
a happy life has led, in part, to the emergence of well-feeling, but
when something as fundamental to human experience as suffering
can be excluded from a eudaemonistic account of the happy life,
compensatory reactions are bound to follow. Rather than question
the assumption that the happy life must exclude all pain, the tradition generated a model of happiness that followed suit and identified it with a dominance of positive affect. This lack of integration
in both accounts creates a divorce between most theories of happiness and the experience of emotional, psychological, and physical
pain. As seen in various rejections of happiness (see chapter 3), this

attitude toward negativity further leads some to conclude that the pursuit of happiness is a frivolous concern.

From Aristotle through Locke and Bentham to the present, the typical picture of the happy life, even through a eudaemonistic lens, has been one in which pain is largely excluded for the happily contented few who by a rare combination of good luck, talent, and effort have succeeded in "having it all." This statement appears to contradict what has already been alluded to about the ability to be happy under torture. If Stoics and Cynics, and even, apparently, Epicureans, could claim happiness under torture, how can one say that their *eudaimonia* excluded pain?

The answer is simple: they managed to retain positive judgments about happiness by keeping pain *external* from their inner domain of virtue and mental tranquillity. In other words, the Stoics keep the meaning of suffering from being integrated into their view of happiness: the goodness of virtue is simply indifferent to the presence of pain. This position was made necessary by their application of the formal criteria of happiness mentioned earlier—completeness and self-sufficiency. Since the happy life lacked nothing, the experience of pain could not be a constitutive part of it. Since Aristotle's notion of the good and completeness includes, rather than excludes, external goods, his version of eudaemonism contains more vulnerability, as exemplified in the tragedy of Priam who is deprived of his happiness by misfortune. Stripped of external goods and conscious of their loss, an individual can retain virtue but not happiness. For Aristotle, thus, the presence of pain is taken into account, but only in a negative fashion.

This is not to say, of course, that happiness is always strictly identified with pleasure. For Aristotle happiness is an activity, not a feeling, but an activity always accompanied by the greatest pleasure.[2] Pain tears at the fabric of Aristotle's happiness with its harmonious interconnection of internal goods, external goods, and good fortune. For example, a person who grudgingly exercises his virtue, or who loses his health or wealth cannot be happy. Happiness belongs to the person who possesses all of life's goods without being deprived of them, because this loss would create obstacles frustrating the exercise of their virtue, diminishing the excellence of an agent's activity. Once the frustration becomes an obstacle to the activity of happiness, it is lost—pain destroys happiness. A truly happy person, for Aristotle, enjoys a high degree of invulnerability against misery, except in cases of the worst ill fortune. The crown of human happiness is the virtue of contemplation because it is delight of the surest kind and the supreme exercise of our highest faculty—the rational mind.

The development of this ideal from Aristotle into the Patristic and Medieval periods adheres closely to the picture of happiness found in the *Nicomachean Ethics*. Some important adjustments were necessary, however, in order to align it with the Christian virtues of faith, hope, and love. As the idea of happiness within the medieval synthesis became weighted heavily toward the perfection of eternal beatitude, the concern of philosophers and theologians for happiness in this world naturally diminished, but it can be asked what effect this transposing of eudaemonism into Christian terms had on the picture of earthly happiness. One might expect that the pain of the present life would be further separated from happiness by the concentration on the life to come.

Augustine's first extant writing, *On the Happy Life*, does reflect clearly classical influence, although it should not be expected to contain his most mature reflections on happiness. In it, Augustine argues that between happiness and misery there exists *no middle ground*. Misery signifies a lack or the frustration of a desire, and since a happy person possesses all the goods that the soul rightly desires, misery must signify unhappiness. Augustine infers from this that happiness consists in *possessing* God, not in *seeking* God, because seeking implies a lack. Augustine explicitly employs the classical criteria of completeness and self-sufficiency in order to come to this conclusion. Indeed, in his later years Augustine refused to apply the term *happiness* (*beatitudo*) to temporal life at all, because only in eternal life can all of the soul's desires be fulfilled in the vision of God. The only happiness we have in this life, he says in *The City of God*, is in the virtue of hope, our present link to the final good of eternal life.[3]

Thus pain, misery, and suffering become a dividing line not only between happiness and unhappiness, but also between life in this world and the happiness of eternity. With his characteristic sense of proportion, Thomas Aquinas, once again a progressive voice in this development, softens this distinction and speaks of a worldly happiness that is imperfect, as well as an eternal, perfect happiness. Pain, however, is still the issue. Any happiness to be enjoyed in this world is imperfect because, following Augustine, it "cannot completely exclude misery," which belongs by necessity to the present life. Here, in this life, "the desire for the good cannot be fully satisfied."[4]

Only in the actual presence of God is all human desire satisfied, all longing stilled, all motion brought to rest, and all pain ceased. What Aristotle only hints at concerning the godlike character of happiness emerges fully in Aquinas's discussion of the grace of beatific vision. Both Aristotle and Aquinas view pleasure as one of the goods of human life. Perfect goodness requires perfect pleasure and dispels all pain. Joy, our delight in possessing what is good, grows to its greatest pitch when we possess God. By being transposed into eternal terms, the invulnerable self-sufficiency of happiness is made complete. Remember that Aristotle took the importance of pleasure as so central that he sneered at the Cynics' argument that a person could be happy even on the torture rack provided he was good, calling it nonsense.[5]

Indeed, one alternative to the problem of pain in happiness is suggested by the Cynics and Stoics who placed happiness entirely in the realm of moral goodness: pleasure, they maintained, has nothing to do with happiness. This fundamental difference between Aristotle's eudaemonism and the Stoics' is found in the second portion of Aristotle's definition of happiness as "activity in accordance with virtue." The remainder of that definition should not go unnoticed: "All the other goods are either necessary prerequisites for happiness, or are by nature co-workers with it and useful instruments for it."[6] Pleasure, as a good of the body, is considered among those other goods, along with such things as wealth, health, honor, and friendship. Pleasure remains, however, a concomitant effect of a virtuously lived life—it is never detached and sought for its own sake.

Epicurus seems to depart from Aristotle dramatically by claiming pleasure as the final good, but ties it so closely to virtue that even the Stoic Seneca praised him. Epicurus emphasized the moral context of happiness to such an extent that despite the fact that he considers pain an evil, he is willing to say, "yet not every pain is of a nature to be avoided on all occasions. . . . [F]or under certain circumstances we treat the good as evil, and again, the evil as good."[7] This recognition of pain as a good reveals the heart of the matter under consideration: can some manner of suffering be considered constitutive of a happy life? Can this connection be made without being guilty of nonsense?

The Cynic position is that pain cannot be constitutive of happiness and cannot participate in the human good. Cynic *eudaimonia* is synonymous only with moral development. The severity of this attitude clashes with the range of fulfillment that most people commonly associate with the idea of the most desirable and choiceworthy of all lives. This view, like that of the Stoics is persuasive only within a civilization in decline, where the only possible domain left open to establishing order and harmony is within one's own soul. Cicero, who debated this issue in the *Tusculan Disputations*, was forced to admit that pleasure was a good, albeit one closely knit into virtue. If ignored too long, well-feeling has a way of asserting its importance, sometimes in explosive fashion, as the hedonism of the eighteenth century was to show.

Excluding pleasure from happiness makes happiness available only to ascetic temperaments, but identifying pleasure with happiness, as did Epicurus and many of the Renaissance and Enlightenment philosophers, leaves the problem of pain still unresolved. Later hedonistic versions of happiness, beginning with Lorenzo de Valla and moving through Locke and Helvetius to Bentham, loosen the connection between virtue and happiness. Happiness becomes contentment or satisfaction with one's life regardless of the acquisition of real moral attainments. For example, as the contentment of the happy life begins to float freely in a world of equally worthwhile objects, one becomes contented by possessing whatever is valued, rather than having choice directed by the judgment of prudence and the other moral virtues. Because of this slippage, Mill finds it necessary to break with Bentham's teaching and posit once again the primacy of prudent choice in the experience of pleasure, even to the point of admitting that pain is sometimes preferable—"better to be a Socrates dissatisfied than a fool satisfied."[8]

It was not long after Mill and the evolutionary philosophy of Herbert Spencer that the large-scale deliberations on happiness dried up and serious minds began to produce the how-to manuals of popular happiness with their brand of twisted Stoicism. The tranquillity of well-feeling results, it is said, not from a mind founded on virtue and in harmony with nature but from the incantation of formulas and slogans—a curious reversal in the direction of resignation. A happy person is not required to live according to the directives of nature and to bear the pain of contact with the world;

his newly acquired thought patterns magically filter out what is negative to consciousness and reshape the world to yield pleasure, regardless of concrete circumstances.

Even Nietzsche, the greatest prophet of self-creation, repeatedly warned against using the desire for happiness as an escape from suffering: "How little you know of human *happiness*, you comfortable and benevolent people, for happiness and unhappiness are sisters and even twins."[9] Nietzsche accused Christians of inventing heaven and its eternal beatitude as an escape from the suffering of the world. Although he admired the power of Christian contemplatives to suffer monastic discipline, Nietzsche regarded their professed intention of preparing for the afterlife as a sign of inner weakness. Happiness was for him "the feeling of power," the "new virtue," which endures the thought of eternal recurrence with the greatest suffering and the richest laughter.[10] In this, Nietzsche undoubtedly represents the culmination of the process of discovering personal freedom that Agnes Heller describes as emerging from the Renaissance. Yet, for Nietzsche the expression of personal preference is not the same as power; the escape into well-feeling is clearly a reactive posture in the face of a tragic world. His overcoming of the self is a powerful refusal of anesthetic happiness.

What these modern versions of happiness have in common is their attempt to emphasize the power of the subject in coping with the external conditions that endanger happiness. They are captured in Camus's startling comment, "One must imagine Sisyphus happy."[11] The apparent paradox of his judgment applied to a mythological character who endlessly rolls a rock to the top of the hill is precisely the antidote that the idea of happiness needs. To imagine Sisyphus happy, we would have to reimagine happiness itself as less static and more tensive, less the achievement of perfection than the straining toward a goal. Camus's comment on Sisyphus provides the direction for reinterpreting the history of happiness from a perspective off the dead end of the pleasure/pain divide. A happy life becomes associated with being committed to a purpose, even if the fulfillment of that purpose is, by its very nature, unrealizable.

Camus's suggestion that we imagine Sisyphus happy implies that there is the need to construct the meaning of his suffering in such a manner that we can call him happy. In other words, the strength of our imagining overcomes the basic absurdity of his, and by implication *our*, position in the world. The ascription of happiness in

Camus's worldview is the assumption of meaningfulness in a meaningless world—suffering is given a purpose, a part to play in the happy life, but only through the effort of imagining.

Given the treatment of pain already seen in the eudaemonist tradition, Camus's suggestion is refreshing, but is it necessary to abandon all realism for the sake of consoling fictions in this way? Returning to the eudaemonist tradition with the problem of pain in mind, some unappreciated nuances begin to appear. Both Boethius and Aquinas, in particular, are seen to have modified their Aristotelian eudaemonism to appreciate the positive role of suffering and passion. For them, a person's aptitude for happiness lies in his capacity for passion, and an ability to suffer the world, not to magically or willfully recreate it.

It was the problem of suffering, of course, that induced Boethius, imprisoned unjustly for treason, to write his *Consolation of Philosophy*. As Aristotle's translator and commentator, Boethius knew his philosophy better than anyone of his time. It is ironic that Boethius found himself, according to Aristotle's standards, deprived of *eudaimonia* by his imprisonment and impending execution. Boethius invents the figure of Lady Philosophy, who visits the prisoner in his cell and rebukes him for his despair. Boethius has obviously forgotten wisdom or he would understand the meaning of his suffering. He must remember his identity as a human being and the "governance" of the world.[12] She echoes Aristotle in reminding Boethius that earthly happiness always remains vulnerable to misfortune. It contains a constant undercurrent of anxiety and bitterness because its enjoyment of external goods cannot be guaranteed.

Lady Philosophy goes well beyond Aristotelian sentiments, however, by contending that people can never be certain of happiness until they have suffered misfortune and, even further, that bad fortune is always better for us than good fortune, because by removing the objects of idolatry, bad fortune "commonly draws them back, as it were with a hook," toward the good.[13] Misfortune thus loses its necessary connection with the destruction of happiness, and is capable of being turned inside out into the fortune of undergoing an ordinate realignment to the good. Suffering, by depriving us of finite goods, provides an opportunity for us to reaffirm the only basis on which our happiness can be securely forged—the relationship between self and God.[14]

This position can make Boethius seem more Stoic than Aristotelian, but it is really an expression of a religious attitude toward pain.

Pain can be a mode of our participation in the providential ordering of the world; thus a happy person should expect to suffer, because in this suffering he or she is reminded of what matters most.
Boethius went so far as to say that God orders pain in such a way
that persons suffer only to the extent that they are able. He argues
that God gives "what is fitting for each individual, and arranges
what is fitting for each individual."[15] Those who need a painful
reminder to steer clear of idolatry receive it; those who would be
led into despair by the same treatment are spared it. This view is
seconded by another religious thinker, Søren Kierkegaard, who remarks that God's judgment falls on those who do not suffer, rather
than on those who do.[16]

The Thomas Aquinas comes to a similar conclusion about the relation of happiness and pain from another route—in his meditation
on the suffering of Christ himself. Like Boethius, he may seem to
accept the separation between pain and happiness, but he actually
attempts to bring about a reconciliation. Aquinas knew very well
that he was breaking with the classical tradition in some of his
questions concerning the passion of Christ. In order to affirm the
teaching that Christ's pain was the greatest that could be suffered,
Aquinas deals with the Stoic and Aristotelian view that the virtuous
suffer very little. Christ, he argues, suffered not only the greatest
bodily pain but also greatest sadness (*tristitia*) at his death. Christ's
suffering extended to his entire soul, even the speculative intellect
that Aristotle maintains suffering cannot reach, but though the intellect suffered, Christ was not hindered from enjoying the perfect
vision of the Father during his death, which did not prevent the full
enjoyment of the beatific vision.[17] Considering Aristotle's objection
that sadness must subvert pleasure and therefore destroy happiness,
Aquinas argues that contrary states of pain and joy coexist with
Christ's earthly beatitude. His pain derived from the soul's connection to the body and his delight from the intellect, which remained
united to the vision of God.[18]

Christ's beatitude, as depicted by Aquinas, can be seen as nothing less than the supreme analogue for the earthly happiness available to the faithful. As such, it represents a significant shift in the
eudaemonistic tradition toward the relationship of happiness to pain.
No longer need suffering be avoided in the pursuit of happiness—
it can be considered integral to that happiness. This is a happiness
that includes pain because it is an expected result of the task to be
completed. To avoid the pain requires that the task be rejected al-

together. Human happiness, as an imitation of Christ, does not reside above the crush of the world, but requires a choice of suffering in a manner specified by his example. Here the Thomistic dictum
that actions are specified by their objects clearly implies that if
Christ is the object of love, then the activity stemming from that
object, that is, happiness, cannot exclude suffering. Aquinas's remarks on the relationship between pleasure and pain support this
interpretation.

Earlier in the *Summa Theologiae* Aquinas foreshadows this interpretation by giving a new twist to the Aristotelian view of pleasure and pain. Aristotle teaches that an intense amount of pain will
drive out pleasure; he pictures the two as if they were on the opposite ends of a seesaw. Aquinas stays close to this picture but amends
it in an important way, one consistent with the presence of affective contraries in the passion of Christ. Sorrow, he says, is contrary
to every pleasure, but the same disposition can give rise to contrary emotions.[19] Even though pleasure and pain are opposite in genus
and species, they can be harmonious if found to be related through
the same disposition to opposite objects. We can simultaneously
rejoice over goodness and sorrow over evil if they are viewed under different formalities.[20] For example, the disposition toward justice can cause grief at the sight of innocent suffering and joy at the
removal of its cause. In this case the pursuit of pleasure and the
avoidance of sorrow—one affirming, one negating—are joined
through the presence of virtue. Thus, Aquinas shows that sorrow
can be a good when the human appetite is distressed by the presence of evil in itself or someone else.[21] "Some sadness is praiseworthy . . . when for example it proceeds from a holy love; this
occurs when a man is saddened over his own, or another's sin."[22]
Sorrow strengthens moral character because its presence reinforces
our recognition and rejection of what is evil.

Aquinas thus widens the scope of a happy life to include not only
pleasure and joy, but a specific range of suffering as well. Greek
pleasure gives way to Christian passion not only in the literal sense
of physical suffering, but also in the generic sense of being acted
on. Here Aquinas takes warrant from Augustine's remark that there
"was no better way to cure our misery than the passion of Christ."[23]
It should be emphasized that Aquinas's concern with happiness in
this world is remarkable for a medieval theologian of the thirteenth
century. He consistently treats the issue of human perfection and
finality in terms of the degrees of happiness available in this life.

For example, in his questions on the spiritual life, he asks whether the rewards described in the Beatitudes belong to the present life. Yes, a Christian should look for divine aid in procuring a happiness *in via*; such a present happiness is naturally to be expected as fruit from a tree when the leaves begin to turn green. "For when a person begins to make progress on the acts of the [infused] virtues and the gifts one can hope that he will attain the perfection which belongs to the journey and that of the destination."[24]

These gifts do not come as pleasures to be enjoyed, however, but as passions accompanied by both joy and sorrow as signs of their reception. Happiness *in patria*, of course, has a perfect character: there, joy is complete and cannot be lost to sorrow. Still, as a realist Aquinas distinguished between the two orders of happiness not simply to glorify what is perfect, but to estimate soberly what can be expected of this life, even at its best. The extremes of hedonism and moralism solved conceptual confusion but did not present a picture of the happy life that would satisfy anyone but an established elite, whether a protected leisure class or an educated, disciplined few. The relation of all this to the classical tradition is plain: for Aristotle a happy man is recognized for the manner in which he found pleasure, but for Aquinas a happy man is also recognized for how he suffers and specifically how he sorrows.

Aquinas's Christian happiness therefore has an advantage over the pagan not only because of the supernatural gifts that aid in its perfection, but also because suffering and sorrow are seen as necessary to the constitution of a happy life. This inclusion gives new meaning to the so-called completeness or wholeness of the happy life. An imperfect life may be properly called happy when the virtues bring order to the mind and the appetites, and when the suffering finds a meaningful place in the perfecting of human life. By choosing to suffer and sorrow in a specific way, the Christian is allowed a greater wholeness that can include the inevitable encounters with misfortune and evil in all their aspects. This can be seen in the etymology of *misericordia*, or mercy. The stimulus for acts of mercy arise from the heart's suffering. If the heart cannot suffer, then the root of mercy is removed. Also, this view gives Christian happiness a greater realism and makes happiness available to more of us who are unable to cultivate the magnanimity of the classical idea.

Christ's passion made clear that the road to beatitude, both perfect and imperfect, has to embrace the sorrow of the world's evil so that it can at the same time delight in its goodness and, eventually, the goodness of God. Living, as we do, amid an unprecedented elevation of wealth over friendship and worldly success over personal integrity, the task of managing life's real goods is itself not always, or even mostly, pleasant, but requires effort, work, and even suffering. Aquinas recognized that suffering can bless us by calling into question our duplicity, our sloth, and our aimlessness and become the refiner's fire through which we can claim a happier life.

It is a pity that such insight into happiness has had such little influence on the generally accepted notions. A look at the history of Christian spirituality uncovers a continuous, deepening reflection in this direction. The great figures of the Reformation and Counter-Reformation have a great deal to say about suffering, about the "dark night of the soul," but the general direction of philosophical reflection about happiness between the fifteenth and eighteenth centuries has already been sampled in the hedonism of Locke and others in the eighteenth century, followed by Kant's rejection and Freud's dismissal. At least in this respect, philosophy was diminished by its modern independence from the enduring insights of religious traditions.

It would be just as absurd to call persons happy who were not satisfied with their lives as it is to describe them as happy while being tortured on the rack. The prudent collecting of life's goods does little justice either to the role of passion in happiness or to the devotion toward a transcendental object that itself is the source of all goodness and human happiness. Aquinas preserved both. By working from the theological data of eternal beatitude and Christ's passion, Aquinas was able to move beyond the limits of Aristotle's eudaemonism. The final objective end of the human person for Aquinas is not eternal or temporal happiness, but God.[25] Thus happiness on earth does not have to carry the impossible weight of perfection, and the desire for immediacy is recognized as an undeniable and universal appetite for the vision of God. For the present we must suffer what Jacques Maritain calls the "anguish of beatitude," which springs from the inescapable circumstance that "the largest and most abounding life will always be something very small, compared with the dimensions of his heart."[26] Worldly happiness will be, as Boethius describes it, "shot through with bitterness" because life in this world is a tragic unfolding toward what is to come.[27]

To argue for a genuine happiness of the journey through life, as Aquinas does, implies that a person may be called happy but still lack qualities belonging to his or her perfection. Obviously, such a happy life does not have to be free of suffering. Suffering will, in fact, be a necessary constituent of any life genuinely committed to a moral purpose. The place of suffering was, in my opinion, never adequately treated in the tradition of classical eudaemonism. The failure of this tradition to give some forms of suffering an *integral* place in the happy life was partially responsible for the disintegration of eudaemonism in the later Renaissance. As long as the summum bonum was conceived to be within our earthly grasp, a happy life excluded any type of misery. Suffering could not meet the criteria of completeness and self-sufficiency. With the exception of Aristotle and the Peripatetics, the classical eudaemonists make happiness available in the face of misfortune but at the cost of a divided human nature.

It is perhaps ironic that the unity of the person is underscored by those philosophers and theologians who begin with the assumption that this world lacks ultimate finality. Suffering is unavoidable, they will say. Far from being invulnerable, the good man will inevitably suffer, likely at the hands of an unregenerate world. Boethius underscores this fragility by both his example and his remark that whatever happiness we enjoy in this world is "never free from worry."[28] Aquinas's metaphysical account of the rational soul's desire to embrace its final end explains the restlessness and dissatisfaction we feel in the wake of our worldly accomplishments. By including these so-called negative states of feeling; a greater realism is added to the eudaemonistic view of happiness. The most desirable earthly life is not a perfect life, and it certainly does not belong to those who can report complete satisfaction with themselves. It does raise the important question, however, of the degree at which suffering becomes crippling, which will be discussed in a later chapter.

The same tragic awareness leads the ancients to debate whether, in addition to intrinsic moral goods, goods of the body and fortune are necessary to happiness. Some accept as a compromise that goods of the body and external goods of fortune can be called advantages to, rather than constituents of, a happy life. We are now in the opposite situation: a good of the body—psychological satisfaction—has become happiness itself. Now we are left to debate whether this satisfaction requires moral justification to be called happiness. In other words, must that satisfaction stem from the dispositions and actions of a morally good person?

Simply to include suffering theoretically in a happy life does not dismiss the fact that pain is capable of destroying hope, of weakening our confidence that good lies in the future. This is a difficult question and can be addressed only individually; there is no utilitarian formula or hedonistic calculus applicable because pain can instruct and chasten; it can remind us to loosen our hold on earthly goods. In the lives of saints, as Maritain remarks, suffering seems transformed paradoxically into a kind of good, a means to union with God.[29] He can say this because once God is seen as the final end of happiness, earthly happiness takes on a "peregrinal aspect." That the happy life should contain happiness, therefore, is no accident. Earthly happiness retains the full dignity of an "infravalent" end, one that should not be imagined along bourgeois lines as "felicity of ease and repose."[30] To talk about a peregrinal happiness does not necessitate resignation, but rather stipulates that human desire will always be frustrated in its enjoyment of finite goods, even the good of happiness itself.

Yet insofar as earthly happiness will contain anguish, Maritain observes within this an inevitable "law of creative conflict" that enables persons to move to "higher forms of active peace and transfiguring integration."[31] Maritain suggests here a way of reimagining happiness without falling prey to its demand for closure and completeness. Of course, there is no insinuation here that one should pursue suffering for its own sake. Rather, his appeal is that we recognize how suffering can be transvalued into an integral part of life on the way to happiness.

Maritain would certainly take issue with Boethius's attitude toward the providential ordering of all individual suffering toward final happiness. He refers to those kinds of sufferings that "fall upon [people] like a beast."[32] People in fact are faced with more than they can bear, and in being crushed by illness, death, and disappointment they cannot only lose their joy, but find their moral rectitude shaken as well. There are examples, of course, of people who withstand misfortunes that would normally crush the rest of us— but it is impossible and inappropriate to seek a formula that would predict or evaluate the ratio of suffering to possible benefit or harm.

Some of those who are religious, at this point, can call it a day and await the promises of eternal life. Those who lack such a consoling perspective find themselves tempted to escape into various postures of denial. Whether one adopts the platitudes of the New Age, with its techniques of ensuring psychological insularity, or the defanged gospel of positive thinking, with its confidence in the efficacy of the mind cure, or the social insularity promised by symbols of the bourgeois dream, or the pie-in-sky denial of the religious enthusiast—all risk blinding themselves to the inherent limitations of happiness in this world. It remains to be asked, if suffering may be included within our happiness, what kind of perfection does the happy life represent? First, some issues about imperfection must be clarified—especially the tragic outcome of suffering.

Notes

1. Herbert Spencer, *The Data of Ethics* (New York: D. Applegate, 1904), and *Social Statics* (New York: A. L. Burt, 1901), and treatment in McGill, *The Idea of Happiness*, ch. 7.

2. Aristotle, *Nicomachean Ethics*, 1099 a 24-25 (21).

3. St. Augustine, "The Happy Life," 71.

4. St. Augustine, *The City of God*, 19.13 (680).

5. *Summa Theologiae*, 1-2.5.a.3. Aquinas explicitly follows Augustine on this point but, as will be discussed, differs from him elsewhere.

6. NE, 1099 b 20-21 (209).

7. NE, 1099 b 25-29 (22-23). Notice the further qualification that these goods should be possessed "not simply at a given moment but to the end of his life," 1101 a 15-16 (26).

8. Epicurus, *Letters, Principal Doctrines and Vatican Sayings*, 129b (56).

9. J. S. Mill, *Utilitarianism and Other Writings*, 14.

10. Friedrich Nietzsche, *The Gay Science*, trans. Walter Kaufmann (New York: Random House, 1974), 270.

11. Friedrich Nietzsche, *Daybreak*, trans. R. J. Hollingdale (Cambridge: Cambridge University Press, 1982), 68.

12. Albert Camus, *The Myth of Sisyphus & Other Essays*, trans. Justin O'Brien (New York: Alfred Knopf, 1955), 91. See comment on Camus's response in his dissertation on St. Augustine's view of happiness and the natural desire for God in Joseph McBride, *Albert Camus: Philosopher and Littérateur* (New York: St. Martin's Press, 1992), 25-40.

13. Boethius, *Consolation of Philosophy*, 1.6 (169).

14. Boethius, 2.8 (225).

15. Comment by C. S. Lewis, "What then can God do in our interests but make 'our own life' less agreeable to us, and take away the plausible sources of false happiness?" in *The Problem of Pain* (New York: Macmillan, 1962), 96.

150 Chapter Eight

16. Boethius, 4.6 (365).

17. Kierkegaard, *Søren Kierkegaard's Journals and Papers*, 7 vols., trans. and ed. Howard V. Hong and Edna H. Hong (Bloomington: Indiana University Press, 1967-78), 4730.

18. ST, 3.46.a.7.

19. ST, 3.46.a.8.

20. ST, 3.46.a.8.

21. ST, 1-2.35.a.4.

22. ST, 1-2.39.a.4.

23. ST, 3.46.a.6.

24. ST, 3.46.a.3.

25. ST, 1-2.69.a.3.

26. ST, 1-2.5.a.3.

27. Jacques Maritain, *Integral Humanism*, trans. Joseph W. Evans (New York: Scribner's, 1986), 56.

28. Boethius, 2.4 (193).

29. Boethius, 2.4, (193).

30. Jacques Maritain, *Moral Philosophy* (London: Geoffrey Bles, 1964), 460.

31. Maritain, *Integral Humanism*, 137.

32. Maritain, 56.

33. Maritain, *Moral Philosophy*, 461.

Chapter 9

Imperfect Happiness

Happiness has been so degraded by its identification with well-feeling that one can appear spiritually callous in rising to its defense. Some of the prophets who warned against the pursuit of psychological happiness have been made welcome, even if their warnings were not heeded for long. One has only to draw a line from Augustine through Luther and Pascal, to Kant and Kierkegaard, to Reinhold Niebuhr and Karl Barth to be reminded of how much respect this dismissal has been afforded. They are heralded for their tough stance against worldliness and an unwillingness to conform to the spirit of the age. In short, they refused to be assimilated for the sake of temporal fulfillment.

The aim of earthly happiness does not, however, have to be rejected in the face of its prophetic dismissal. Thinking about human happiness can be renewed by supplying a shift of contexts—from the maintenance of well-feeling to the struggle of forging well-being. Rather than expecting a happy life to offer freedom from suffering and disturbance, we not only continue to expect vulnerability to misfortune, but to anticipate the difficulties of seeking order in a disordered world.

Yet to see suffering as constitutive of happiness raises another danger, the danger of a pessimism that can subvert our concern for the whole human good. The restoration of happiness as a worthy human aim must begin by rejecting its present use as a mechanism to escape suffering and to avoid self-criticism and involvement in the lives of others, but even this recommendation, which seems so obvious and necessary, can be distorted—it can result in wishes that

151

run contrary to the fundamental principle of friendship and love of neighbor—wishing the good for others.

Yes, as Aquinas says, earthly happiness is imperfect; and, yes, as Boethius says, it always contains bitterness; but it is also obvious to anyone that suffering can and does really cripple us—it is not always instructive or redemptive. To say "Blessed are the poor" (Luke 6.20) outside the theological context of grace and repentence is to state a maxim with cruel social implications. What results when this principle is applied in the political sphere? Should we be less disturbed by the presence of an economic underclass—perhaps their poverty blesses them? Is it not one thing to maintain that happiness is imperfect, yet quite another to say that the imperfection itself is a blessing? This line of reasoning suggests a need to discuss the tragic dimensions of suffering.

It seems strange, in the first place, to mention happiness and suffering in the same breath. We all know that suffering comes regardless of what we think about it or what framework we place it in. Even those possessed of the prophetic spirit about these matters must admit that the idea of happiness naturally aligns itself with pleasure and other states of well-feeling, not pain. This association is not a philosophical or a theological mistake; it does not necessarily lead to hedonism or utilitarianism—the enjoyment of pleasure, as Aristotle has said, is necessary for the virtues to be deeply embedded.[1] Given ordinate desires, pleasure and enjoyment can indicate the possession of something good. The mistake, according to Aristotle, comes when we ignore the object of pleasure and the activities giving rise to pleasure and treat pleasure as a value in itself.[2] As Callicles reminded Socrates, enjoyments can arise from the grain of any character; it is getting what one wants that reaps the reward of satisfaction.[3]

Although pleasure more quickly comes to mind when we imagine happiness, once we turn our attention to the question of the objects and activities constitutive of a happy life, distress comes into view. Socrates himself left a powerful image of this association with his image of the leaky jars.[4] A good life retains its satisfactions because they share in the durability of virtue; a bad life enjoys its conquests, but not for very long. It was Augustine, however, who, in the *The City of God*, challenged the entire tradition of classical eudaemonism by arguing that pagans sought the happy life as an idol to be worshiped in the place of God. His own prophetic critique of happiness arises out of a meditation on his life, as he says in the *Confessions*—"I loved the happy life, *but I feared to find it in your abode*, and I fled from it, even as I sought it."[5] For him, a basic human infirmity subverts all human attempts to follow the simple and wise injunction to seek happiness without idolatry.[6]

The substance of his critique, then, has two poles: not only are we wrong about the object of our happiness, but we are also naturally disposed, because of original sin, toward embracing something less and treating it as final. Ordinate desire, therefore, requires both an appropriate object and the willingness to suffer the loss of familiar delectations, but while we are in the habit of seeking to satisfy an infinite desire with finite objects we are cut off from anything that Augustine, or any Christian in the premodern tradition, would call true happiness. True happiness can be nothing less than eternal blessedness with God.

Since imperfection is unavoidable, no aspect of our terrestrial journey to that blessedness can be called happy, with the exception of our hope.[7] The suffering of the present life makes it impossible for any life to fulfill the eudaemonistic criteria of completeness and self-sufficiency. Augustine's religious reconsideration of *beatitudo* and *felicitas* led him to add spiritual distress to the suffering of misfortune. This is due to four factors: (1) resistance to relinquishing entrenched delights; (2) guilty awareness of falling short, i.e., sin; (3) imperfection attendant even to the most sanctified life; and (4) the undergoing, or suffering, of divine help. This is a far cry from the happy life free from all regret and repentence found in Cicero.[8] What these meanings of suffering have in common is a description of disproportion in an individual's being and the self-awareness often belonging to those states. Suffering, therefore, can be for good or ill, depending on the nature of the disproportion. If persons suffer by receiving from another an ability beyond their own power, then the suffering is beneficial. If the suffering gives evidence of diminished potency, as in blindness or deafness, it is destructive.

Augustine's one qualification in his rejection of earthly happiness—that one can participate in happiness in this world through the virtue of hope—seems to have foreshadowed the emergence of psychological happiness. Hope, for him, is not simply an unfounded attitude; hope is a belief, a knowledge of sorts, that goodwill lies in the future. So, from an Augustinian point of view, subjective adjustment is not enough for happiness. In Augustine the object of eudaemonistic happiness has been transposed to eternity, and the hope that is its final earthly vestige can be misconstrued as an invitation to pursue happiness as a psychological state alone. Augustine, of course, would reject this construal as idolatry, whereas figures of the more secular ages to come would find in psychological happiness one more affirmation of individual autonomy.

It is easy to see that when the object of happiness, God, is placed out of reach in this life, how human self-consciousness would offer itself as the last domain for the possession of a good that could be called happiness.[9] Augustine's critique of happiness has been described as the problem of consciousness and satisfaction—in particular, the inability to achieve an integration of satisfactions in this life: in short, the inadequacy of terrestrial experience to live up to the eudaemonistic standard of completeness. Thus, it can be said that Augustine unintentionally set the scene for the dominant value of well-feeling in modernity by eliminating all the other options.

The idea of earthly happiness at the end of the Patristic period stood rejected in favor of a belief in a transcendent object and the problem of egocentric desire. Helped by its strong ratification in Boethius's *Consolation of Philosophy*, this rejection stood unchallenged until the twelfth century, when discussions of "imperfect happiness" began to appear, probably in response to the earliest Latin translations of Aristotle's *Nicomachean Ethics*.[10]

For Aquinas the fact of human imperfection became a qualifier of happiness, not a destroyer. This challenge to Augustine's otherworldliness, made possible by the Aristotelian revival, was inspired in Aquinas by his teacher Albertus Magnus, who commented on the whole of the *Ethics*. The admittedly modest notion of earthly happiness found in Aquinas's writings comes as a much-needed counterbalance to the Augustinian dualism, especially in the realm of politics. Though in his treatments of happiness Aquinas cites Augustine and Boethius on the lack of earthly happiness, he proceeds in an almost off-handed way with his proposal of a *beatitudo imperfecta*, seemingly unaware of the significance of his distinction.

Aquinas, fully aware of the tendency to idolize temporal goods, includes them in earthly happiness anyway, without any of the dramatic warnings typical of Augustine. For Aquinas, the wholeness of the human good remains what it is, even in the face of possible idolatry. The Aristotelian external goods and bodily goods, the subject of so much controversy among the classical schools, are reinstated as necessary to earthly happiness.[11] Their necessity as instrumental goods, serving the goods of the soul, is not treated as optional. Health, for example, helps secure higher goods in life, such as knowledge. His treatment of temporal happiness as a mixed concept, that is, different goods, is always carefully subsumed to eternal beatitude—there are not two final ends, but one. Even with an explicit awareness of the true summum bonum, Aquinas is unwilling to shape his account of earthly happiness to fit into a spiritual mold.

It is legitimate to question whether turning the spotlight on this theme accords with Aquinas's intentions. After all, he explicitly alludes to the Augustinian rejection of pagan eudaemonism, so any reconstruction of *beatitudo imperfecta* must be carried out in the spirit of the prophetic critique, or it ignores Aquinas's own use of authority.

This can be done, but it is not enough to interpret just the relevant texts. They can be enriched by related themes in Aquinas's thought itself and the work of his later interpreters. There are important aspects of Aquinas's view of earthly happiness that are not developed and need to be drawn out. Aquinas thought that he reserved a place in his ethics for Aristotle's *eudaimonia* while he was obviously superceding it with the beatitude of the beatific vision. It seems that Aquinas's attention was so strongly focused on shaping the immeasurably larger outer edge of happiness that he did not notice the extent to which it was reshaping the Aristotelian nucleus.

Aquinas's use of the concept of imperfect happiness is a deliberately minimal notion set beneath the maximal conception of the beatific vision. It is minimal in the sense that Aquinas is willing to predicate happiness of a life less than perfectly actualized in the presence of God. It is a happiness that can be gained and lost. Since pagans are capable of it, imperfect happiness can be acquired through the exercise of natural powers, unaided by divine grace.[12] It is based mainly on the classical exercise of practical reason, but at its most perfect it is contemplative.[13] The classical primacy of contemplation in happiness remains, but in a qualified way.

Most startling, however, is that Aquinas predicates happiness of lives perhaps destined for eternal damnation. This fact reveals the distance that Aquinas has moved away from the theories of the classical eudaemonists and their criteria of completeness, self-sufficiency, and choiceworthiness. Rather than an all-or-nothing state,

Aquinas conceives happiness across a scale of act and potency—"a thing is perfect in so far as it is actual."[14]

> Since happiness signifies some final perfection; according as various things capable of happiness can attain to various degrees of perfection, so there be various meanings applied to happiness.[15]

> For when a person begins to make progress in the acts of the virtues and gifts, one can hope that he will attain both the perfection which belongs to the journey and that of the destination.[16]

Earthly happiness *is* the blessedness of the journey. Aquinas considers the ends of human life as twofold. To say that the human end is twofold is not to say that these are separate; they are related as last to proximate. It is crucial to notice that the two happinesses differ in species—imperfect happiness is an imperfect operation subject to man's natural power taking its species from its object, which is an imperfect good.[17] The difference between the perfect good, God, and imperfect good—the universal good—also distinguishes the ends of human law and divine law, but it remains what Aquinas calls a *participation* in the sovereign good, which does not destroy the nature of temporal happiness. The notion of participation, therefore, ensures the connections of the proximate to the final end.[18]

Given these distinctions, temporal happiness can consist of roughly four kinds—the active and contemplative pagan type and the active and contemplative Christian type: the former measured by prudence, the latter by charity. What complicates any kind of division is that any typology can be subdivided in terms of act and potency, as the life of charity can be enriched even further by the infused gifts and beatitudes. The diversity of the happy life on earth resembles the degrees of beatitude of the blessed in heaven.

The most significant aspect of imperfect happiness to be underscored is its status as an act of willing, or love, rather than an act of knowing. The reasons given explicitly by Aquinas for this are two: (1) imperfect happiness consists first and principally as an operation of the practical intellect directing human actions and passion; (2) in this life the will can gain a closer relation to the good than the intellect.[19] Although Aquinas says the presence of the other virtues is necessary to support the activity of contemplation, the summit of imperfect happiness, this instrumental role is not their sole function. The virtues establish an ordinate relation of all human desires to the good.

Indeed, there is an unresolvable tension between loving and knowing in earthly happiness. Aquinas and other medievals addressed this issue under the rubric of whether happiness consists in an act of the intellect or the will. Aquinas uses this format to show that terrestrial happiness is a kind of loving, but not one that rejects the demands of finality in the name of individual freedom. Aquinas's view of imperfect happiness, in spite of his claims about contemplation, can also explain how the happy life remains *in via* and in a tensive passion toward the final end.

There is no doubt, however, that Aquinas would claim the intellectualism that is so often laid at his feet. If we look at the insistence of Aquinas on the importance of the intellect in happiness, we notice not only his insistence on a human fulfillment that must somehow satisfy our rational nature as *homo sapiens* but also that the intellect guides the will to a happiness that is true rather than false. The will moves toward an end presented to it by the intellect.[20] Thus his explanations of happiness usually begin with the particular need of a rational nature to seek out the causes of things and move to a consideration of the relation of the will to the intellect, emphasizing the role of the intellect in discriminating between the will's choices.

As Thomas argues in the *Summa Contra Gentiles*, from the perspective of the will alone all forms of happiness look identical.[21] Like Aristotle, Boethius, and Augustine before him, Thomas recognizes that competing forms of happiness bear a strong resemblance if regarded only in respect of the passions and delight each elicits. The will moves toward the absent good or rejoices in present good, whether the good is apparent or real, but Aquinas holds the intellect responsible for distinguishing between true and false happiness,[22] which the will is not equipped to do. It is precisely the dynamism of the will's motion toward the "absent good," however, that gives happiness in this life its special character.

The intellect can claim, however, a superior mode of possessing its object—knowledge. The will must go outside of itself for what it does not yet have, while the knower contains the known within himself, and so for Aquinas this more intimate mode of possession—actual subjective attainment—qualifies intellection as the primary activity of happiness. The will cannot possess anything on its own, since it represents "the hunting power rather than the catching power."[23] When Thomas said that "happiness is in the one who is happy," his intent was not to make happiness wholly subjective, but to stress that only through rationally directed activity can we find a place of happy rest. In this life the intellect can possess the only object that can satisfy its natural desire—God.[24]

For all his intellectualism, by some considered a blessing and by others a curse, Aquinas was extremely careful in not claiming more for human knowledge in this life than could be maintained in the light of sin, grace, and our need for the theological virtues. In fact, it is under the force of these theological data that Aquinas provides his account of earthly happiness with the superiority of the will over the intellect in earthly happiness. Here he diverges significantly from Aristotle, because the object of happiness, God, was not to be found within the realization of any human potency, but beyond it.

A stronger account of the role of loving in earthly happiness can be made than is explicitly stated by these texts, however. The reason for this follows directly from Aquinas's own dictum that in this life human love can attain a closer relation to the good than can the intellect. It is in terms of the loving and the partial realization of the good, therefore, that the activity of earthly happiness must be described.

In Aquinas there are basically three kinds of love. First, there is natural love, called *amor*, which is the natural tendency of anything for its natural end, and there are the voluntary loves of rational beings of objects of their own choosing. Second, voluntary loves, or elected love, which contain an element that Aquinas calls *delectio*, can be divided into two types—acquired and infused. Friendship is the primary example of an acquired love, but it, like all the acquired virtues, is capable of being infused with divine grace. Third, the love of charity (*caritas*) is always an infused virtue since it is the bond of friendship that unites human beings to God.

It is clear in Aquinas that perfect happiness consists of friendship with God—it is a perfected state in which knowing and loving reach a perfect accord; but the happiness of the journey is a kind of loving as well, one that replaces the contemplative ideal of the ancients. It is a loving that seeks the whole good for human beings, a good including goods of the body, fortune, and the common good. In other words, Aquinas's account of imperfect happiness, precisely because it is designed to be subordinated to the beatific vision, actually tones down the theorizing emphasis of Aristotle's account. Aquinas's terrestrial happiness requires the voluntary disposition of a person to love rightly.

This love that comes as a result of a person's moral choice unified into character can be called *amor* in the sense that it becomes part of a person's second nature. Aquinas distinguished between first and second nature; the former is an individual's natural potency as a human being, the latter is his or her acquired potency. The direction of the will in an acquired character can also be called *amor*, or tendential love, if the distinction is kept clear, in spite of the fact that it results from an element of choice or *delectio*.

With this more dynamic characterization of earthly happiness, Aquinas's turn toward modernity is obvious—he moves beyond the Augustinian happiness in hope, a happiness that lies ahead only in heaven, but he also moves within range of the prophetic critique. It could now be asked whether Aquinas tempts the moral fates by reintroducing happiness into the finite order. In response it can be said that he surely knew its temptations, its utter centrality. After all, he depicted the fall of Lucifer as a willful choice of happiness before God, while in the prologue to the second part of the *Summa Theologiae*, he says that the aversion of human life from God is nothing less than a rejection of the object of happiness.[25]

From an Augustinian viewpoint Aquinas seems to be setting up an idol with his view of imperfect happiness. Is Aquinas guilty? This question gets us closer to the point of the prophet's critique. We have already seen that Augustine himself would predicate the happiness of Christians in terms of their hope. It can be inferred from this that he, and the other prophets, would not object to Aquinas calling Christians happy if they participate in God by the bond of charity. After all, Catholics come to the altar at every Mass on hearing the words, "Happy are those who are called to His Supper." It goes without saying, of course, that we are far away from the common parlance of happiness that concerns itself only with measuring the degree of subjective well-feeling.

What about Aquinas's imperfect pagan happiness, the earthly happiness of the unbeliever? At its best it is the Aristotelian life of moral virtue supported by the basic goods of the body and fortune. How could we call a life happy that may never know and love its true final end? At such an assertion the prophet must object that we only encourage the making of idols—whether virtue itself, even worse the infused gift of charity, or the more likely candidates of wealth, power, and pleasure.

It also can be said on behalf of the prophet that the entire history of happiness supports his critique—the gradual elimination of virtue from the equation and, as a consequence, the ordering of goods without reference to the genuine final end. In the place of God various candidates have emerged to claim the title of summum bonum—from freedom to power, wealth, and psychological satisfaction. All of these idols have come to inhabit the American pursuit of happiness and its imitators. Given this historical perspective, perhaps Augustine—not Aquinas—was right!

As a consequence, it may be the case that Maritain and other contemporary Thomists, who following Aquinas, see the right to the pursuit of happiness as integral to the political order:

> When you know that we are all made for blessedness, death no longer holds any terror; but you cannot become resigned to the oppression and enslavement of your brothers, and you aspire, for the earthly life of humanity, to a state of emancipation consonant with the dignity of this life.[26]

Is this perspective vulnerable to a powerful rebuttal? Since the idea of happiness contains an implicit recommendation and an obligation of whatever it is associated with, it should be either banished or saved for what is truly ultimate. From the prophet's perspective one should be recommending a life of suffering love, a life that places the well-being of others first, since the word happiness has precisely the opposite effect and connotation.

Thus the prophet here has much in common with conservative religious thinkers who have objected to the political association of Catholicism with democracy and by implication with the "pursuit of happiness."[27] Happiness, they argue, as total human fulfillment, promises too much in the political order. For example, it stimulates an invasion of privacy and gives government too much power, too much of a mandate and mission and leads to utopianism. Indeed, the prophet can remind us of how it helped justify a theocracy, how it can lead to different forms of ideological domination—all in the name of promoting human happiness.

So the prophet and the politician can each denounce happiness: the former because it sets our sights too low, the latter because it sets the sights of government too high. It is thus no surprise that these prophets and these politicians have often been allies and have even belonged to the same church and the same political party.

Although one can sympathize with elements of both the religious and political critique, a moderate account of earthly happiness must be defended. First, it challenges the dualistic separation of the cities of God and man by viewing human beings, as Aquinas does, as being wayfarers, from the beginning of life on a journey to God. For the *homo viator,* happiness or unhappiness is always in the process of becoming. The happiness sought in this life, through the exercise of natural reason and the guide of virtue, with the support of political warrant, is participation in perfect happiness. This distinction is not a contemporary twist, not an attempt to force Aquinas to speak in a more modern idiom. This is Aquinas's own image employed to describe both pagan and Christian happiness in this life, one upheld by the notion of the resurrected body and the fundamental continuity of subjective happiness in this life and the next.

Second, the love of neighbor or political friendship requires our wishing the whole good for others. This wish includes not only God, but also the goods of fortune, the body, and external goods—in short, all aspects of our well-being encompassed by political happiness, that is, earthly life. To wish that someone might lack any aspect of that well-being falls short of love's full obligation. Aquinas's emphasis on the nature of earthly happiness as loving and achieving the real human good opposes the tendency of the well-intentioned prophets to misapply "blessed are the poor" to the political sphere.

Before moving to the next point, however, it is necessary to look at an objection from Aquinas himself. He says that we are bound by charity to hate sin,[28] and that the love of neighbor does not extend to sin and lack of justice—hatred of fault is equivalent to desire for good.[29] Hatred of what is evil is simply the flip side of loving the good; it indicates a desire to remove impediments to a good life. The question then becomes what if those impediments are external goods of various forms?—wealth, honor, and so forth.

This issue arises in another context where Aquinas asks whether the Church should receive those who revert from heresy? His answer poses a serious problem. He argues that the Church extends its charity to all, including its enemies, by wishing and working for their good. The good is twofold, spiritual and temporal. According to the spiritual good, the Church can receive them—for their salvation. We are not required by charity to will the temporal goods

except in relation to the eternal salvation of them and others. Hence if the presence of one of these goods in one individual might be an obsta-

cle to eternal salvation in many, we are not bound out of charity to
wish such a good to that person, rather should we desire him to be
without it, both because eternal salvation takes precedence of temporal
good, and because the good of the many is to be preferred to the good
of one.[30]

The only way to meet this objection directly is to point out that
this comment, and others like it, are made within a theological
context—they belong to judgments made with the benefit of charity. Thus they are not suitable as recommendations in the political sphere, in the domain of earthly happiness. In other words,
Aquinas's position does not warrant our wishing that the mass of
humanity remain in poverty so that they can avoid the temptation
to greed.

Such judgments in charity are far too difficult to make to be the
province of the philosopher and the citizen. They require greater
intimacy than that of acquaintances and fellow citizens. Most im-
portantly, employing such a maxim politically ignores the distinction between the end of natural law and the end of divine law. The
Beatitudes are instituted, according to Aquinas, for removing the
obstacle of "sensual happiness"—excess riches and bodily pleasure,
inordinate passions[31]—but these are blessings that are in part voluntary, not imposed, as a spiritual poverty is voluntary.[32]

The third reason for defending imperfect happiness is the meaning of political friendship—it demands that we wish for prosperity,
not suffering. While we know from experience that suffering may
lead to God, we should also remember that it leads to despair and
cynicism: suffering can break and cripple as well as redeem. There
is no way to say in advance what will cripple, any more than we
can predict what will redeem. Too often, however, prospective wishes are made on the basis of a retrospective appraisal. In other words,
we see that suffering has reoriented our life in the past, so we wish
suffering for someone who we think needs a similar reorientation.
Such wishes can become formulated into principles about the various lessons that suffering can teach.

Boethius makes this point when he has Lady Philosophy state
that God imparts suffering and joy in the degree that most benefits
each,[33] but the way any individual is going to respond to good or
bad fortune is a matter of mystery. Because of this unpredictability,
joy must be seen as the better bet for leading people to their proper end. After all, human beings were made for joy—the *frui* of the

beatific vision. Our wishes should be for a reorientation to what is good and should leave the choice of means to a greater wisdom.

It is easy for those inspired by the religious vision of providentially ordered suffering to assume the place of active agents in the divine economy. The argument that punishment makes a wicked person happier goes back to Socrates.[34] The coherence of the position depends on the identification of the human good, and therefore happiness, with virtue alone. Boethius employs the same argument but broadens its implications to include the whole of our lives with God applying the paddle, as it were, as needed.[35] Like those of Socrates, his claims are large: the wicked are happier when punished, the victims are happier than the criminals, and the actions of evil people actually make all people better.

Do such theological convictions provide license for any kind of intentional participation at a political level in such an economy? In other words, does a confidence in the outcome of punishment provide us a free hand in handing out some of our own to those we think deserving? It is not my intention to address the issue of the results sought by society in punishing lawbreakers, in spite of the fact that rehabilitation is still one of those stated outcomes, but the danger of bringing the weight of religious authority to our attitudes toward punishment as well as suffering must be recognized. Certainly Lady Philosophy is correct in instructing the despairing Boethius that there is something to be learned from his suffering,[36] but to turn this bit of common sense into a generalized attitude toward the material goods of life is to mistake the political order for the religious and to mistake human agency for God's.

Thus, fourth, a revealed knowledge of original and actual sin, or even our commonsense knowledge of human weakness, should not make us wish for suffering—for example, poverty—in order to compensate for the inability of the city to teach virtue. Again, to build one's case on the cases of a few individuals who have responded heroically to misfortune is to ignore the tragedies of ordinary life. Once again, friendship does not counsel shortcuts, especially those based on the efforts of an extraordinary few.

Neither should such a knowledge narrow the heart against sinners, which, of course, includes ourselves. One prophetic spirit has criticized the increased social involvement of the Church, as reflected in Maritain's progressive social thought, saying that we have "to choose between the politics of our religion or the religion of our politics."[37] This statement betrays a misunderstanding of the *poli-*

tics of his religion, which calls for a full recognition of the relation of all goods to their originating source. Indeed, the advantage of the Catholic tradition over the dissenting traditions is the legacy of philosophy that provides a way of mediating the claims of the political and spiritual orders while preserving their integrity. Catholics can, therefore, have a philosophy of politics that does not seek its warrant in an ambiguous association with principles drawn directly from sacred writings.

Fifth, the fundamental danger of viewing earthly happiness—regarding external goods, bodily goods, and acquired virtues—as irrelevant to Christian happiness is an indifference to real suffering and a retreat into subjective well-feeling, whether religious enthusiasms or bourgeois pig-happiness. The happiness of well-feeling is one that many of us can afford to extoll precisely because we belong to a class that already claims a good share of the material goods that we think *other* people do not really need because of *our* religious beliefs!

This is the danger of using an ascetic model of spirituality to inform our criticisms of attempts at, for example, financial success, one instance of the struggle to attend to real needs, to the built-in teleologies, of human nature. To think the poor blessed in this manner is precisely what Maritain warns against when he says that the Christian must not "take for his pillow the very love which he has received."[38] The division separating political happiness and earthly infused happiness is large compared to that which distinguishes the latter and eternal happiness. Since the difference is one of species, the political realm does not have to be treated as if it were *only* the staging area of eternal salvation.

As Maritain writes, in his own reflections on the eighth beatitude, the saints know why they suffer, "they know that persecution is good for them."[39] There are those, however, for whom persecution follows in the pursuit of earthly justice. He sees a common purpose uniting them:

> The latter threatens to drive a man out of his mind unless it is accompanied by the former; the former requires and awakens and sanctifies the latter. How could men who daily ask that the will of the Father be done on earth as it is in heaven not thirst after justice on earth and within the human community? . . . So long as abysmal poverty and slavery and injustice exist in the lives of men and in their mortal societies, there will be no rest for the Christian.[40]

Maritain recognizes that there is some reorienting purpose to suffering of this kind but, turning to the example of the Jewish Holocaust and other atrocities, he writes, "Blessed are they that suffer persecution . . . these words are not for them. . . ."[41] This is not the suffering, in short, recommended by the Beatitudes; this is blind, inarticulate, and involuntary suffering. Although it can be said in faith that this suffering forecasts God's mercy, who can say that this experience does not break the spirit?

> In the throes of death, in the moment when they pass to the other side of the veil and the soul is on the point of leaving a flesh for which the world had no use, is there not yet time enough to say to them: Thou shalt be with Me in paradise? For them there are no signs, for them hope is stripped bare as they are themselves; for them, to the bitter end, nothing, even from the direction of God, has shone forth in men's eyes.[42]

The beneficence of suffering love is the innermost gesture of our happiness with God, but it is a gesture that also encompasses our neighbors and their desire for happiness both in this world and the next. Thus to defend an ordinate understanding of earthly happiness is no less spiritually earnest than to prophetically denounce it. When the prophet turns away from the miseries of the world to proclaim the eternal vision of God, heed should be paid to Maritain's warning that God can be seen, or not seen, in the face of one's neighbors. Indeed, those who wish the whole happiness of their neighbor may be casting their own net of suffering much wider than those who minister solely to the inner spirit.

Notes

1. Aristotle, *Nicomachean Ethics*, 1099 a 12-21 (21).
2. NE, 1174 a 14-1174b (279-80).
3. Plato, *Gorgias*, 491e5-492c (61).
4. *Gorgias*, 493d5-494a5 (63).
5. St. Augustine, *Confessions*, trans. John K. Ryan (New York: Doubleday, 1960), 6.11 (150).
6. In "The Happy Life," 2.10, Augustine asks whether "Everyone who possesses what he wants is happy?" His mother Monica answers, "If he wishes and possesses good things, he is happy; if he desires evil things—no matter if he possesses them—he is wretched"; see translation by Ludwig Schopp (St. Louis: B. Herder, 1974), 56.

7. St. Augustine, *City of God*, 19.20 (669).

8. Cicero, *Tusculan Dispuations*, 5.18 (479).

9. Charles Norris Cochrane, *Christianity and Classical Culture: A Study of Thought and Action from Augustus to Augustine* (New York: Oxford University Press, 1944), 389-92.

10. See the series of articles by Antony J. Celano: "The Concept of Worldly Beatitude in the Writings of Thomas Aquinas," *Journal of the History of Philosophy* 25 (1987): 215-226; "Act of the Intellect or Act of the Will: The Critical Reception of Aristotle's Idea of Human Perfection in the 13th and Early 14th Centuries," *Archives d'histoire doctrinale et littéraire du moyen âge* 65 (1990): 93-119; "The Understanding of the Concept of *Felicitas* in the Pre-1250 Commentaries on the *Ethica Nicomachea*," *Medioevo* 12 (1986): 29-53; "Peter of Auvergne's Questions on Books I and II of his *Ethica Nicomachea*: A Study; "The *Finis Hominis* in the Thirteenth-Century Commentaries on Aristotle's *Nicomachean Ethics*," *Archives d'histoire doctrinale et litteraire du moyen âge* (1986): 23-53.

11. *Summa Theologiae*, 1-2.4.a.5,7.

12. ST, 1-2.5.a.5.

13. ST, 1-2.3.a.5, 2-2.186.a.4. ad 4.

14. ST, 1-2.3.a.2.

15. ST, 1-2.3.a.2.ad 4.

16. ST, 1-2.69.a.2, 2-2.9.4.ad 3. United to God by faith, we enjoy happiness imperfectly in this life; we can be called happy by reason of being on our way to God. Like happiness, charity is imperfect here (ST, 2-2.23.a.1)—this is what he called the charity of the wayfarer (ST, 2-2.24.a.4).

17. ST, 1-2.5.a.3, 1-2.98.a.1.

18. ST, 1-2.5.a.3.ad 2; for the same reason he calls the act of wisdom a beginning or participation of future happiness (ST, 1-2.66.a.5.ad 2).

19. "But sometimes it is possible to attain it, yet it is raised above the capacity of the attainer, so that he cannot have it forthwith; and this is the relation of one that hopes, to that which he hopes for, and this relation alone causes a search for the end" (ST, 1-2.4.a.3).

20. The intellect is present to the will in all its willing. Aquinas repeatedly argued that the will's object, as supplied by the intellect, is "naturally prior to its act" (*Summa Contra Gentiles*, 3.2.105; hereafter cited as SCG). Translation is taken from St. Thomas Aquinas, *Summa Contra Gentiles*, 4 vols., trans. Anton C. Pegis, James F. Anderson, Vernon J. Bourke, and Charles J. O'Neile. (Notre Dame: University of Notre Dame Press, 1975).

21. SCG, 3.2.105.

22. SCG, 3.2.104.

23. Thomas Gilby, O. P., vol. 16, Blackfriars ed. of *Summa Theologiae* (New York: McGraw-Hill, 1969), 72, n. 4.

24. Although intellect is essentially superior to will, it is not superior in relation to God, particularly in this life since we lack the light of glory through which we can gain knowledge of God in eternity. Intellectual apprehension of God necessarily scales Him down, while the approach of love working

outwardly from our intellectual appetite preserves the nobility of his Being. Thus Aquinas could also argue that the love of God is better than knowledge of God (ST, 1-2.82.a.3), explaining that it is better to love things higher than us but better to know the things that are lower.

This does not present a problem in understanding Aquinas's repeated insistence on the primacy of the intellect in the Beatific Vision. The emphasis on the intellectual act of seeing God affirms grace, meeting the inclination of rational human nature through God's own illumination of the mind by the *lumen gloriae*. By His act of love God relieves human love of its task of outstripping the limited intellect. In making Himself immediately known through His essence, not by any likeness of an intelligible species, God rescinds a portion of the primacy that love enjoys in imperfect happiness. But God's accommodation of Himself to the rational creature has enabled the mind to satisfy its hunger for vision and knowledge of the first cause (ST, 1.12.a.2.5). Love and joy are each perfected as a result of what God has accomplished for the human mind (ST,1-2.11.a.2.ad 3).

25. ST, 1-2. *prologus.* Also, "But he [Lucifer] desired resemblance with God in this respect,—by desiring, as his last end of beatitude, something which he could attain by the virtue of his own nature, turning his appetite away from supernatural beatitude, which is attained by God's grace" (ST, 1.63.a.3).

26. Jacques Maritain, *Christianity and Democracy*, trans. Doris C. Anson (London: Geoffrey Bles, 1945), 35-36. Readers of Maritain will recognize this remark as typical of his social thought. See also Yves R. Simon, *Philosophy of Democratic Government*, rev. ed. (Notre Dame: University of Notre Dame Press, 1993), 288-96.

27. For example, critics of Maritain's program of *Integral Humanism* and his political legacy; see Gerry Lessard, "The Critics of *Integral Humanism*: A Survey" in *Thomistic Papers*, vol. 3, ed. Leonard Kennedy, C. S. B. (Houston: Center for Thomistic Study, 1987), 117-40.

28. ST, 2-2.25.a.11.

29. ST, 2-2.34.a.3.

30. ST, 2-2.34.a.3.

31. ST, 1-2.69.a.3.ad 6.

32. ST, 1-2.69.a.3.ad 6.

33. Boethius, *The Consolation of Philosophy*, 4.6 (365).

34. *Gorgias*, 476-78 (41-45).

35. Boethius, 4.4, *passim*.

36. Boethius, 2.6 (211) and the comment that bad fortune instructs, 2.8 (225).

37. Thomas Molnar, "Seed and Harvest," *Modern Age* (Summer 1968): 319.

38. Jacques Maritain, *Integral Humanism*, trans. Joseph W. Evans (New York: Scribner's, 1986), 44.

39. Jacques Maritain, "That Suffer Persecution," *A Maritain Reader*, ed. Donald and Idella Gallagher (New York: Image Books, 1966), 315-25. First published in *Commonweal* 44:26 (11 October 1946).

40. "That Suffer Persecution," 320-21.

41. "That Suffer Persecution," 321. Maritain continues, "They did not give their lives, their lives were taken from them, and under the shadow of horror. They suffered with having wanted to suffer. They did not know they died. Those who know why they die are greatly privileged" (323).

42. "That Suffer Persecution," 324.

Chapter 10

The Passion of Happiness

At the beginning of this study the question was posed as to whether we must choose between the happiness of well-feeling and that of well-being, or whether some mediation was possible between them. The present dominance of well-feeling has been seen to be indisputably dangerous, but at the same time the flaws in traditional eudaemonistic accounts of well-being have been seen as partly to blame. The bargain that can be struck between the two conceptions of happiness involves making room within eudaemonism for a greater appreciation of well-feeling in all its complexity, without making subjective states the sole norm of individual happiness. The meaning of these states for our judgments about happiness has to be seen in the context of a whole life. So-called positive and negative states should not be understood in isolation from a life's larger projects. In this way, the totality of our affectivity, including experiences of suffering and pain, *can* be integrated into happiness.

The description of happiness as an activity of loving and realizing the real human good to an extent reasonably consonant with an individual's natural capacity and historical circumstances was traditional in eudaemonism, except for the emphasis on loving as opposed to knowing. Integral to the making of a happy life, the love of goodness is an acquired virtue of the will disposing the whole person toward an envisioned goal of realization. This makes the *activity* of happiness—the gradual, interminable realization of the earthly good—an activity of a complicated sort. These complications, as have already been seen in the last two chapters, give eudaemonism a more human face and greater realism without sacrificing its moral foundations.

Happiness, we must confess, cannot be a perfect activity since that would require not only attaining perfection but also becoming a perfect being, a being whose very essence was to be in perfect act. No, the activity of human happiness enfolds some forms of suffering, certain imperfections, and, it will be argued, requires passion.

Obviously, a happy life includes the so-called passions of the soul—emotions—from the averting of fear and hate to the affirmations of joy. No one in the present age needs to be convinced of this, but there is a passion in the activity of happiness that runs much deeper, a fundamental *undergoing, responsiveness,* and *receptive agency* at the heart of earthly happiness. It is an undergoing, that once made explicit, gives a eudaemonistic account of happiness a long-needed flexibility to include greater attention to suffering, subjectivity, desires, emotions, and love.

Passion does not always mean painful suffering—its generic meaning is simply being passive, that which is in the state of being acted on, and it is in this sense of passion that we meet another conceptual problem within eudaemonism, particularly of the Aristotelian type employed by Aquinas. When Aristotle stated that happiness was an *activity* of the soul in conformity with virtue he was explicitly distinguishing the activity of happiness from a state (*hexis*) and from passion (*pathos*).[1] Happiness cannot be a state, or a set of them, because a person can possess them while not acting, as in the case of someone sleeping.

Happiness as an activity specifies a person whose potential is being actualized: a happy person is a human being in act. For a similar reason, Aristotle cannot call happiness a passion. Passion as the state of being acted upon is directly opposed to the category of activity. To place happiness in the category of a passion might suggest that happiness has nothing to do with an individual's effort or actions. Happiness, as a consequence, would fail the criterion of being choiceworthy, since we most admire those good lives that are good because of a person's effort. The self-made millionaire is more admirable than the lazy recipient of a trust fund. It is crucial to eudaemonism that a happy person not only possess good, but be active in doing so.

Aquinas's language about happiness, especially imperfect or earthly happiness, parallels Aristotle: happiness consists in activity or *operation,* the immanent activity through which human potency is reduced to act and reaches its specific perfection, its ultimate actuality.[2] Among creatures in this world, only the perfection of rational animals is called happiness, because only such animals are capable of self-conscious knowledge of and voluntary action toward the final end. Thus, for Aquinas, the form of happiness consists in the voluntary operation of knowing and loving God as befits our nature.[3] We are not happy insofar as we exist, although to exist is good; we are happy insofar as what is potential to our existence becomes actual through activities that fulfill our natural desire. In other words, our happiness is determined by the way we respond to the gift of human existence. The response is called an activity since it, again following Aristotle, perfects the agent inwardly.

Consequently, for Aquinas and Aristotle, notions such as passion and action are not, first of all, facts about human psychology or behavior; they are not used primarily to describe states of mind, or consciousness, or emotions and feelings, or physical motion. Passion and action are concepts whose meaning is applicable to objects throughout the natural world, including but not restricted to human beings. This does not exclude the range of meanings that we associate automatically with these words. What separates us from the worlds of Aristotle and Aquinas is not a denial of what we would normally associate with passion and action, but rather the metaphysical framework that undergirds every aspect of this account. In order to answer the questions posed above about Aquinas's account of earthly happiness, we will have to take a closer look at the metaphysics underlying his view of human nature. What will be seen, surprisingly, is that a *passion of happiness* begins to emerge within the account.

For Aquinas, natural desire (*desiderium*) belongs to everything that is, whether inanimate, vegetative, sentient, or intelligent. It can be found in all things overflowing from the fact of their natures or essences. Dogs and cats, snails and magnolias, all contain a principle of activity through which they are inclined and ordered in their ends and the actions necessary to reach them. To say that the nature of a thing has desires is to say that it is inclined in a specific direction, that there are necessary limits to what a thing may become—flowers cannot avoid their smells or dogs their bark.

If one asks how Aquinas, or Aristotle, knows the nature of things, the answer is observation and reflection. Concepts about what is natural arise from a reflection on sense experience—they are not projected onto beings. The idea of things having a nature is made plausible when we observe that similar things have similar traits.

The order and predictability of these traits suggest that they are held together by a principle of action that is called their nature. Thus, we can know natures, what things are, and we can know their desire by discerning the patterns of their motion toward absent objects. When a rock falls to the ground, or a flower bends toward the light, or termites eat a back porch, or a child is dazzled by her first picture book we are witnessing expressions of natural desire. It must be added, however, that the nature of an individual thing provides far from exhaustive knowledge of it.

These natural desires are not restrictive or limiting in any negative sense; they serve to benefit their subjects because nature supplies an inclination toward movement and action not only for its own sake but also for the perfected wholeness of the thing itself.[4] Things are guided from within by the inner necessity of what they are; it is the fullness, wholeness, and perfection that they desire naturally. Natural desire ensures that things will find their way through the world, where, as Aquinas says repeatedly, following Aristotle, that "natural desire cannot be in vain."[5]

In saying this, Aquinas was not pretending that the world was perfect or that the natural order was devoid of death and catastrophe. His optimism was qualified by recognizing that obstacles often stand in the way of desire reaching its end—after all, squirrels eat acorns before the acorns can become oak trees.[6] Aquinas's point is that natural desire represents an aspect of nature that cannot be put under human control—because the natural desire of a finite thing precedes our understanding and use of it. In short, nature and its desires are intractably given. The pursuit of happiness, in his terms, is an active and ordinate *response* to natural desire.

For Aquinas's description of natural desire to be plausible, we must accept the analogical use of terms. The meaning of desire must differ somewhat depending on whether it is found in a stone, a flower, a squirrel, or a child. Indeed, Aquinas discovers a hierarchy in these desires depending on the degree to which the subject is the principle cause of the resulting action.[7] Viewed from this perspective, the desire to act is not the same in all things. Aquinas's favorite example of movement caused by purely extrinsic factors is that of an arrow shot by an archer; the movement of the arrow is supplied by sources outside the arrow, that is, the archer and the bow. In an analysis of desire and motion in inanimate matter, the vegetable and animal worlds will uncover a greater variation in motion, which can only be explained by more complicated relations of intrinsic and extrinsic causality.

For example, the natural desire of human beings includes desires of other natures: like a rock we will fall to the ground if pushed; like a plant we need the sun and fresh air; like an animal we must eat and sleep; but we are unique in needing to know the causes of things. Thus, humans lay claim to the most intrinsic or immanent of moving principles, a rational soul that, for Aquinas, is the seat of intelligence, will, and freedom. As a consequence of this uniqueness, Aquinas uses special terms to describe its end—*beatitudo* or *felicitas*—which we will call happiness. No other earthly being can be said to be pursuing happiness, though they do seek ends, because no other thing pursues its end freely and knowingly.[8]

Yet, like all other natural desires and ends, the desire for human happiness is a given: what we are, what we are to become, the ordinate range of means, all are outlined by our nature. Our original question can now be brought to a sharper focus: does the attainment of human happiness belong to the individual, to the integrity of his or her agency, or are humans like the arrow being shot by the archer?

Before we treat that question directly, there are further complications to consider. For example, nature and desire have been described, but it has not yet been asked what gives natural desire its end. In Aquinas, the first intelligent agent, God, gives creatures their permanent intrinsic principle of movement and inscribes on them their inclinations toward actions and ends. A thing's nature, which includes its inclinations, are in scholastic terms its first actuality. It is useful to call the first actuality a thing's passive urge in order to emphasize both that natural desire is a given and that finite natural desire requires the action of other agents to reach perfection.[9] In short, all things need to be acted upon. For Aquinas, "All entities are passive to something, with the exception of the first agent [God]."[10] How a subject responds to this actuality, how a subject brings this potency to act, through the efforts of its own agency, is called its second actuality.

This dynamism of responsiveness is illustrated in the film *Awakenings*, based on the book by Oliver Sachs. In this movie a physician attempts to find some way of "awakening" the life of his seemingly comatose patients, each suffering the long-term catatonic effects of childhood encephalitis. The doctor senses life inside his zombie-like patients, but it is not until he happens to toss a ball toward one of them that this life is made visible as the patient's hand springs up to catch the ball. After repeating the behavior with patients throughout his ward, he attempts to explain it to the hospital's director by saying, "They take the will of the ball."

The director of the hospital is of course skeptical, but the doctor continues to search for objects that will actuate the passive potencies of his patients, for he knows that human action, which we normally call human life, requires objects or ends to help cause those actions. To "take the will of the ball" illustrates the way the cosmos of created natures are united in their individual actions toward their own perfection and fulfillment. Within the teleological give and take of Aquinas's world, things are perfected not only by the pull of a final end, but also by the interplay of finite things prompted by each other toward growth: we are, in short, spurred toward fulfillment by a "great chain of being." In spite of being described as an activity, eudaemonistic happiness turns out, in fact, to require a great web of dependencies and interrelationships, which begins with natural desire, and the response to existence itself, but comes to include family, friends, tradition, education, institutions, and so on.

Sachs describes the "awakenings" observed in his patients, treated with L-dopa, as a response to being, a change of one's relation to the world. The patient

> ceases to feel the presence of illness and the absence of the world, and comes to feel the absence of his illness and the full presence of the world. . . . Thus the awakened patient turns to the world, no longer occupied and preoccupied by his sickness. He turns an eager and ardent attention on the world, a loving and joyous and innocent attention. . . . He falls in love with reality itself.[11]

This perfect satisfaction that his patients temporarily experience raises the problem of happiness in its full metaphysical context. Sachs describes this side-effect of L-dopa as a kind of sudden and explosive realization of natural potency in his patients, and he asks "How much we can summon [from] one world."[12] He argues that their awakening was doomed to be lost for the simple reason that the totality and complexity of their relationships made it impossible that they all remain satisfied. Illness becomes a metaphor for the intractability of human finitude.

The desire for happiness thus picks its way through a tangle of particularity, never finding among the gamut of limited objects and experiences any one that satisfies, and even though we might make an idol of romantic love, wealth, or success, we do not seek to possess them except as a means to our happiness. Thus, it is impossible to choose unhappiness directly—the desire for happiness irresistibly drives the will.[13] Apart from misfortune, unhappiness results from our mistakes about what we freely choose under the form of goodness. Since the will's determination toward the universal good underlies and makes possible all choice, we cannot escape from the mire of false happiness by forsaking its pursuit.[14]

It is clear, then, that Aquinas was heir to the teleology of Aristotle, but with the addition of God as Creator, the meaning of act and potency was transformed. No longer are finite beings in an eternal world viewed as acted upon by the attraction of unmoved movers, the pure actuality of an intellectual being. For Aquinas, both nature and existence are given by God in creation. This focus of existence itself multiplies the ontological dependence of finitude on the divine, so that the intent of Aquinas's metaphysics is no longer merely tracing the dynamism of natures but eliciting wonder and gratitude for the very existence of those natures and their desires.

As a result, between Aristotle and Aquinas we straddle two versions of act and potency and two versions of final causality; Aristotle's divinity remains within the span of finite being, while Aquinas's infinite God, the very act of existing, becomes unique in kind rather than simply in degree. We can ask, however, whether Aquinas heightens the dependency of the finite on the divine to such an extent that it threatens human freedom. It is one thing to affirm the need for objects and purposive action; it is quite another to accept the inner necessity of a passive urge.

With God as first, last, and efficient cause of existence little room seems left for nature to act. So we are back at the beginning with a metaphysical version of passion and desire, one strongly informed by the doctrine of the real distinction between essence and existence, that appears to squelch an important fact about free human agency, especially in regard to happiness. How can one make room for anything other than a divinely given happiness?

Turning to Aquinas's treatment of passion and happiness, we see that he was well aware of the need to underscore human freedom. Free and voluntary action, Aquinas insisted, is the necessary but not sufficient condition of happiness. A happy life is one that we must freely contribute to, for the simple reason that among those goods belonging to human happiness is the fact of our effort at attaining it.

With all that is given as constitutive of our happiness, however, it is difficult to imagine that Thomistic happiness is not a state of being acted on, a passion of some sort. First, human nature itself, and its natural desire, is a product of divine art. Second, the ordinate pursuit of earthly happiness is a way mapped out by that nature. Third, it is by gratuitous divine action, not human effort alone, that a person possesses perfect, eternal happiness. It is by the grace of the light of glory that we are enabled to see God. By his own act of love God relieves human love of its task of surpassing the capacity of human nature.

In making himself immediately known through his essence, not by any likeness of an intelligible species, God accommodates himself to his rational creatures by raising the power of their intellect to the vision of God.[15] It seems, therefore, as if both in the order of grace and in the order of created nature our human efforts are dwarfed by God's own efforts, without which rational animals would neither exist nor be inclined toward an infinite object and, moreover, would be unable to satisfy entirely that desire. Happiness must require a passion of some sort.

Aquinas was always expert at anticipating objections. He in fact admits that the happiness of seeing God, during which the soul passively receives the effects of divine grace, can be called a passion. This infusion of grace in the intellectual part of the soul can be called a passion in the sense in which "every reception is called a passion,"[16] but this acknowledgment stands in apparent contradiction to the principle that happiness is an activity. How does Aquinas repair the inconsistency? He does so by consigning the passionate element to the background of his happiness treatises while keeping the active principle well in the foreground. His reasons for preserving the active nature of happiness, when there is so much metaphysical and theological pressure to the contrary, is Aquinas's axiom that God's actions are always respectful of created natures. In other words, God does not hot-wire the gap between first and second actuality, between natural desire and happiness. To appreciate Aquinas's position fully we must take a closer look at the different meanings of passion.

The first, or general, meaning is that already mentioned, the reception of something in any way at all. Thus, perfect happiness insofar as it requires the reception of grace is a passion. The second meaning, its proper or strict sense, is motion, "inasmuch as it is by way of motion that reception in a patient takes place."[17] Passion occurs in this sense when an agent produces an alteration in something, for example, if you are saddened by a poorly made pizza.[18] Whether sadness or joy, Aquinas in fact groups all emotions (*passiones animae*) under this category. It is the third meaning of passion which is passion in its most proper sense—a loss or defect on the part of the patient caused by the agent. A common example of this would include our suffering the loss a good, such as the good of friendship, which we need to flourish. Obviously, a bad pizza would not qualify here, unless someone was either poisoned or lacked friends to eat it with.

So, given the three meanings of passion, only the general meaning of passion applies to happiness, just as it applies to the whole of creation as well,[19] but Aquinas does not consider this simple presence of potentiality, which can be found in every created thing, as passion in the proper or the most proper sense. It is interesting, then, to notice how little attention Aquinas seems to pay to the significance of the general sense; his passion scale, so to speak, extends in the direction of emotion and the extremity of his scale, passion *propriisimus*, designates passion as the enemy of natural desire. What is most properly called a passion is that which results from our losing a real good.

When Aquinas contrasts receiving health and receiving illness, both are said to be passions, but only the latter is passion *propriisimus*.[20] His reasoning seems to be that passion most properly applies "when something that naturally goes with a thing or is properly inclined to it is taken away."[21] Sickness and sadness both fall into that category of passion if they are responses to the loss of something good, say, sadness over the loss of a friend.

It is surprising that for Aquinas passion and desire become antagonists.[22] The two words that we so often use in the same breath, often as synonyms, are found here to be fundamentally at odds. In spite of a vast metaphysical background in which so much is given to human existence, Aquinas downplays the passive for the sake of fortifying the activity of genuine human agency.

Perhaps the most obvious reason that passion is systematically dissociated from happiness in Aquinas is the relation of emotion, our second sense of passion, to the freedom of action. Aquinas views emotions as belonging more to the body than to the mind. Intellect and will command and direct human actions while sensuality has its own instinctual necessity.[23] Indeed, Aquinas assumes that emotions do not qualify as voluntary since they are not in our power; they arise spontaneously in response to sensitive perceptions.[24] Emotions, therefore, are not directly worthy of praise, except those, presumably moderate, emotions that do not diminish our freedom of choice, which itself is the condition of our moral agency.[25] Aquinas comes surprisingly close to Kant in saying that emotions that precede a choice diminish the direction given by reason and thereby detract from its merit, even though the object of emotions may be good.[26]

Presumably, emotions, regardless of how they fall within the ordering of virtuous dispositions, always remain outside (or consequent to) what we can legitimately call our moral agency. Emotions that follow from choice add to merit as an indication of an intense movement of the will. Aquinas writes, "It is true, then, that acting from passion [emotion] lessens praise and blame, but with passion [emotion] can increase both of them." [27] Thus, we may admire the fervent passion of a social reformer, for example, but we should be aware that if her exuberance is not rooted in her commitments, but vice versa, then her zeal cannot be trusted.

Notice, however, that Aquinas does not follow the Stoics in separating emotion from virtue and happiness. As has been suggested, there is good reason for his focus on the willing prior to the emotions. What might be found to be missing, though, is an appreciation of the role that habituation plays in shaping those antecedent emotions in the first place. Aristotle himself said that the happy man was one who would learn not simply to control the passions but to order them toward the good. A person who can be called happy must have learned to enjoy pleasure at the right time and in the right things; but then, Aquinas is following Aristotle in denying that the emotional states can be virtues.[28] Thus, emotions in themselves have no moral value, because virtues reach down, so to speak, from reason to embrace the body and its appetites, while emotions begin in the body and move toward reason.[29]

There is another distinction to be made that reasserts the passionate nature of becoming happy in the Thomistic sense, the happiness of the journey. It has been pointed out that Aquinas trades on a dual use of the term *nature*.[30] For him, nature has two kinds of potencies, active and passive: what it does by virtue of its own activity and what it does by influence of a higher nature. As Jan

Aertsen points out, much of the debate over whether or not there is a natural desire for God in Aquinas could be resolved if it was noticed that his view of a nature's inclination toward an end includes its capacity to be acted on as well as its capacity to act.[31] Human happiness, therefore, occurs because of a "concursus" of powers, those belonging to human nature and those belonging the divine nature.[32] Our capacity for passion, for receptive agency, makes these converging actions possible. It also provides testimony to the real distinction between human existence and existence itself—only the latter can be totally active and devoid of passion.

Aquinas plainly acknowledges this sense of ontological dependence: all finite creatures receive existence and are, therefore, in potentiality; only God is pure actuality. Aquinas, therefore, could have brooded on this fact to the point of absorbing everything into the godhead, or—and this is what he did—he could have attempted a philosophical explanation of how the finite existences enjoy their own finite act of existence, in spite of their being finite. This is the reason he keeps the general meaning of passion in the background: it threatens to swallow up the motions of finite things, robbing them of their second actuality and, in our case, of our personal efforts at happiness.

Aquinas was aware of the alternate explanation, one that would have portrayed the entire drama of the exit of human creation and our return to God as passively dominated by the forces of natural and supernatural love. He explicitly rejects this as violating his basic principle of cooperation between nature and grace.[33] Aquinas insists that human happiness *belongs* to the creature, not to any higher power, whether angels or God. "Happiness is in the one who is happy."[34] Although its cause and its object belong to God, happiness must still be regarded as something made.[35] Human action remains because the meaning of fulfillment, when applied to rational creatures, includes the fact of our agency. He rejects a view of happiness that would have robbed rational creatures of their free and proper activity. In keeping passion, passivity, and the affections themselves assigned to the background, Aquinas underscores the integrity that God preserves in his creatures, even in the face of divine power.

What has happened, though, to the subjective experience of personal emotion? Does Aquinas offer a tonic to the emotive self-scrutiny mentioned earlier? His treatment of the emotions seems limited by the standard classical view of the emotions. One wonders, for example, about the strict inability of the passions to become domesticated, so to speak, by virtue and to carry rationality forward in their own domain.

For Aquinas, however, the emotions themselves belong to the whole person; they are grounded in natural desire and express the same finality belonging to the intellect and the will toward the extrinsic final end that is God. Emotions, then, help dispose us toward happiness in this life and the next. These emotions are left behind, however; they are provisional and preparatory, just as the material body is preparatory. The eternal happiness of the whole person, the composite of soul and spiritualized body, will experience a spiritualized joy and delight. Yet, in this life, these emotions remain subordinated to the act of vision while being responsive to it; thus a happy person can undergo both sadness and joy while struggling toward an arduous goal. For Aquinas, the activity of the intellect and will remain primary, suggesting a realistic intellectualism that reaffirms the distinctiveness of human nature while appreciating the subsidiary function of human emotion.

Character no doubt includes the disposing habits of a person's desires and feelings, but for Aquinas, once again, the mere presence of an affective state or wish, as in the case of emotion, does not justify it. What can feel natural (his word is *connatural*) to us, or instinctive in a certain way, can be out of sync with our natural desires. Thus, our popular notion of desire as a felt impulse or craving can be scrutinized for its relation to deeper desires. Aquinas would allow that the freedom to pursue happiness through the making of our character inevitably provides us with the occasion to develop inordinate desires. Our experience of falling in love with a person who feels right may in fact be an instance of desiring the wrong person with whom to share the all-important good of friendship.

Aquinas would agree that a table of virtues is a flexible moral norm, one best suited to the particularity of human lives, but this flexibility does not extend to the breaking point of redefining human nature. Aquinas's obvious point is that rational creatures cannot create natures. Thus, one might ask whether the insistence on a happiness stemming from natural desire and requiring human action looks like the assertion of a rather tragic fact about human nature: are we trapped between an irresistible desire for a supernatural end and a natural inability, compounded by human weakness, to reach it? Here we are, compounds of created nature and infinite desire, stuck with an unsolicited appetite, requiring us to draw on a power we do not have, to quench a thirst that left unsatisfied—as we all know too well from Beckett's Godot—presents the likelihood of despair. For Aquinas, however, the alternative of despair belongs only to those who freely refuse the promptings of nature and grace or, in the language of *Awakenings*, refuse to "take the will of the ball."

Conclusion

The passion of happiness intends the complete human good. A good life is not simple, however, and a eudaemonist must give priority to goods of the soul and the common good, since without them, other goods, those of the body and external goods, are misused, and the whole good suffers as a result. Part of the complexity of the good is that judgments about achieving happiness, should be made relative to individual differences in capacity and circumstance. These advantages and disadvantages in the pursuit of happiness include factors of native endowments, family and community nurturing, education, wealth, and economic opportunity. Happiness, once again, can be said to belong to those who, given their humanity and their circumstances, have distinguished themselves for their steadfast and successful commitment to the life they envision, for overcoming different kinds of obstacles in seeking their goal.

The meaning of the human good is notoriously difficult to discuss for a number of reasons, not the least of which is the lack of public consensus on ethical issues. This particular problem can be overcome, however, by stressing the level of generality and formality in descriptions of human goodness. In other words, any principles one might propose to direct a happy life are necessarily several steps removed from application to individual situations. For example, agreement that happiness requires justice does not imply agreement about the justice of an actual state of affairs. The same slippage between principle and instantiation modifies all recommendations for happiness.

It is impossible to provide, therefore, at an abstract level how a happy life will look in the concrete—since happy lives will belong to different people and reflect the diversity of their individual characteristics, experience, and backgrounds. Yet happy people will bear a definite resemblance—they will be, as Tolstoy said, alike in dis-

tinctive ways. For example, it has been argued that the happy life
is the loving and imperfect realization of the good for human beings—that it involves the possession and enjoyment of different kinds
of goods, those of the soul, the body, and fortune—but it would be
a mistake at this point simply to portray happiness as a virtuous
collecting of real goods or to conclude that the limits of satisfaction are supplied by the ordinate desire. (Yet, even this conclusion
is sufficient to unseat the dominance of well-feeling.)

The most significant issue left for comment is whether this human good be can considered a summum bonum or a totum bonum?
Is the end of human life dominated by a single overriding good, or
is it an aggregate of all the human goods? The classical dispute
between dominant-end and inclusive-end theorists focuses on Aristotle's treatment of contemplation in Book 10 of his *Ethics*—the
question being whether happiness consists in possessing the highest
of the human goods or whether it consists in an orderly collection,
or totalizing, of all the goods. A recent reading of Aristotle has
shown that this particular dichotomy is not really representative of
his eudaemonism.[36]

Aristotle's argument is that if happiness is life lived in conformity with virtue, then it should conform with the excellence of the
highest of all human powers, that is, the contemplative intellect.
Theoria is the activity of the mind exercised for its own sake, as
opposed to making or doing something. Since contemplation is the
only activity that is done strictly for its own sake, it qualifies as a
complete and self-sufficient activity par excellence; the contemplative is less vulnerable to misfortune than others since he will care
less about external goods and will need less of them to express his
particular excellence.[37]

For Aristotle, persons whose excellence is confined to the practical, nontheoretical sphere must be content with a happiness that
is second best, but the dichotomy of the dominant-end/inclusive-end
debate is reduced if one sees that the basis of their happiness remains the same. Both active and contemplative happiness are se-
cured through the exercise of reason, the highest human faculty, but
since the mind is being exercised through the virtue of prudence
(*phronesis*) toward practical action, active happiness lacks the self-
sufficiency of reason being exercised for its own sake.

Even the second best happiness is difficult to enjoy. To qualify
for active happiness one must first of all be virtuous, secondly, be

moderately prosperous, and, thirdly, maintain both of these over a long span of time; but to be completely happy, one must add to these qualifications an active disposition of the mind toward thinking for its own sake—theorizing. To make the happy life even more difficult to obtain: Aristotle seems to think that the only sure way to learn virtue is to learn it in the home as a youth.[38] This adds another aspect of good fortune that impinges directly on the very foundation of *eudaimonia*—a morally virtuous life.

Aquinas, it has been said, overcame the tragic consequences of Aristotle's position by his identifying of the final end with something preexistent, that is—God, as opposed to an end to be made. Obviously, the existence of God is not subject to tragic circumstances, and the access to God is made available equally through the means of grace, especially revelation. These amendments make eternal happiness available in principle to everyone.[39] Certainly such arguments enter into theological disputes about predestination and election, but the present concern is for the consequences of this transformation in the earthly sphere. As has been seen, Aquinas saw earthly happiness as something more imperfect than Aristotle and, consequently, more accessible to a variety of people.

For Aquinas, the end of eternal happiness already exists; it is not waiting to be made, as it is in Aristotle. In effect, the concepts provided by Aristotle are employed by Aquinas to describe a kind of happiness that the Philosopher, in the eyes of Aquinas, only hints at. Indeed, the distinction between these ways of conceiving the object of happiness can better be understood by considering it in relation to theology. God as the summum bonum is totally distinctive in comparison with all other options. God is not one good thing that is to be possessed among others—God alone is what is necessary to eternal happiness. The vision of God does not need to include anything else but God. God is a highest good in a manner that no other object can be a highest good, because all other objects of happiness require other goods that do not exist in the manner in which God exists.

In other words, one might argue that happiness consists in the contemplative gazing at the unchanging first principles of reality— metaphysical truth. These principles, although they provide real knowledge of being, do not exist independently of the mind that thinks about them. A similar analysis applied to other possible objects of happiness would reveal that, whether it is virtue or plea-

sure or honor, all other objects of happiness depend for their existence on the one who is happy. God alone can be a possible object
of happiness yet remain a distinctive existence.[40]

God is also distinctive as an object of happiness because of divine simplicity. God is not a bundle of goods but goodness itself.
Lady Philosophy tells Boethius that by loving divine goodness he
possesses all the goods that he lost on earth—the goods are perfectly unified into a single goodness.[41] Thus when temporal and
eternal happiness are contrasted, we notice that the object of earthly happiness remains a mixed good. This tendency has already been
seen even among those eudaemonists who tried to limit it to one
good or the other. Aristotle affirms that theorizing requires other
goods of life to support it. Epicurus seeks the happiness that pleasure brings through the exercise of virtue. The Stoics play the ver-
bal game of calling the goods of the body and fortune advantages.
The Cynics, who are at least consistent in declaring virtue the sole
highest good, have to be dismissed on the grounds of ignoring the
other needs of human life. The object of temporal happiness remains
a mixed good precisely because there is no single object in this life
that is capable of satisfying needs to that extent.

Thus, it appears difficult to avoid some sort of inclusivist or
hybrid approach to the human good. A multifaceted good corre-
sponds to the differing levels of desires and fulfillments required
by the body, mind, and will of a human being, but the question then
arises as to how the goods are ordered: is life a kind of smorgas-
bord in which we go from bowl to bowl and simply serve up on
our plate whatever looks good to us, as long as we don't overeat?
Is there some more unifying object or vision to the pursuit of a
happy life than this?

The possibility for some sort of unifying vision, of something
real, beyond the recognition of basic human goods arises when issues of pluralism and incommensurability are raised. How do we
respond in concrete situations when choices have to be made between acting virtuously and acquiring wealth, enjoying pleasure, or
safeguarding health? What criterion is applied when differing goods
come into a seeming conflict and we cannot choose both? The happy life, thus, is not as simple as the inclusivist might lead one to
think. There must be some factor that enables us to make choices
concerning our character and identity—to shape our lives as a whole.
Happiness is not a mere collecting of goods: human action requires
that there be a dominant end—even if it is only the vision of the

kind of person you want to be, the kind of life you want to have. It is a vision such as this that acts on us and enables us to resolve dilemmas of this sort. In a sense one could say that a happy life is one that is passionate about the good that one sees lying ahead, a vision that enables us to make choices among goods, since we cannot have everything. The vision not only guides our choices, but also informs us of the meaning of their consequences, including the pleasures and pains they bring.

To speak of an integrating vision in directing our lives does not necessarily imply—though it could—some form of mystical experience. We need look no farther than the virtue of prudence to find that the vision of the human good is implicit in our voluntary action. Aquinas describes prudence as the wisdom of being able to order the whole of life.[42] It is the characteristic of the wise person to order parts into a whole; prudence, as right reason applied to action, brings a vision of human goodness to bear upon the choice of means in individual circumstances.[43] Prudence, while directing the making of a happy life, does not create the final measure of the human good—prudence is a making that responds, in part, to an existence that is already there.[44] If its guiding and integrating vision bears no realistic resemblance to that existence, then disorder will result, although, as we have seen, it may be glazed over with layers of self-satisfaction.

An ordinate response to one's human existence includes the recognition that self-satisfaction in any form represents a dangerous temptation. At the most basic level, it can create an obstacle to the moments of self-recognition constitutive of a happy life. Self-satisfaction also creates the illusion of autonomy, of a happiness entirely produced by the self, a happiness without passion or dependence—in other words, the happiness of a god. The passion for happiness begins as a response to the unsolicited gift of one's existence. The only satisfaction prudent to expect must result from an encounter with the *source* of our existence. But for that we must, as the poet Milton said, stand and wait.

Notes

1. *Nicomachean Ethics*, 1098 b 29-1099 a 7.
2. *Summa Theologiae*, 1-2.3.a.2.
3. ST, 1-2.1.a.8.

4. St. Thomas Aquinas, *Truth*, 22.1, trans. R. W. Mulligan, J. V. McGlynn, and R. W. Schmidt (Chicago: Regnery, 1952-54); hereafter cited as T.

5. ST, 1.75.a.6 is one of the many places Aquinas invokes this principle.

6. Aristotle's account of natural desire can be found in his *Physics* 192b and 255b.

7. Antonius Finili, O. P., "Natural Desire," *Dominican Studies* 1 (1948): 337-9, 313-59; see also his "New Light on Natural Desire," *Dominican Studies* 5 (1952) 159-84.

8. ST, 1-2.1.a.8.

9. Finili, 344.

10. ST, 1.60.a.1.2.

11. Oliver Sacks, *Awakenings* (New York: Vintage Books, 1976), 282-83.

12. Sacks, 309.

13. ST, 1-2.13.a.6.

14. ST, 1.82.a.2.

15. SCG, 3.53; ST, 1.12.a.2,5.

16. T, 26.3.

17. T, 26.1.

18. T, 26.1 and ST, 1-2.1.a.3.

19. T, 26.1.

20. ST, 1-2.22.a.1.

21. ST, 1-2.79.a.2.

22. T, 26.8.

23. ST, 1.81.a.2.

24. T, 26.6.

25. T, 26.7.

26. T, 26.7.

27. T, 26.7.

28. ST, 1-2.41.a.1.ad 2.

29. ST, 1-2.41.a.1.ad 2.

30. Jan Aertsen, *Nature and Creature: The Way of Thomas Aquinas's Thought* (Leiden: E. J. Brill 1988), 369.

31. Aertsen, 370.

32. ST, 1-2.2.a.3.

33. ST, 1-2.23.a.2-3.

34. ST, 1-2.2.a.2.

35. ST, 1-2.3.a.1.

36. See Don Asselin, *Human Nature and* Eudaimonia *in Aristotle* (New York: Peter Lang Publishing, Inc., 1989).

37. NE, 1177 a 12-1179 a 33; 1178 a 233-30.

38. NE, 1095 b 3-9.

39. Alan Donagan, *Human Ends and Human Action: An Exploration in St. Thomas's Treatment* (Milwaukee: Marquette University Press, 1988), 38.

40. The only counterexamples of this are absurdities such as considering the possession of a material thing. Yes, these are objects that have their own independent existence, but they fail to qualify on other grounds.

41. Boethius, *Consolation of Philosophy*, 3.9 (265).

42. ST, 1.1.a.6.

43. ST, 2-2.47.a.2.

44. Aquinas describes a prudent person as possessing vision, as "one who sees as it were from afar, for his sight is keen. . . . [Who] considers things afar off, in so far as they tend to be a help or hindrance to that which has to be done at the present time" (ST, 2-2.47.a.1; 2-2.47.a.1.ad 2). Thus Aquinas calls prudence wisdom about human affairs, for being prudent is about the human good—the highest causes in this order (ST, 2-2.47.a.2.ad 1).

Bibliography

Abelard, Peter. *Dialogue of a Philosopher with a Jew and a Christian.* Trans. Pierre J. Payers. Toronto: Pontifical Institute of Medieval Studies, 1979.

Achtenberg, Deborah. "Human Being, Beast and God: The Place of Human Happiness According to Aristotle and Some Twentieth-Century Philosophers." *The St. John's Review* 38 (1988) 21-47.

Adler, Mortimer J. *A Dialectic of Morals: Towards the Foundations of Political Philosophy.* New York: Frederick Ungar, 1941.

Adler, Mortimer J. *Ten Philosophical Mistakes.* New York: Macmillan, 1985.

Adler, Mortimer J. and Walter Farrell, O. P. "The Theory of Democracy—Part III." *The Thomist* 4 (January 1942) 121-81.

Adler, Mortimer J., *The Time of Our Lives: The Ethics of Common Sense.* New York: Holt, Rinehart and Winston, 1970.

Addison, Joseph, and Richard Steele. *The Spectator.* 4 vols. New York: E. P. Dutton & Co., 1951.

Adkins, Arthur W. H. *Merit and Responsibility: A Study in Greek Values.* Chicago: University of Chicago Press, 1960.

Aertsen, Jan. *Nature and Creature: Thomas Aquinas's Way of Thought.* Leiden: E. J. Brill, 1988.

Alain. *Alain On Happiness.* Trans. Robert D. and Jane E. Cottrell. New York: Frederick Ungar, 1973.

Annas, Julia. "Epicurus on Pleasure and Happiness." *Philosophical Topics* 15:22 (Fall 1987) 5-21.

Annas, Julia. *The Morality of Happiness*. New York: Oxford University Press, 1993.

Anscombe, G. E. M. "Modern Moral Philosophy." *Philosophy* 33 (1958) 1-19.

Aquinas, St. Thomas. *Commentary on the Nicomachean Ethics of Aristotle*. 2 vols. Trans. C. I. Letzinger. Chicago: Regnery, 1964.

Aquinas, St. Thomas, *Physics*. Trans. R. J. Blackwell. New Haven, CT: Yale University Press, 1963.

Aquinas, St. Thomas, *Truth*. Trans. R. W. Mulligan, J. V. McGlynn, and R. W. Schmidt. Chicago: Regnery, 1952-54.

Aquinas, St. Thomas. *Summa Contra Gentiles*. 4 vols. Trans. Anton C. Pegis, James F. Anderson, Vernon J. Bourke, Charles J. O'Neil. Notre Dame: University of Notre Dame Press, 1975.

Aquinas, St. Thomas, *Summa Theologiae*. 3 vols. Trans. English Dominican Fathers. New York: Benziger Brothers, Inc. 1947.

Aquinas, St. Thomas. *Treatise on Happiness*. Trans. John A. Osterle. Notre Dame: University of Notre Dame Press, 1983.

Aristotle. *Eudemian Ethics: Books I, II, and VIII*. Trans. Michael Woods. Oxford: Clarendon Press, 1982.

Aristotle. *Nicomachean Ethics*. Trans. Martin Ostwald. Indianapolis: The Bobbs-Merrill Co., Inc., 1962.

Aristotle. *The Rhetoric and the Poetics of Aristotle*. Trans. W. Rhys Roberts and Ingram Bywater. New York: Random House, Inc., 1954.

Argyle, Michael. *The Psychology of Happiness*. New York: Methuen, 1987.

Arendt, Hannah. *On Revolution*. New York: Penguin Books, 1963.

Artfield, Robin. "On Being Human." *Inquiry* 17 (Summer 1974) 175-92.

Asselin, Don. *Human Nature and Eudaimonia in Aristotle*. New York: Peter Lang Publishing Inc., 1989.

Augustine. *The City of God*. Trans. Marcus Dods. New York: Random House, Inc., 1950.

Augustine. *Confessions*. Trans. John K. Ryan. New York: Doubleday, 1960.

Augustine. "The Happy Life." Trans. Ludwig Schopp. St. Louis: B. Herder Book Co., 1974, 43-84.

Augustine. *The Trinity.* Trans. Edmund Hill, O. P. Brooklyn: New City Press, 1990.

Austin, Jean. "Pleasure and Happiness." *Philosophy* 43 (Jan. 1968) 51-62.

Barnouw, Jeffrey. "Pursuit of Happiness in Jefferson." *Interpretation* 11 (May 1983) 225-48.

Barrow, Robin. *Happiness and Schooling.* New York: St. Martin's Press, 1980.

Barrow, Robin. *Plato, Utilitarianism, and Education.* Boston: Routledge & Kegan Paul, 1975.

Beccaria. *On Crimes and Punishments.* Trans. David Young. Indianapolis: Hackett Publishing Company, 1986.

Becker, Carl L. *The Declaration of Independence: A Study in the History of Political Ideas.* New York: Vintage Books, 1922.

Becker, Carl L. *The Heavenly City of the Eighteenth-Century Philosophers.* New Haven: Yale University Press, 1932.

Bellah, Robert, Richard Madsen, William M. Sullivan, Ann Swindler, and Stephen M. Tipton. *Habits of the Heart: Individualism and Commitment in American Life.* New York: Harper & Row, Publishers, 1985.

Beierwaltes, Werner. *Regio Beatitudinis: Augustine's Concept of Happiness.* Philadelphia: Villanova University Press, 1981.

Benditt, Theodore M. "Happiness." *Philosophical Studies* 25 (January 1974) 1-20.

Benditt, Theodore M. "Happiness and Satisfaction—A Rejoinder to Carson." *The Personalist* 59 (January 1978) 108-09.

Besterman, Theodore, ed. *Studies on Voltaire and the Eighteenth Century.* Vol. 134. London: Cheney and Sons, Ltd., 1975.

Boas, George. *The Happy Beast.* Baltimore, MD: The Johns Hopkins University Press, 1933.

Boethius. *The Consolation of Philosophy.* Trans. S. J. Tester. Cambridge: Harvard University Press, 1918.

Bossi de Kirchner, Beatriz. "Aquinas as an Interpreter of Aristotle on the End of Human Life." *The Review of Metaphysics* 40 (Spring 1986) 41-54.

Bourke, Vernon. *Joy in St. Augustine's Ethics.* Villanova: Villanova University Press, 1979.

Bourke, Vernon. "The Nicomaechean Ethics and Thomas Aquinas." *St. Thomas Aquinas 1274-1974 Commemorative Studies.* Toronto, 1974.

Buckley, Joseph, *Man's Last End.* St. Louis: B. Herder Book Co., 1949.

Bradburn, Norman M., and David Caplovits. *Reports on Happiness.* Chicago: Aldine Publishing Company, 1965.

Bradburn, Norman M. *Structure of Psychological Well-Being.* Chicago: Aldine Publishing Company, 1969.

Bradley, F. H. *Ethical Studies.* New York: The Liberal Arts Press, 1951.

Brandt, R. B. "Fairness to Happiness." *Social Theory & Practise* 15 (Spring 1989) 33-58.

Braybrooke, David. "Thoughtful Happiness." *Ethics* 99 (April 1989) 625-36.

Brito, E. "God's Happiness: Hegel and Aquinas." *American Catholic Philosophical Quarterly* 64:4 (Autumn 1990) 491-508.

Brochman, George. *Happiness and Humanity.* Trans. Frank G. Nelson. New York: Viking, 1950.

Butler, Joseph. *Five Sermons.* Indianapolis, IN: The Bobbs-Merrill Company, Inc., 1950.

Campbell, A. *The Sense of Well-Being in America: Recent Patterns and Trends.* New York: McGraw-Hill, 1981.

Campbell, A., P. E. Converse, and W. L. Rodgers. *The Quality of American Life: Perceptions, Evaluations, and Satisfaction.* New York: Russell Sage Foundation, 1976.

Campbell, Richard. "The Pursuit of Happiness." *The Personalist* 59 (January 1978) 325-39.

Camus, Albert. *The Myth of Sisyphus and Other Essays.* Trans. Justin O'Brien. New York: Alfred A. Knopf, Inc., 1955.

Carriere, Gaston. "Plotinus' Quest of Happiness." *The Thomist* 14 (April 1951) 217-37.

Carson, Thomas. "Happiness and Contentment: A Reply to Benditt." *The Personalist* 59 (January 1978) 101-07.

Carson, Thomas. "Happiness and the Good Life." *Southwestern Journal of Philosophy* 9 (Fall 1978) 73-88.

Carson, Thomas. "Happiness and the Good Life: A Rejoinder to Mele." *Southwestern Journal of Philosophy* 10 (Summer 1979) 189-92.

Carson, Thomas. "Happiness, Contentment, and the Good Life." *Pacific Philosophic Quarterly* 62 (October 1981) 378-92.

Cassirer, Ernst. *The Philosophy of the Enlightenment.* Trans. Frits C. A. Koelln and James P. Pettegrove. Princeton: Princeton University Press, 1951.

Celano, Anthony J. "The Concept of Worldly Beatitude in the Writings of Thomas Aquinas." *Journal of the History of Philosophy* 25 (1987) 215-26.

Celano, Anthony J. "Act of the Intellect or Act of the Will: The Critical Reception of Aristotle's Idea of Human Perfection in the 13th and Early 14th Centuries." *Archives d'histoire doctrinale et littéraire du moyen âge* 65 (1990) 93-119.

Celano, Anthony J. "The Understanding of the Concept of *Felicitas* in the Pre-1250 Commentaries on the *Ethica Nicomachea.*" *Medioevo* 12 (1986) 29-53.

Celano, Anthony J. "Peter of Auvergne's Questions on Books I and II of his *Ethica Nicomachea*: A Study and Critical Edition." *Medieval Studies* 48 (1986) 1-110.

Celano, Anthony J. "The *Finis Hominis* in the Thirteenth-Century Commentaries on Aristotle's *Nicomachean Ethics.*" *Archives d'histoire doctrinale et littéraire du moyen âge* (1986) 23-53

Celano, Anthony J. "Aristotle on Beatitude." *Ancient Philosophy* 5 (Fall 1985) 202-14.

Chekola, M. C. *The Concept of Happiness.* Ph.D. dissertation, University of Michigan, 1974.

Cicero. *Tusculan Disputations.* Trans. J. E. King. Cambridge: Harvard University Press, 1927.

Clark, Stephen R. L. *Aristotle's Man: Speculations upon Aristotelian Anthropology.* Oxford: Clarendon Press, 1975.

Cohen, Richard A. "Emmanuel Levinas: Happiness is a Sensational Time." *Philosophy Today* 25 (Fall 1981) 196-203.

Cooper, John M. *Reason and the Human Good in Aristotle.* Cambridge: Harvard University Press, 1975.

Cooper, John M. "Aristotle and the Goods of Fortune." *The Philosophical Review* 94 (April 1985) 173-96.

Creel, R. E. "Eudology: The Science of Happiness." *New Ideas in Psychology* 1 (1983) 303-12.

Crocker, Lester G. *An Age of Crisis: Man and World in Eighteenth-Century French Thought.* Baltimore: The Johns Hopkins University Press, 1959.

Csikszentmihalyi, Mihaly. *Flow: The Psychology of Optimum Experience.* New York: Harper & Row, 1990.

Davis, Wayne. "A Theory of Happiness." *American Philosophical Quarterly* 18 (April 1981) 111-20.

Diener, Ed. "Subjective Well-Being." *Psychological Bulletin* 95 (1984) 542-75.

Den Uyl, Douglas, and Tibor R. Machan. "Recent Work on the Concept of Happiness." *American Philosophical Quarterly* 20 (April 1983) 115-33.

Diogenes, Laertius. *Lives of Eminent Philosophers.* 2 vols. Trans. R. D. Hicks. Cambridge: Harvard University Press, 1925.

Donagan, Alan, *Human Ends and Human Action: An Exploration in St. Thomas's Treatment.* Milwaukee: Marquette University Press, 1988.

Driscoll, Edward A. "The Influence of Gassendi on Locke's Hedonism." *International Philosophical Quarterly* 12 (March 1961) 87-110.

Dybikowski, J. "Is Aristotelian Eudiamonia Happiness?" *Dialogue* 81 (1981) 185-200.

Edel, Abraham. "Happiness and Pleasure." *Dictionary of the History of Ideas,* 374-87. New York: Charles Scribners's Sons, 1973.

Elster, Jon and John E. Roemer. *Interpersonal Comparisons of Well-Being.* Cambridge: Cambridge University Press, 1991.

Epicurus, *Letters, Principal Doctrines, and Vatican Sayings.* Trans. Russel M. Geer. Indianapolis, IN: Bobbs-Merrill, 1964.

Ficino, Marsilio. *The Book of Life*. Trans. Charles Boer. Irving: Spring Publications, Inc., 1980.

Ficino, Marsilio. "Letter 115 to Lorenzo di Medici." *Letters of Marsilio Ficino*. Vol. 1, 171-78. London: Shepheard-Walwyn, 1975.

Ficino, Marsilio. *Marsilio Ficino and the Phaedran Charioteer*. Trans. Michael J. B. Allen. Berkeley: University of California Press, 1981.

Ficino, Marsilio. *The Philebus Commentary*. Trans. Michael J. B. Allen. Berkeley: University of California Press, 1975.

Ficino, Marsilio. "Platonic Theology." Trans. Josephine L. Burroughs. *Journal of the History of Ideas* 5 (April 1944) 227-42.

Fine, Reuben. "The Protestant Ethic and the Analytic Ideal." *Political Psychology* 4 (1983) 245-64.

Finnis, John. "Practical Reasoning, Human Goods, and the End of Man." *Proceedings of the American Catholic Philosophical Association* 58 (1985) 23-36.

Freedman, Jonathan. *Happy People: What Happiness Is, Who Has It, and Why*. New York: Harcourt, Brace, Jovanovich, 1978.

Friedman, R. Z. "Virtue and Happiness: Kant and Three Critics." *Canadian Journal of Philosophy* 11 (March 1981) 95-110.

Freud, Sigmund. *Civilization and Its Discontents*. Trans. James Strachey. New York: W. W. Norton & Company, Inc., 1961.

Freud, Sigmund. *The Future of an Illusion*. Trans. W. D. Robson-Scott. New York: Anchor Books, 1964.

Freund, Michael. "Toward a Critical Theory of Happiness: Philosophical Background and Methodological Significance." *New Ideas on Psychology* 3 (1985) 3-12.

Freund, Michael. *An Empirical Investigation of Happiness and Its Determinants*. Ph.D. dissertation, Columbia University, 1978.

Gay, Peter. *The Enlightenment: An Interpretation*. New York: Alfred A. Knopf, 1967.

Gilson, Etienne. *Dante and Philosophy*. Trans. David Moore. Gloucester, Mass.: Peter Smith, 1968.

Gilson, Etienne. *The Christian Philosophy of St. Thomas Aquinas*. Trans. L. K. Shook. New York: Random House, 1956.

Glidden, David K. "Hellenistic Background for Gassendi's Theory of Ideas." *Journal of the History of Ideas* 49 (July/September 1988) 415-24.

Godfrey, Joseph J. *A Philosophy of Human Hope.* Boston: Martinus Nijhoff Publishers, 1987.

Goldstein, Irwin. "Happiness: The Role of Non-Hedonic Criteria in Its Evaluation." *International Philosophical Quarterly* 13 (1973) 523-34.

Gordon, Robert M. "The Passivity of Emotions." *The Philosophical Review* 45 (July 1986) 371-92.

Gordon, Robert M. *The Structure of Emotions.* Cambridge: Cambridge Universtiy Press, 1987.

Gosling, J. C. B., and C. C. W. Taylor. *The Greeks on Pleasure.* Oxford: Clarendon Press, 1982.

Gray, John. *A Lecture on Human Happiness.* London: Sherwood, Jones, & Co., 1825.

Green, Ronald M. *Religious Reason: The Rational and Moral Basis of Religious Belief.* New York: Oxford University Press, 1978.

Grean, Stanley. *Shaftesbury's Philosophy of Religion and Ethics.* Athens, OH: Ohio University Press, 1967.

Green, T. M. "Life, Value, Happiness." *Journal of Philosophy* 53 (1956) 317-30.

Greene, Jack P. *Pursuits of Happiness: The Social Development of Early Modern British Colonies and the Formation of American Culture.* Chapel Hill: University of North Carolina Press, 1988.

Griffin, James. *Well-Being: Its Meaning, Measurement, and Moral Importance.* Oxford: Clarendon Press, 1986.

Grisez, Germain, Joseph Boyle, and John Finnis. "Practical Principles, Moral Truth and Ultimate Ends." *American Journal of Jurisprudence* 32 (1987) 99-151.

Habermas, Jurgen. "Moral Development and Ego Identity." *Communication and the Evolution of Society,* 69-94. Trans. Thomas McCarthy. Boston: Beacon Press, 1979.

Hackett, Jeremiah. "Practical Wisdom and Happiness in the Moral Philosophy of Roger Bacon." *Medioevo* 12 (1986) 29-53.

Hagberg, Garry. "Understanding Happiness." *Mind* 93 (October 1984) 589-91.

Hamowy, Ronald. "Jefferson and the Scottish Enlightenment: A Critique of Garry Wills' *Inventing America: Jefferson's Declaration of Independence*. *William & Mary Quarterly* (1979) 503-23.

Hansen, Marlene R. "Sex and Love, Marriage and Friendship: A Feminist Reading of the Quest for Happiness in *Rasselas*." *English Studies* 6 (1986) 513-25.

Hardie, W. F. R. *Aristotle's Ethical Theory*. Oxford: Clarendon Press, 1980.

Hare, Richard. *Freedom and Reason*. Oxford: Clarendon Press, 1963.

Harris, James. *Three Treatises*. London: F. Wingrave, 1742.

Hartley, David. *Observations on Man: His Frame, His Duty, and His Expectations*. 2 vols. Gainesville, FL: Scholars' Facsimiles & Reprints, 1966.

Harwood, John T. *The Early Essays and Ethics of Robert Boyle*. Carbondale: Southern Illinois University Press, 1992.

Hazard, Paul. *The European Mind (1680-1715)*. Cleveland: World Publishing Company, 1963.

Hazard, Paul. *European Thought in the Eighteenth Century: From Montesquieu to Lessing*. Trans. J. Lewis May. Cleveland: World Publishing Company, 1963.

Heer, Cornelis, de. *Makar, Eudaimon, Olbios, Eutyches: A Study of the Semantic Field Denoting Happiness in Ancient Greek to the End of the 5th Century B.C.* Amsterdam: University of Western Australia Press/A.M. Hakkert, 1968.

Hegel, G. W. F. *The Phenomenology of Mind*. Trans. J. Baillie. New York: Harper & Row, 1967.

Hegel, G. W. F. *The Philosophical Propaedeutic*. Trans. A. Miller. New York: Basil Blackwell, 1986.

Heller, Agnes. *Renaissance Man*. Trans. Richard E. Allen. New York: Schocken Books, 1978.

Henry, A. M., ed. *Man and His Happiness*. New York: Fides, 1956.

Heywood, Ellis. *Il Moro: Dialogue in Memory of Thomas More*. Trans. Roger Lee Deakins. Cambridge: Harvard University Press, 1972.

Hilber, Richard M. *Happiness Through Tranquility: The School of Epicurus*. Lanham: University Press of America, 1984.

Hoag, Robert W. "Happiness and Freedom: Recent Work on John Stuart Mill." *Philosophy and Public Affairs* 15 (Spring 1985) 188-99.

Hobbes, Thomas. *Leviathan*. Oxford: Clarendon Press, 1958.

Hutcheson, Francis. *Inquiry into the Original of Our Ideas of Beauty and Virtue*. 4th ed. London: 1738.

Horley, James. "Life Satisfaction, Happiness, and Morale: Two Problems with the Use of Subjective Well-Being Indicators." *The Gerontologist* 24 (1984) 124-27.

Ignatieff, Michael. *The Needs of Strangers: An Essay on Privacy, Solidarity, and the Politics of Being Human*. New York: Viking Penguin, Inc., 1984.

Ionescu, Ghita. *Politics and the Pursuit of Happiness: An Enquiry into the Involvement of Human Beings in the Politics of Industrial Society*. New York: Longman Inc., 1984.

Irwin, T. H. "Stoic and Aristotelian Conceptions of Happiness." *The Norms of Nature*. Ed. Malcolm Schofield and Gisela Striker, 205-44. Cambridge: Cambridge University Press, 1986.

Irwin, T. H. "Permanent Happiness: Aristotle and Solon." *Oxford Studies in Ancient Philosophy*, vol. 3. Ed. Julia Annas, 89-124. Oxford: Clarendon Press, 1985.

Jaffa, Harry V. *American Conservatives and the American Founding*. Durham, NC: Carolina Academic Press, 1984.

Jaffa, Harry V. *Thomism and Aristotelianism: A Study of the Commentary by Thomas Aquinas on the Nicomachean Ethics*. Chicago: The University of Chicago Press, 1952.

Johnson, Samuel. *The History of Rasselas Prince of Abyssinia*. Woodbury, NY: Barron's Educational Series, 1962.

Jones, Howard Mumford. *The Pursuit of Happiness*. Cambridge: Harvard University Press, 1953.

Jones, James F., Jr. "Prolegomena to a History of Happiness in the Eighteenth Century." *French-American Review* 6 (1982) 283-95.

Kalin, Martin G. *The Utopian Flight from Unhappiness: Freud Against Marx on Social Progress*. Chicago: Nelson-Hall, 1974.

Kant, Immanuel. *Critique of Practical Reason*. Trans. Lewis White Beck. Indianapolis: The Bobbs-Merrill Company, Inc., 1956.

Kant, Immanuel. *Foundations of the Metaphysics of Morals.* Trans. Lewis White Beck. Indianapolis: The Bobbs-Merrill Company, Inc., 1959.

Kant, Immanuel. *The Doctrine of Virtue.* Trans. Mary J. Gregor. New York: Harper & Row, 1964.

Kant, Immanuel. *Religion Within the Limits of Reason Alone.* Trans. Theodore M. Greene & Hoyt H. Hudson. New York: Harper & Row, 1960.

Kekes, John. "Happiness." *Mind* 91 (July 1982) 358-76.

Kekes, John. "Human Nature and Moral Theories." *Inquiry* 28 (June 1985) 231-45.

Kekes, John. *Moral Tradition and Individuality.* Princeton: Princeton University Press, 1989.

Kenny, Anthony. "Happiness." *Proceedings of the Aristotelian Society* 46 (1965-6) 93-102.

Kenny, Anthony. *The Aristotelian Ethics: A Study of the Relationship Between the Eudemian and Nicomachean Ethics of Aristotle.* Oxford: Clarendon Press, 1978.

Kerr, Walter. *The Decline of Pleasure.* New York: Simon and Schuster, 1962.

Khan, Abraham H. *Salighed as Happiness?: Kierkegaard on the Concept Salighed.* Ontario, Canada: Wilfrid Laurier University Press, 1985.

Kierkegaard, Søren. *Søren Kierkegaard's Journals and Papers.* 7 Vols. Trans. and ed. Howard V. and Edna H. Hong. Bloomington, IN: Indiana University Press, 1967-78.

Finili, Antonius, O. P. "Natural Desire." *Dominican Studies* I (1948) 313-59.

Finili, Antonius, O. P. "New Light On Natural Desire." *Dominican Studies* V (1952) 159-84.

Kirk, G. S., and Raven, J. E. *The Presocratic Philosophers.* Cambridge: Cambridge University Press, 1969.

Kirk, Kenneth. *The Vision of God: The Christian Doctrine of the Summum Bonum.* Greenwood: The Attic Press, Inc., 1977.

Koch, Adrienne. *The Philosophy of Thomas Jefferson.* Gloucester: Peter Smith, 1957.

Kosman, L. A. "Being Properly Affected: Virtues and Feelings." *Essays on Aristotle's Ethics.* Ed. Amelie Rorty, 103-16. Berkeley: University of California Press, 1980.

Kraut, Richard. "Two Conceptions of Happiness." *The Philosophical Review* 138 (April 1979) 167-97.

Kristeller, Paul Oscar. "A Thomist Critique of Marsilio Ficino's Theory of Will and Intellect." *Harry Austryn Wolfson Jubilee Volume,* 563-94. Jerusalem: American Academy for Jewish Research, 1985.

Korsmeyer, C. "Is Pangloss Leibniz?" *Philosophy and Literature* 1 (1977) 201-8.

Kurtz, Paul. *Exuberance: A Philosophy of Happiness.* Buffalo: Prometheus Books, 1977.

Lewis, Jan. *The Pursuit of Happiness: Family and Values in Jefferson's Virginia.* Cambridge: Cambridge University Press, 1983.

Lieb, Irwin C. "Happiness and the Good Life." *The Good Life and Its Pursuit.* Ed. Jude P. Dougherty, 19-43. New York: Paragon House, 1982.

Locke, John. *An Essay Concerning Human Understanding.* Ed. Peter Nidditch, Oxford: Clarendon Press, 1975.

Locke, John. *Essays on the Law of Nature.* Ed. W. von Leyden. Oxford: Oxford University Press, 1954.

Long, A. A., and D. N. Sedley. *The Hellenistic Philosophers.* vol. 1. Cambridge: Cambridge University Press, 1988.

McDonald, Forrest. *Novo Ordo Seclorum: The Intellectual Origins of the Constitution.* Lawrence: University of Kansas Press, 1985.

MacIntyre, Alasdair. *After Virtue.* Notre Dame: University of Notre Dame Press, 1984.

MacIntyre, Alasdair. *A Short History of Ethics.* New York: Macmillan, 1973.

MacIntyre, Alasdair. *Herbert Marcuse.* New York: The Viking Press, 1970.

MacIntyre, Alasdair. *Whose Justice? Which Rationality?* Notre Dame: University of Notre Dame Press, 1988.

Maritain, Jacques. *Christianity and Democracy.* Trans. Doris C. Anson. London: Geoffrey Bles, 1945.

Maritain, Jacques. *Integral Humanism.* Trans. Joseph W. Evans. New York: Scribner's, 1986.

Maritain, Jacques. *Moral Philosophy.* London: Geoffrey Bles, 1964.

Maritain, Jacques. "That Suffer Persecution." *A Maritain Reader.* Eds. Donald and Idella Gallagher, 315-25. New York: Image Books, 1966.

Mauzi, Robert. *L'Idée du bonheur dans la littérature et la pensée françaises au XVIII siècle.* Paris: A. Colin, 1960.

McCown, Chester C. "The Beatitudes in the Light of Ancient Ideals." *Journal of Biblical Literature* 46 (1927) 50-61.

McDonald, R. C. "Pursuing Happiness." *The Personalist* 58 (April 1977) 179-81.

McFall, Lynn. "Happiness, Rationality, and Individual Ideals." *The Review of Metaphysics* 37 (March 1984) 595-613.

McFall, Lynne. *Happiness.* New York: Peter Lang, 1989.

McGill, V. J. *The Idea of Happiness.* New York: Frederick A. Praeger, 1967.

McNaughton, Robert. "A Metrical Concept of Happiness." *Philosophy and Phenomenological Research* 14 (1953) 172-83.

McShea, Robert J. "Human Nature Ethical Theory." *Philosophy and Phenomenological Research* 39 (March 1979) 386-401.

Mahrer, Alvin R. "Is Human Destiny Tragic? Psychoanalytic and Humanistic Answers." *The Humanistic Psychologist* 14 (Summer 1986) 73-86.

Mandeville, Bernard. *Free Thoughts on Religion, the Church, and National Happiness (1720).* New York: Scholars' Facsimiles & Reprints, 1981.

Marra, William A. *Happiness and Christian Hope.* Chicago: Franciscan Herald Press, 1979.

Mele, Alfred R. "On Happiness and the Good Life." *Southwestern Journal of Philosophy* 10 (Summer 1979) 181-87.

Meyer, Donald. *The Positive Thinkers: A Study of the American Quest for Health, Wealth, and Personal Power from Mary Baker Eddy to Norman Vincent Peale and Ronald Reagan.* Revised Edition. Middletown, CT: Wesleyan University Press, 1988.

Meynell, Hugo. "Human Flourishing." *Religious Studies* 5 (1969) 147-54.

Midgley, Mary. "Human Ideals and Human Needs." *Philosophy* 58 (January 1983) 89-94.

Mill, John Stuart. *Autobiography.* Indianapolis: The Bobbs-Merrill Company, Inc., 1957.

Mill, John Stuart. *Utilitarianism and Other Writings.* New York: New American Library, 1974.

Mitchell, Timothy A. *Hedonism and Eudaemonism in Aquinas—Not the Same as Happiness.* Chicago: Franciscan Herald, 1983.

Mitsis, Phillip. *Epicurus' Ethical Theory: The Pleasures of Invulnerability.* Ithaca: Cornell University Press, 1988.

Montague, Roger. "Happiness." *Proceedings of the Aristotelian Society* 67 (1967) 87-102.

Moore, Barrington, Jr. *Reflections on the Causes of Human Misery and upon Certain Proposals to Eliminate Them.* Boston: Beacon Press, 1973.

Moravcsik, J. M. E. "On What We Aim At and How We Live." in *The Greeks and the Good Life.* Ed. David Depew, 198-235. Indianapolis: Hackett, 1981.

Murray, Charles. *In Pursuit of Happiness and Good Government.* New York: Simon & Schuster, 1984.

Myers, David G. *The Pursuit of Happiness: Who is Happy—and Why.* New York: William Morrow and Co., 1992.

Nietzsche, Friedrich. *Beyond Good and Evil.* Trans. Walter Kaufman. New York: Vintage Books, 1966.

Nietzche, Friedrich. *Daybreak.* Trans. R. J. Hollingdale. Cambridge: Cambridge University Press, 1982.

Nietzsche, Friedrich. *The Gay Science.* Trans. Walter Kaufman. New York: Random House, 1974.

Nietzsche, Friedrich. *Human, All Too Human: A Book for Free Spirits.* Trans. Marion Faber and Stephen Lehmann. Lincoln: University of Nebraska Press, 1984.

Nietzsche, Friedrich. *Thus Spake Zarathustra.* Trans. R. J. Hollingdale. New York: Penguin Books, 1961.

Nietzsche, Friedrich. *The Will to Power.* Trans. Walter Kaufman and R. J. Hollingdale. New York: Vintage Books, 1968.

Nietzsche, Friedrich. *Untimely Meditations.* Trans. R. J. Hollingdale. Cambridge/New York: Cambridge University Press, 1983.

Norton, David L. *Personal Destinies: A Philosophy of Ethical Individualism.* Princeton: Princeton University Press, 1976.

Nussbaum, Martha C. *The Fragility of Goodness: Luck and Ethics in Greek Tragedy and Philosophy.* Cambridge: Cambridge University Press, 1986.

O'Connor, William. *The Eternal Quest: The Teaching of St. Thomas Aquinas on the Natural Desire for God.* New York: Longmans, Green and Co., 1947.

O'Connor, William. "The Natural Desire for Happiness." *The Modern Schoolman* 26 (January 1949) 91-112.

O'Donovan, Oliver. *The Problem of Self-Love in St. Augustine.* New Haven: Yale University Press, 1980.

Okun, Morris A. and William A. Stock. "The Construct Validity of Subjective Well-Being Measures: An Assessment Via Quantitative Research Synthesis." *Journal of Community Psychology* 15 (October 1987) 481-92.

Pangle, Thomas. *The Spirit of Modern Republicanism: The Moral Vision of the American Founders.* Chicago: University of Chicago Press, 1988.

Parker, Dorothy. *The Portable Dorothy Parker.* New York: The Viking Press, 1973.

Pascal, Blaise. *Pensées.* Trans. A. J. Krailsheimer. Harmondsworth: Penguin, 1970.

Passmore, John. *The Perfectibility of Man.* London: Duckworth, 1970.

Peale, Norman Vincent, and Smiley Blanton. *The Art of Real Happiness.* New York: Prentice-Hall, 1950.

Pieper, Josef. *Happiness and Contemplation.* Trans. Richard and Clara Winston. New York: Pantheon Press, 1958.

Plato. *Gorgias.* Trans. W. C. Hembold. Indianapolis: The Bobbs-Merrill Company, Inc., 1952.

Plato. *Gorgias*. Trans. Terence Irwin. Oxford: Clarendon Press, 1979.

Ple, Albert. *Duty or Pleasure?: A New Appraisal of Christian Ethics*. Trans. Matthew J. O'Connell. New York: Paragon House Publishers, 1987.

Plotinus. *Enneads*. Trans. A. H. Armstrong. vol. 1. Cambridge: Harvard University Press, 1968.

Porter, Jean. "Desire for God: Ground of the Moral Life in Aquinas." *Theological Studies* 47 (March 1986) 48-68.

Powys, John Cowper. *The Art of Happiness*. New York: Simon & Schuster, 1935.

Quennell, Peter. *The Pursuit of Happiness*. Boston: Little, Brown and Company, 1988.

Rapaczynski, Andrezj. *Nature and Politics: Liberalism in the Philosophies of Hobbes, Locke, and Rousseau*. Ithaca: Cornell University Press, 1987.

Raphael, D. D. *British Moralists: Sixteen Fifty to Eighteen Hundred*. 2 vols. Oxford: Oxford University Press, 1969.

Raschke, Carl A. "The Human Potential Movement." *Theology Today* 33 (October 1976) 253-62.

Reale, Giovanni. *A History of Ancient Philosophy: III. The Systems of the Hellenistic Age*. Trans. John R. Catan. Albany: State University of New York Press, 1985.

Rescher, Nicholas. "Technological Progress and Human Happiness." *Unpopular Essays*. Pittsburg: Pittsburg University Press, 1980.

Rieff, Philip. *Freud: The Mind of the Moralist*. New York: Doubleday & Company, Inc., 1961.

Ring, Merrill. "Aristotle and the Concept of Happiness." *The Greeks and the Good Life*. Ed. D. Depew, 69-71. Indianapolis: Hackett, 1981.

Roche, Timothy D. "The Perfect Happiness." *Southwestern Journal of Philosophy Supplement* 27 (1988) 103-25.

Roche, Timothy D. "Ergon and Eudaimonia in Nicomachean Ethics I: Reconsidering the intellectualist interpretation." *Journal of the History of Philosophy* 26 (April 1988) 175-94.

Robbins, Caroline. *The Pursuit of Happiness*. Washington DC: American Enterprize Institute for Public Policy Research, 1974.

Rostvig, Maren-Sofie. *The Happy Man: Studies in the Metamorphoses of a Classical Ideal*, Vol. I: 1600-1700. Revised edition. Oslo: Norwegian Universities Press, 1962.

Rousseau, Jean Jacques. *Emile*. Trans. Allan Bloom. New York: Basic Books, 1969.

Russell, Bertrand. *The Conquest of Happiness*. New York: Liverwright, 1930.

Ruttenberg, Howard S. "Modern Psychoanalysis as Philosophy." *Modern Psychoanalysis* 7 (1982) 7-27.

Sacks, Oliver. *Awakenings*. New York: Vintage Books, 1976.

Sandbach, F. H. *Aristotle and the Stoics*. Cambridge: Cambridge Philological Society, Supp. vol. 10, 1985.

Sandbach, F. H. *The Stoics*. New York: W. W. Norton, 1975.

Salkever, Stephen G. "Rousseau and the Concept of Happiness." *Polity* 11 (1978) 27-45.

Schaar, John H. ". . . And the Pursuit of Happiness." *The Virginia Quarterly Review* 46 (Winter 1970) 1-26.

Shackleton, Robert. "The Greatest Happiness of the Greatest Number: the History of Bentham's Phrase." *Studies on Voltaire and the 18th Century* 90 (1972) 1461-82.

Scheler, Max. *Formalism in Ethics and Non-Formal Ethics of Value*. Trans. Manfred S. Frings and Roger L. Funk. Evanston: Northwestern University Press, 1973.

Schelling, F. W. J. *Of Human Freedom*. Trans. James Gutmann. Chicago: Open Court Publishing Company, 1936.

Schlesinger, Arthur. "The Lost Meaning of the 'Pursuit of Happiness,'" *William & Mary Quarterly* 3rd Series 21 (1964) 325-7.

Schofield, Malcolm, and Gisela Striker, eds. *The Norms of Nature*. New York: Cambridge University Press, 1987.

Schopenhauer, Arthur. *The World as Will and Idea*. Vol. 3. Trans. R. B. Haldane and J. Kemp, 1883 (eleventh impression, 1964).

Schopenhauer, Arthur. *Parega and Paralipomena*. Trans. E. F. J. Payne. Oxford: Clarendon Press, 1974.

Scruton, Roger. "Reason and Happiness." *Nature and Conduct*. In *Nature and Conduct*. Ed. R. S. Peters, 139-61. New York: Macmillan, 1975.

Shields, David S. "Happiness in Society: The Development of an Eighteenth-Century American Poetic Ideal." *American Literature* 55 (December 1983) 541-59.

Seigel, Jerrold E. *Rhetoric and Philosophy in Renaissance Humanism.* Princeton, New Jersey: Princeton University Press, 1968.

Shea, Joseph. "Two Conceptions of the Structure of Happiness." *Dialogue* 26 (1987) 453-64.

Silber, John R. "The Copernican Revolution in Ethics: The Good Reexamined." *Kant: A Collection of Critical Essays.* Ed. Robert Paul Wolff, 266-90. New York: Doubleday, 1967.

Silberman, Isidor. "On Happiness." *The Psychoanalytic Study of the Child* 40 (1985) 457-72.

Simmel, Georg. *Schopenhauer and Nietzsche.* Trans. Helmut Loiskanell, Deena Weinstein, and Michael Weinstein. Amherst: The University of Massachusetts Press, 1986.

Simon, Yves R. *Freedom of Choice.* Ed. and trans. Peter Wolff. New York: Fordham University Press, 1969.

Simon, Yves R. "The Pursuit of Happiness and the Lust for Power" *Philosophy of Democratic Government.* Rev. ed. Notre Dame: University of Notre Dame Press, 1993.

Simpson, Robert. "Happiness." *American Philosophical Quarterly* 12 (April 1975) 169-76.

Slote, Michael. "Goods and Lives." *Pacific Philosophical Quarterly* 63 (October 1982) 311-26.

Smart, Ninian. "What is Happiness?" *The Good Life and Its Pursuit.* Ed. Jude P. Dougherty, 35-50. New York: Paragon House, 1982.

Smith, Steven G. "Worthiness To Be Happy and Kant's Concept of the Highest Good." *Kantstudien Journal* 75 (1984).

Snell, Bruno. *The Discovery of Mind: The Greek Origins of European Thought.* Trans. T. G. Rosenmeyer, New York: Harper & Row, 1960.

Sokolowski, Robert. *Moral Action: A Phenomenological Study.* Bloomington: Indiana University Press, 1985.

Sontag, Frederick. "Happy/Unhappy." *Concepts and Alternatives in Kierkegaard.* Copenhagen: C. A. Reitzels Boghandel, 1980.

Solzhenitsyn, Aleksandr I. *The Cancer Ward*. Trans. Rebecca Frank. New York: Dell Publishing Co., Inc., 1980.

Spencer, Herbert. *The Data of Ethics*. New York: D. Applegate & Co., 1904.

Spencer, Herbert. *The Principles of Ethics*. 2 vols. Indianapolis: Liberty Classics, 1978.

Spencer, Herbert. *Social Static: or the Conditions Essential to Human Happiness Specified and the First of Them Developed*. New York: A. M. Kelley, 1969.

Staley, Kevin M. "Happiness: the Natural End of Man?" *The Thomist* 53 (April 1989) 215-234.

Steiner, George. *In Bluebeard's Castle: Some Notes Towards the Redefinition of Culture*. New Haven: Yale University Press, 1971.

Tatarkiewicz, Wladyslaw. *Analysis of Happiness*. Trans. Edward Rothert and Danuta Zielinskn. The Hague: Martinus Nijhoff, 1976.

Taylor, Richard. "Ancient Wisdom and Modern Folly." *Midwest Studies in Philosophy* XIII (1988) 54-63.

Taylor, Shelley E., and Jonathan D. Brown. "Illusion and Well-Being: A Social Science Perspective on Mental Health." *Psychological Bulletin* 103:2 (1988) 193-210.

Telfer, Elizabeth. *Happiness*. New York: St. Martins, 1980.

Theron, Stephen. "Happiness and Transcendent Happiness." *Religious Studies* 21 (September 1985) 349-67.

Theron, Stephen. "The Impossibility of Altruism." *The Downside Review* 104 (October 1986) 242-52.

Thomas, D. A. L. "Happiness." *Philosophical Quarterly* 18 (1968) 97-113.

Tolstoy, Leo. *Anna Karenina*. Trans. Constance Garrett (New York: Bobbs-Merrill Co., Inc, no date.

Trinkhaus, C. E. *Adversity's Noblemen: The Italian Humanists on Happiness*. New York: Columbia University Press, 1940.

Trippett, F. "The Scientific Pursuit of Happiness." *Time* (19 March 1979) 100, 102.

Unamuno, Miguel de. *The Tragic Sense of Life in Men and Nations*. Trans. Anthony Kerrigan. Princeton: Princeton University Press, 1972.

Undset, Sigrid. *Images in a Mirror.* Trans. Arthur G. Chater. New York: Alfred A. Knopf, 1938.

Valiunas, Algis. "Tolstoy and the Pursuit of Happiness." Commentary 87:6 (June 1988) 33-41.

Valla, Lorenzo. *On Pleasure, de voluptate.* Trans. A. Kent Hieatt and Maristella Lorch. New York: Abaris Books, Inc., 1977.

Veatch, Henry. *Human Rights: Fact or Fancy?.* Baton Rouge: Louisiana University Press, 1985.

Veenhoven, Ruut. *Conditions of Happiness.* Dordrecht: D. Reidel Publishing Co., 1984.

Veenhoven, Ruut. *Data-Book of Happiness.* Dordrecht: D. Reidel Publishing Co., 1984.

Veenhoven, Ruut. "The Utility of Happiness." *Social Indicators Research* 20 (1988) 333-54.

Vlastos, Gregory. "Happiness and Virtue in Socrates' Moral Theory." *Proceedings of the Cambridge Philological Society* 30 (1984) 181-213.

Vlastos, Gregory. "Justice and Happiness in the *Republic.*" *Plato, II: Ethics, Politics, and Philosophy of Art and Religion: A Collection of Critical Essays.* Ed. Gregory Vlastos, 66-95. Garden City, New York: Doubleday & Co., 1971.

Voegelin, Eric. *From Enlightenment to Revolution.* Chapel Hill, NC: Duke University Press, 1975.

Voegelin, Eric. *Science, Politics & Gnosticism.* Chicago: Henry Regnery Company, 1968.

Voegelin, Eric. *The New Science of Politics: An Introduction.* Chicago: The University of Chicago Press, 1952.

Voltaire. *Candide or Optimism.* Trans. Lowell Blair. New York: Bantam Books, Inc., 1962.

Von Wright, G. H. *The Varieties of Goodness.* London: Routledge & Kegan Paul, 1963.

Walhout, Donald. "Human Nature and Value Theory." *Thomist* 44 (April 1980) 278-97.

Wallin, Jeffrey D. "John Locke and the American Founding." *Natural Right and Political Right: Essays in Honor of Harry Jaffa.* Ed. Thomas B. Siver and Peter W. Schramm. Durham, NC: Carolina Academic Press, 1984.

Walter, Edward. "A Concept of Happiness." *Philosophical Research Archives* 13 (1987-88) 137-50.

Warner, Richard. *Freedom, Enjoyment, and Happiness: An Essay On Moral Psychology.* Ithaca: Cornell University Press, 1987.

Warner, Richard. "Grice on Happiness." *Philosophical Grounds of Rationality.* Ed. Richard Warner and Richard E. Grandy, 475-93. Oxford: Oxford University Press, 1986.

Waterman, Alan S. "Personal Expressiveness: Philosophical and Psychological Foundations." *Journal of Mind and Behavior* 11 (Winter 1990) 47-74.

Waterman, Alan S. "Two Conceptions of Happiness: Contrasts of Personal Expressiveness (Eudaimonia) and Hedonic Enjoyment." *Journal of Personality and Social Psychology* 64:4 (1993).

Weiland, George. "The Reception and Interpretation of Aristotle's *Ethics.*" *The Cambridge History of Later Medieval Philosophy.* Eds. Norman Kretzmann, Anthony Kenny, and Jan Pinborg, 657-72. Cambridge: Cambridge University Press, 1982.

Weiland, George. "Happiness: The Perfection of Man." *The Cambridge History of Later Medieval Philosophy.* Eds. Norman Kretzmann, Anthony Kenny, and Jan Pinborg, 673-86. Cambridge: Cambridge University Press, 1982.

Weyant, Robert G. "Helvetius and Jefferson: Studies of Human Nature and Government in the Eighteenth Century." *Journal of the History of Behavioral Sciences* 9 (1973) 29-41.

White, Morton. *The Philosophy of the American Revolution.* New York: Oxford University Press, 1978.

White, Nicholas P. "Happiness and External Contingencies in Plato's *Republic.*" *Moral Philosophy: Historical and Contemporary Essays.* Milwaukee: Marquette University Press, 1989.

Whitebook, Joel. "Reason and Happiness: Some Psychoanalytic Themes in Critical Theory." *Habermas and Modernity.* Ed. Richard Bernstein. Cambridge: MIT Press, 1985.

Wholey, Dennis. *Are You Happy? Some Answers to the Most Important Question in Your Life.* Boston: Houghton Mifflin Company, 1986.

Wike, Victoria S. "Kant On Happiness." *Philosophy Research Archives* 13 (1987-88) 79-90.

Wike, Victoria S. "The Role of Happiness in Kant's *Groundwork*." *Journal of Value Inquiry* 21 (1987) 73-78.

Willey, Basil. *The Eighteenth-Century Background: Studies on the Idea of Nature in the Thought of the Period*. London: Chatto and Windus, 1944.

Wills, Garry. *Inventing America: Jefferson's Declaration of Independence*. Garden City, NY: Doubleday & Company, Inc., 1978.

Wilson, John. "Happiness." *Analysis* 29 (January 1968) 13-21.

Wilson, John. *Preface to the Philosophy of Education*. Boston: Routledge and Kegan Paul, 1979.

Wittshire, S. F. "Boethius and the *summum bonum*." *Classical Journal* 6 (1972).

Wiltse, Charles M. *The Jeffersonian Tradition in American Democracy*. Chapel Hill: University of North Carolina Press, 1937.

Wolfe, Tom. *The Pump House Gang*. New York: Farrar, Straus & Giroux, 1968.

Wollaston, William. *The Religion of Nature Delineated* (1724). New York: Scholars' Facsimiles & Reprints, 1974.

Wright, William Kellog. *The Ethical Significance of Feeling, Pleasure, and Happiness in Modern Non-Hedonistic Systems*. Chicago: University of Chicago Press, 1907.

Zeyl, Donald. "Socratic Virtue and Happiness." *Archiv fur Geschichte der Philosophie* 64 (1982) 225-38.

Index

About the Author

Deal W. Hudson is the editor of CRISIS magazine in Washington D.C. Dr. Hudson has been an associate professor of philosophy at Fordham University and Mercer University Atlanta. He has previously edited *Jacques Maritain: Philosopher and Friend, The Future of Thomism*, and *Sigrid Undset on Saints and Sinners*. Dr. Hudson presently serves as president of the American Maritain Association, chair of the Yves R. Simon Institute, and director of Programs for the American Academy of Liberal Education.